simple secrets to
a happy life

Luci Swindoll

THOMAS NELSON
Since 1798

NASHVILLE   DALLAS   MEXICO CITY   RIO DE JANEIRO

Published in Nashville, Tennessee, by Thomas Nelson. Thomas Nelson is a registered trademark of Thomas Nelson, Inc.

Thomas Nelson, Inc., titles may be purchased in bulk for educational, business, fund-raising, or sales promotional use. For information, please e-mail SpecialMarkets@ ThomasNelson.com.

Page design by Mandi Cofer.

Unless otherwise indicated, Scripture quotations are taken from *The Message* by Eugene H. Peterson. © 1993, 1994, 1995, 1996, 2000. Used by permission of NavPress Publishing Group. All rights reserved.

Scripture quotations marked KJV are from the KING JAMES VERSION.

Scripture quotations marked NASB are from the NEW AMERICAN STANDARD BIBLE®, © The Lockman Foundation 1960, 1962, 1963, 1968, 1971, 1972, 1973, 1975, 1977, 1995. Used by permission.

Scripture quotations marked NIV are from HOLY BIBLE: NEW INTERNATIONAL VERSION®. © 1973, 1978, 1984 by International Bible Society. Used by permission of Zondervan Publishing House. All rights reserved.

Scripture quotations marked NLT are from *Holy Bible*, New Living Translation. © 1996. Used by permission of Tyndale House Publishers, Inc., Wheaton, Illinois 60189. All rights reserved.

Scripture quotations marked NKJV are from THE NEW KING JAMES VERSION. © 1982 by Thomas Nelson, Inc. Used by permission. All rights reserved.

The source of some of the maxims and statements quoted in this volume are not known. Readers who can document the source are asked to contact the publisher so correct attribution can be added to future printings.

Library of Congress Cataloging-in-Publication Data

Swindoll, Luci, 1932-

Simple secrets to a happy life / Luci Swindoll.
p. cm.
ISBN 978-1-4002-0353-6
1. Christian life. 2. Conduct of life. 3. Happiness--Religious aspects--Christianity. I. Title.
BV4501.3.S965 2012
248.4--dc23

2011038357

Printed in the United States of America

12 13 14 15 16 QGF 6 5 4 3 2

To my mother, Lovell Lundy Swindoll, who died forty years ago at the age of sixty-three while writing a book she never finished. In her honor, I dedicate this book to her. In the front of Mother's Bible, which she read every day, was this verse: "That our sons may be as plants grown up in their youth; that our daughters may be as corner stones, polished after the similitude of a palace" (Psalm 144:12 KJV). She prayed and believed that for both of my brothers and me.

Contents

Part Four: Living a Good Life

Part Five: Staying Connected

{ FOREWORD }

An Immersion in Matters of the Soul

If you knew Luci Swindoll, you would know that there is no way to capture her in a way that does justice to that crystalline mind of hers, her exuberance and wild spirit, her great huge tender heart. I'm not going to try, even on the occasion of *Simple Secrets to a Happy Life*, her marvelous, rich new book. But there are a few things I can share with you about her.

I have known her intimately for a dozen or so years. I adore her, and yes, that profound faith of hers is one thing I love, something that has, in her books, helped me more over the years than I can say. Yes, her hilarious sense of humor and timing are so delightful—sometimes gentle, sometimes acerbic—that they cause me to feel simultaneously blessed and jealous. There's no one kinder. And of course, she can casually recite to you one of the world's most significant poems, render it elegant and accessible at the same time, blow you away with her ability to have memorized so many of the great poems of all time, which you've just *got* to love in a person—especially if you yourself have grown to be someone who can barely remember to take your socks off before getting in the shower. Here she is, reciting "Sailing to Byzantium," or a Shakespearean sonnet, without being a show-off about it—but instead because she is a giver of light, and the poem maybe amplifies a point of faith or history that you were talking about.

Now, normally, I do not like to be around people who are quite so highly accomplished, because it makes me feel somewhat inadequate. I'm a drop-out, while here she was a cartographer for Mobil Oil, and sang opera professionally, and has read every single literary classic, and can discuss them, and make you laugh during this discussion, plus throw the lights on for you, AND on top of it all, speaks to gigantic audiences as a member of the Women of Faith, and has written a dozen books of her own, and blah blah blah. What *ev*, as the teenagers say. But I forgive Luci's accomplishments because while she's a classicist, she's also totally cool, actively cool—and I don't just mean the haircut. She's *au courant* with the great music, poetry, and issues of our time, even while rattling off Edna St. Vincent Millay. The thing is that around Luci, you're not with someone who is giving herself airs, but rather someone who is an agent for the life-giving artistic coolness of God, the way a clarinet is an agent for the Mozart concerto.

So, here's the problem: we met a dozen or so years ago, when I had lunch with the Women of Faith, and of course I fell in love with them all because, I tell you, they make a girl weak in the knees, and I wanted to follow them around for the rest of my life like a little dog, lapping up their joyful, contagious Christian wisdom. And then there was Luci. She's sturdy, maybe zaftig, stylishly white haired, beautiful as a model, a font of knowledge and faith, and yet one of life's great listeners, who made me laugh and who clearly thought I was the funniest, snappiest piece of cheese in the world.

Naturally, I thought it meant we were soul mates.

And I have felt this ever since I met her, that we have a special connection of the heart and soul, as women who love to read and laugh and write and dance and be silly, who both love to hide in their studies and travel the world, who love their friends and their solitude, more than anything on earth, except for our guy Jesus. We've become dear friends. I know I could call her from anywhere in the world and ask her for help—to wire me funds, or simply listen, to pray with me and share the exact right line of Scripture, or make me laugh about our shared humanity and occasional ridiculousness. But the soul mate thing is ever so slightly more complicated because it turns out she has this effect on *everyone*. Everyone falls in love with her. Everyone reads one of her books and wants to know this woman personally. Everyone, upon meeting her or hearing her talk onstage, feels that sweet sense of connection, where it seems that she is sharing from her plainest, deepest self, and seeing into yours, and seeing who you are, and loving that, as is, without needing to change you, or fix you, or set you straight. She's the world's soul mate. She is best friends with Jesus, so she shares from abundance, and lives from her core, of tenderness and humor and curiosity. She just wants to share her amazement and gratitude for Christ's love, and the light with which He imbues our earth and our lives.

Of course, when I first realized that she has this effect on everyone, I grew bitter. But only for a few minutes. The truth is that

I do get to have Luci as my soul mate in this life, and that a person can't be with Luci or read her work without feeling immersed in matters of the soul: our joys and sorrow; our opportunities to live big and wild and alive; our freedom; our salvation.

—Anne Lamott

Start with What You Know

It was a long time before I figured this out.

When I was a child, growing up with my two brothers (one about a year older than I and the other two years younger), our mother had a way of giving us specific instructions that enabled her to get things done and encouraged us to live a certain way. I don't believe she was aware of it at the time, but as I've become a full-fledged adult and thought back on the things she wanted us to do or ways she wanted us to be, I've come to realize that Mother spoke to us more often than not in five-word sentences, always starting with a verb. Since the verb is the part of speech that requires action (and that's what Mother wanted), that verb held the key to making her desires known, so we'd get on with it—make tracks, do our chores, think right thoughts, behave in the manner she asked of us. And note that the verb had to be imperative because Mother was expressing a command or request.

For example, as children, when the boys were quiet (too quiet, according to Mother's antenna), she would say to me in all seriousness, "Go look for the boys," and just as I would take the first step to begin my search, she'd continue over her shoulder, "Tell 'em to quit it." It didn't matter what they were doing. The very notion that they were too quiet caused Mother to believe things were amiss, and she wanted me to check it out. (More often than not, they were wrestling or, as Mother would say, "rasslin'.")

As I grew a bit older, I'd often complain to Mother that I was bored. I wanted something to do but didn't know what. Very lovingly, she'd say, "Make something with your hands," and to this day that's one of my favorite things in life—inventing handmade things. Years later, as a college student packing for school, when I wasn't sure what to take, Mother said, "Start with what you know." And I now use that as a guideline for almost every undertaking: saving money, building a house, making a decision, or writing a book.

It's strange how one can go through the major part of life and not see certain patterns that have evolved through years of simply living. Then, when we're virtually "over the hill," it hits us out of the blue. That's what happened to me a couple of years ago, and it's out of those learned patterns that I'm writing this book. I've looked back over the various decades I've lived, loved, lost, learned, languished, and laughed and have compiled fifty simple chapters, sorted into five parts, that I trust will be helpful to you. I certainly don't know all the answers to a happy life, but I can tell you for a fact that there are a few simple secrets. Once we become acquainted with those, life is a lot richer and more fun.

Every chapter title starts with an imperative verb and is five words long. It's a simple premise that I trust will be easy to read and apply in your life. I'm suggesting we start with what we know. Then, as we move along we'll finally come to the chapter on living with an attitude of gratitude, no matter our circumstances. Basically, life is what we make it: the risks we take, the people we love, the battles we survive, the joys we share, and the instructions we take to heart. As Ralph Waldo Emerson said: "Life is a series of lessons which must be lived in order to be understood."

PART ONE

Beginning with the Basics

{ ONE }

Honor Your Father and Mother

Most of us know it by heart even if we can't remember where we first heard it. It's the beginning of the fifth commandment listed in Exodus 20. You may have learned it as a child, but knowing this verse from memory and practicing it are two different things. Yet it's a basic tenet when it comes to enjoying a happy life. Interestingly, the commandment is to children, not parents, and since we are all children of parents, this verse applies to every one of us.

Initially, I interpreted the verse to mean "respect your mom and dad," but I now realize that *showing honor* to them is much weightier than *respect*. The word in the original Hebrew language meant "to be heavy, rich, honorable, and glorious," and it was most commonly used in reference to God's glory. Therefore, to give one's father and mother honor is to say that we (the children) understand the weighty responsibilities that come with parenting.

The apostle Paul repeats this commandment in Ephesians 6:2 and 3: "Honor your father and mother (which is the first commandment with a promise) so that it may be well with you, and that you may live long on the earth" (NASB). And the Greek word for *honor* here means "to show high regard for; to revere." I find that very thought provoking and have come to understand there are several reasons why this powerful instruction is one of the Ten Commandments.

First of all, this commandment upholds the principle of authority, without which we would not have a society that works. The first time a child sees authority is in the home, and if this authority is negated or neglected, the child will likely grow up to be irresponsible—and irresponsibility leads to a chaotic life and society.

Second, let's say you had very little love for your parents when you were growing up. Loving someone is not the same as giving them honor. All *honor* asks is to respect the position parents hold even if we don't like their personalities, lifestyles, or politics. It's similar to respecting the president of the United States simply because of the office he or she holds. The position itself commands honor.

And third, when there is honor on the part of the offspring, that honor will manifest itself in actions that protect, give care and goodness, exhibit generosity, and go the extra mile even though there may be no reciprocity on the part of the parent. In other words, when your parents grow older and cannot take care of themselves, you (as their child) will honor them by seeing that they are taken care of in a manner that is safe and healthy. Even if your parents are unbelievers, it's possible when you honor them in this manner that

4

a door into their hearts will open to God because of your kindness and desire to regard them highly.

I have a dear friend who is a believer. She's an only child and her mother is a reprobate in every sense of the word and a rank *un*believer. To my knowledge, she's never taken personal responsibility for her daughter, herself, or anyone else. Ever. She's currently living in a care facility. Nevertheless, my friend has not missed a moment of seeing after her mother's needs in her old age. That is honoring to her mother, even though they couldn't be further apart in their beliefs and lifestyles. The daughter cares for her mother out of obedience to God. She's created careful and wise boundaries around the care she provides, doing what her mother needs without permitting her to control the money, time, or relationship.

In so many ways, I see God's provision for them both. As my friend cares for her mother, God cares for my friend and it "goes well with her," although it can be painful and confusing at times. I believe it's very possible, through my friend's kindness, that her mother may ultimately see her need for God and invite Christ into her heart. Who's to say? God works in mysterious ways to bring us into his kingdom. Anything is possible.

{ TWO }

Be On Time for Everything

When I graduated from college in the spring of 1955, I went to work at an orphans' home, teaching water sports in the summer and art in the fall. Most of the teachers were still wet behind the ears from graduation, but we became good friends since we all lived in a nearby apartment house affiliated with the school. It was a fun time in life when each of us was just getting our moorings regarding careers and how they might play out in the future. There was always lots of input from everybody. We had the world by the tail and were ready to answer all questions when asked.

One evening Beverly, the music teacher, and I were casually chatting when she threw out an invitation for me to come to breakfast in her apartment the following Saturday. Beverly said something like, "Come to my house, and I'll make you a fancy breakfast."

Without giving it much thought, I responded, "Sure," never really intending to go—or not go. The invitation went in one ear and out the other. So on Saturday, when it wasn't all that convenient for me to actually get there for breakfast, I just stayed home. Later in the day I dropped by Beverly's place, and when she answered the door I could see she'd been crying.

"Where've you been, Luci?" she asked. She proceeded to tell me she'd prepared a gourmet recipe that morning, something she thought I would especially like, and all week she had been looking forward to our time together. When I didn't come, she wondered if I'd gotten sick or been hurt or had just forgotten about it. Embarrassed and chagrined, I apologized. Then I confessed that I remembered her invitation but simply hadn't taken it seriously. I was in the wrong. She accepted my apology and was kind in her response, but I could tell she was very hurt.

That experience taught me a huge lesson about keeping my word. I knew better than to just not show up. After all, my father had always insisted his children be prompt, courteous, and on time for everything. But for some reason, it hadn't seemed to matter that day. The thought that has really stuck with me through the years, though, was Beverly's question, "Where've you been, Luci?"

It made me realize how important it is to pay attention. It taught me to listen to what is being said and how I'm responding. If I'm not serious or paying attention, even in a casual conversation, it's not fair to the other person—who might just be inviting me to do something fun or interesting! I never want to disappoint someone again the way I disappointed Beverly, and I don't want them to wait on me, wondering, *She said she was coming . . . but is she?*

To help ensure that I'm on time for everything to which I've committed, I make it a habit to listen, to be focused in a personal conversation, to really hear another's words, to clarify when I don't understand, and to fully engage in whatever I'm doing and whoever is with me. Always. All the time.

Eventually, what started as a conscious effort has become a natural pattern and a personal habit; today it serves as a corollary secret that helps me be on time for everything. Focusing firmly on what's being said to me isn't always easy, but it's always kind.

Here's my A-list for being fully present in a conversation:

- Be sure I listen.
- Be sure I understand what's being communicated.
- Be sure I'm clear about what's involved before I commit to something.
- Be sure I can do what I say I will do.
- Be sure I show up on time!

I remember this list because it started with Beverly, a name that begins with a *B*, and that reminds me of the word *be*. That little verb carries a lot of weight. *Be* has movement in it. It means being alive, inside and out. But it's up to us as to *how* alive we want to be—how responsible, how engaged, and, ultimately, how trustworthy.

Shakespeare got it right: "To be or not to be: That is the question." One of the simple secrets of a happy life is *to be* on time for everything.

{ THREE }

Take Jesus with You Everywhere

I can hardly remember a day in my childhood when my mother wasn't somewhere in the house singing. She had a beautiful soprano voice and would spontaneously break into song. Not only would she sing, but also on occasion she'd dance down the hallway to music on the radio or grab the broom and waltz with it as her partner around the kitchen. Sometimes as she sang she would motion for one of us kids to add harmony. She knew many hymns by heart and sang them frequently and heartily as she did her chores or cooked a meal.

I well remember a favorite of hers was an old hymn called "Take the Name of Jesus with You." Mother believed every word she sang:

Take the name of Jesus with you,
Child of sorrow and of woe;
It will joy and comfort give you—
Take it, then, wher-e'er you go.

Precious name, O how sweet!
Hope of earth and joy of heav'n,
Precious name, O how sweet!
Hope of earth and joy of heav'n.

Interestingly, just writing those words forms a picture in my mind of something that happened more than sixty years ago. I can see it clearly in my head. I remember leaving for school with Mother singing that at the kitchen sink, and when I said good-bye, she looked over her shoulder and said, "Take Jesus with you today, honey."

I knew instinctively that Mother wanted to assure me Jesus would be with me regardless of what happened that day for good or bad. He would be in my thoughts and actions—with me on my walk to school, down the hallways, in my classrooms, when I talked with my friends, or answered questions from the teacher. He'd be with me on the court when I played volleyball after school or met with the swim team. And Mother wanted me to know that on my way home, Jesus would go before me, protecting me and bringing me home safely. She didn't want me to spend a minute of the day without the consciousness of his presence. Although I was walking out the door that morning, I was not alone. I was never alone.

Now that I look back over many years of living, I can tell you it's one of the best lessons Mother ever taught me. She had no idea when she casually threw that phrase over her shoulder what a valuable tool she was giving me.

Or maybe she did.

Trusting that God was with her (and with her family) seemed second nature to Mother. She was a student of his Word and rested in his faithfulness. She didn't worry, fret, or fear. She believed God and knew he could be trusted completely. She didn't just "preach" it, she lived it and sang of it with confidence. What I first saw in my mother, I came to experience on my own; I don't struggle with the sovereignty of God or his faithfulness, and I've never seen doubt in either of my brothers. How do I explain it? There may be many reasons, but certainly one is the assurance of faith in God that our mother demonstrated, both in her words and her example. She reflected the truth of Colossians 3:16 and 17:

> Let the word of Christ—the Message—have the run of the house. Give it plenty of room in your lives. Instruct and direct one another using good common sense. And sing, sing your hearts out to God! Let every detail in your lives—words, actions, whatever—be done in the name of the Master, Jesus, thanking God the Father every step of the way.

{ FOUR }

Let People Know You Care

Several months ago, Mary Graham and I were talking about kindness, having a tender spirit, and caring about other people, and I asked her to tell me the most caring individual she's ever encountered in life. Since Mary's in her sixties and has lived a long, full life of reaching out to thousands of people all over the world through Campus Crusade and now as the president of Women of Faith, I could hardly wait for her answer. After a couple of minutes she said, "I'd have to say Thidwick."

"Who?"

"*Thidwick, the Big-hearted Moose* by Dr. Seuss."

"You've gotta be kiddin' me! There's a moose named Thidwick?"

"Yes! Dr. Seuss wrote a book about him sixty years ago. I memorized it when I was a freshman in high school. It's a poem that tells the story of Thidwick letting all these little animals live in his antlers for free. There's a bug, a spider, a couple of birds, four squirrels, a bobcat, a turtle, on and on. Even a fox, a big bear, and a whole swarm of bees. Thidwick had such a big heart he couldn't say no, so everybody moved in and took over. I've quoted that poem to all my nieces and nephews through the years as I babysat them because it has such a good moral—although in the end, Thidwick took the concept a little too far."

I loved the fact Mary knew that book and answered my question with a moose. (Never look a gift-moose in the mouth!) Being generous, softhearted, and sweet to others is almost a lost art in today's world. Even though there are lots of Scriptures that make reference to caring, it takes time to care, and few people want to give that kind of time. Matthew 5:7 says, "You're blessed when you care." And in 1 Corinthians 13 we're reminded, "Love cares more for others than for self."

But the story of Thidwick teaches another truth about caring that might be more important and leads to an even happier life. It's learning how to say no to those who want to take advantage of us when we care. The bevy of animals living in Thidwick's antlers wanted too much. They called the shots, told him where to go and what to do, and invited more "guests" to live with them.

Some of us are like that. We move in and invite others to come along. Or we allow others to move in and invite guests.

Where's the balance between caring and being careful? Where's the boundary line? As caring people, when we let others run over us and take advantage of us, we're in a pickle before we know it. That's what happened to Thidwick:

> *You couldn't say "Skat!" 'cause that wouldn't be right.*
> *You couldn't shout "Scram!" 'cause that isn't polite.*

So when should a boundary line be drawn? When the degree of caring negatively affects our quality of life and inadvertently invites carelessness on the part of the other person. Dr. Seuss himself once said, "Unless someone like you cares a whole awful lot, nothing is going to get better."

That's true, but as he beautifully illustrated in the life of Thidwick, balance is required. In order to do the two simultaneously (and it *can* be done), we need to turn the whole ball of wax over to God, who gives us balance. For guidance, look to the promise in Psalm 91:14–15: "I'll give you the best of care if you'll only get to know and trust me. Call me and I'll answer, be at your side in bad times; I'll rescue you, then throw you a party."

As Christians, we're to show kindness to others and care for them. But while God's Word teaches us to put others' needs before our own, it also reminds us to care for ourselves as well—as his cherished children whom he created with love. That means striking a balance as we care—with caution.

{ FIVE }

Learn to Organize Your Stuff

If your stuff isn't organized, it has the potential to drive you crazy. For me, I simply can't concentrate when things are out of whack: my files are a mess, my closet's in chaos, or dirty dishes wait in the sink. I may try to ignore out-of-place things, but they're so distracting. All I can think about is straightening things up. Call me crazy, but it's the truth. People often ask how I manage to keep "order in my court." If you're one of those people, here are half a dozen ideas that might help:

1. Decide what you want organized and find time to do it.
  Take time to figure out what's important to keep—and what can be stored or given away. Start there. Don't rush.

Look through what you've treasured all these years and make sure it's still important in your life. Even if this chore takes weeks or months to finish, it'll be worth the effort. If you decide to keep it, find a place for it right there and then. Don't put it off.

2. *Make lists and follow them carefully, marking off what gets done.*

Lists keep you on track and your sanity intact in this chaotic world. Write down where you put things, what you want to keep, and what means something to you. You can store the list in your iPhone or BlackBerry, but write it down somewhere. In a busy life, how do we remember things without lists?

3. *Clean up smaller areas first to give yourself a sense of accomplishment.*

This is by far one of my favorite ways to organize, and even more so as I get older. Here's why: little by little it all gets done. And what doesn't get done probably wasn't that important anyway. When we look too far ahead, it's discouraging. So work awhile and then stop and savor your small accomplishment.

4. *Create a place for specific things and return them there after using them.*

Let's say your jewelry drawer is a mess. Buy plastic boxes with compartments and separate the gold from the silver or handmade from machine made or sort any other way that makes sense to you. Put your jewelry in those boxes, and put the boxes back in the drawer. When you wear a pair of earrings, put them back where they go when you take them off. The same goes for books, CDs, photographs, letters—whatever. If it's important to you, give it a spot to call its own.

5. *Forgive yourself for days you're not organized, but don't get used to that state.*

Since you're a human being in a broken world, you're not going to be organized every day of your life. Give yourself grace. It's like riding a bicycle. Even if you fall off, you never think, *Well, this just doesn't work for me. I'll never try it again.* You get back on track, knowing it's all part of the process. Keep going, and in time, you'll fall less and less.

Here's the point: if we get low and stay there, we'll never get organized because the fun of accomplishment will get buried under the burden of procrastination or depression.

6. *Celebrate and rejoice over the messes you've straightened up.*

I'm a big fan of having fun as I go along in life. Without parties or shouting or dancing or visiting or laughing now and then, life is too hard. After cleaning up a mess, invite friends or family over to see what you've done. Take pictures of "before" and "after" and stick them in your journal, your Bible, or on the mirror. Cleaning up something is a huge reason to throw a party. When I have a big project to organize, I put on great music and whistle or dance while I work.

Here's the biblical encouragement to being organized: "Be sure that everything is done properly and in order" (1 Corinthians 14:40 NLT). Not only that, but the Bible even specifies paying taxes as a step toward living an organized life. Look at Romans 13:5–6, which says, "You must live responsibly—not just to avoid punishment but also because it's the right way to live. That's also why you pay taxes—so that an orderly way of life can be maintained."

{ SIX }

Keep Your Word Every Time

Keeping your word every time depends upon the amount of integrity you have within yourself—and integrity is a two-sided coin: one side reflects the respect you have toward another individual, and the other side shows how much you respect yourself. The two sides are reflected in Jesus's words in Luke 6:31: "Do to others as you would have them do to you" (NIV).

Keeping your word means you're going to do what you say you'll do. And isn't that what we want of others too? If a friend or business contact promises to do something, we want him or her to keep that promise.

The importance of being a woman of my word was confirmed for me when, after I had worked for twenty years as a draftsman-artist with Mobil Oil Corporation (long before it became Exxon Mobil), I was promoted to an executive position as manager of rights of way and claims for their West Coast pipeline division. While I was honored and thrilled about this offer, I have to admit I also was scared to death of what a job of that magnitude would entail.

Could I do it? Did I have the brains to run a division? Was I qualified enough to make decisions that would affect the entire company, not just my own standards?

I knew I was a good employee because there's no way I could have been given that opportunity had I not demonstrated years of punctuality and dedication. But an executive? That was a whole new ballgame.

As I was contemplating Mobil's offer, I decided to phone my friend Martha, a public relations professional, and ask her opinion of my taking the new job. Martha was a seasoned Mobil employee whose life showed a great deal of integrity. I trusted her judgment and knew she'd give me an honest response.

She listened as I laid out the situation, and then she enthusiastically encouraged me to take the job. "It's right up your alley," she said. "You enjoy people, you're a hard worker, you're not afraid of change, you love a challenge, and you'll be the first woman in a management position in that division. Do it!" Then she added this clincher: "Just remember two things: don't be afraid to ask questions, and never sign anything until you're sure."

I've never been shy about asking questions, so that was a no-brainer. It was the second part of Martha's advice that resonated within me: *never sign anything until you're sure.* She was reminding me that when I signed something, I would be giving my word. I would be saying, "Yes, I will do this." Or in this case, "I will see that my company does this." I needed to be sure I understood what I was promising so that I made good on that promise every time.

It all sounded a lot like my own philosophy that I'd lived by all my adult life: "Say what you mean and *do* what you say."

Putting all those thoughts together, I felt a surge of confidence, knowing *I can do this job.*

And I did. That job opened a whole new world to me, both in my work life and in my personal life. I loved it! But whenever a contract or agreement was to be finalized, I made sure I understood everything involved because I was giving my word, and I wanted to keep my word every time.

Even today, long retired, I am very cautious before I sign a document of any sort. I read it thoroughly and determine if I fully understand and trust it before I sign my name. After all, it's my name that gives credence to the agreement. If I sign it, that means I will keep my word.

You won't be surprised to read the source of this simple but powerful secret. It's right there in Psalm 15:5: "Keep your word even when it costs you, make an honest living, never take a bribe. You'll never get blacklisted if you live like this."

{ SEVEN }

Make Something with Your Hands

If I remember correctly, it started in the sixth grade. For Christmas that year, I got a set of Lincoln Logs, one of the best gifts I've ever received. From those logs I built bridges, buildings, and roadways. I was in heaven!

Seeing my dedication to Lincoln Logs, my family and friends gave me paint sets, model airplanes and ships, Legos, scrapbooks, and reams of paper I could make into kites or use for drawing. Making something with my hands was a fascinating way to grow up. And I still feel that way today—sixty-eight years after my first set of Lincoln Logs.

What is it about handmade things that gives me such a thrill?

First, I love the sense of accomplishment, and nothing provides that satisfaction like making something with my hands.

Second, it's a challenge. I want to see if I can do it.

Third, I enjoy figuring things out . . . feeling the thrill of knowing how parts come together to move or squeak or react.

Would you believe that a few years ago, three different friends gave me the *same* book for my birthday: *The Way Things Work* by David Macaulay? I've read it from cover to cover and *love* that book. (And for Christmas that same year, I was given two copies of *The Way Things Really Work*.)

I'd give anything to take off a whole year and do nothing but make gifts so that every time I handed a friend or family member a present, it'd be one I'd made. Oh, gosh! I'd love that. Maybe that idea comes from an incident many years ago when I gave my friend Ruth a birthday present and the moment she received it, she said very sincerely, "Did you make this, Luci?"

I replied, "What if I didn't?"

With all the seriousness in the world, and knowing full well I hadn't made it, she said, "I'll give you another chance."

My mother taught me to make things, and she was a fabulous teacher: artistic, thorough, fun, and extremely creative. Mother had a reputation for making everything. I was standing by her in church one Sunday when a woman next to her told Mother how much she loved the perfume she was wearing. "I'll bet you made it, didn't you?"

Our family got a good laugh out of that, not only because it was such a telling question but because there was enough truth to it that Mother *could* have made it, had she set her mind to it.

And my father was a fabulous builder of things and teacher as well: patient, experimental, clever, and encouraging. He'd draw cartoons on a little pad and then would ask me to draw one. He lettered beautifully and taught me how to do it before I ever entered the first grade. To this day, I print notes all the time rather than write them in cursive.

My dad also gave me my first little toolbox—to match his big one. Again, I was in heaven. Together, Daddy and I repaired clocks, toilets, garage doors, skates, and various gadgets around the house.

In 1983 the very first message I gave publicly as a professional was about a young man who (with a friend) made something with his hands in his parents' garage. That man was the late Steve Jobs, and that something was the first Apple computer. Look where that design took him.

And what about God? Look at what *he* made by hand: everything! And he's the ultimate teacher. His creativity is limitless. Isaiah 48:13 tells us, "Earth is my work, handmade. And the skies—I made them, too, horizon to horizon. When I speak, they're on their feet, at attention."

We have no way of knowing what God has in store for us if we simply use our hands to plant ideas and dreams and then watch them take root.

{ EIGHT }

Do All Your Homework First

Did you know there's actually a website called Cramster.com? At this site you can insert any question about your homework and it'll give you the answer. Honestly!

You might be thinking, *I wish I'd known that a long time ago when I was . . .* Not I. Even as a child in school, there would've been no temptation for me to bypass homework. I loved it. I'm not kidding. I had a passion to learn, research, read, write, and study. It was in my DNA. I'd start the minute I got home from school and not move until it was completely finished.

While I loved learning, then and now, my enjoyment of homework was more than that. As a child, I was primarily motivated just

{ NINE }

Treat Other People
with Kindness

A number of years ago I was standing out in front of the car wash in my neighborhood in California, idly watching traffic in the thoroughfare while waiting for my car to be serviced, wiped down, and detailed, when a beat-up, dirty old SUV pulled into the driveway, driven by a guy who hadn't shaved in weeks, hadn't had a haircut in months, and was totally unkempt in every sense of the word. In the backseats of his Land Rover were five kids, all looking pretty much like the driver (only without beards). There were three boys and two girls ranging in ages from about four to ten or eleven. It's hard to see that many children (especially with a man) and not have your attention completely captured.

When the SUV stopped, the driver got out and walked around behind it, opened the back and began taking the kids out of the car one by one. I carefully watched this whole procedure and was utterly amazed at this guy and his children. Every one of them called him "Daddy," and I never in my life saw a person kinder than he. He cuddled the little ones as they laughed and kissed him on the cheek. And the older children teased and giggled and were exceedingly obedient. I stood there enchanted by their interaction. It melted my heart, and my first thought was, *Don't judge a book by its cover, Luci*—a lesson I'd learned from my father as a child.

After a bit, when all the children were out of the car, they sat by one another on a long bench, with each of them wanting "the best seat" next to their dad. The SUV had moved into the car-wash area by this time, and while the family waited, they all began to sing a little ditty they'd memorized. Never once did the father raise his hand or his voice. He was so gentle with those kids, yet he kept them in line by being totally present and engaged with each child. And his engagement overflowed to their interaction with one another. They were what we used to call a happy family.

I'll never forget that scene. It captured a place in my heart forever. I was mesmerized by how the dad treated those kids. And his kindness to them must have been contagious because they were so thoughtful and sweet to each other. When do you see that kind of behavior in public?

My favorite attribute in people is kindness. It melts me every time, and I do find it contagious. I like seeing it more than humility, compassion, forgiveness, self-control, or even (spare me if this is your favorite) love. While I recognize all these characteristics come from God and I'm everlastingly grateful they're ours by virtue of a relationship with Christ, kindness still wins my heart, hands down!

Kindness embodies so many of those other attributes because it's a compilation that's experienced (and seen) in one's attitude toward other people. It's a package deal.

God is kindness personified. In 1 Peter 2:3, we're invited to "drink deep of God's pure kindness. Then you'll grow up mature and whole in God." That's quite a statement. What Christian doesn't want to be "mature and whole in God"? We get that way by seeing and recognizing God's kindness to us and then passing it on.

Remembering that little family at the car wash makes me think of another verse, Ephesians 4:32: "Be kind and compassionate to one another, forgiving each other, just as in Christ God forgave you" (NIV). Watching those kids and their dad show kindness to one another was a great incentive for me to be kind to everybody I meet—and I still am reminded of that incentive by the memory. Kindness is a gift to receive and a joy to give.

{ TEN }

Read Your Bible
Every Day

Aristotle once wrote, "Good habits formed at youth make all the difference." But what if we start good habits once we're past youth? Will they still make a difference?

I think they will. It's never too late to start a good habit. Take Bible reading, for example. Reading your Bible every day is a bit like reading a weight scale. Most of us have bathroom scales in our home, so we're familiar with the process of weighing ourselves. There are two things we need in order to weigh: a private place and a scale. How simple is that?

And if we mean business, we follow certain guidelines. For instance, we might:

- Weigh at the same time every day.
- Remove our clothing and shoes.
- Step on the scale.
- Focus on the process without getting hung up on the weight.

In the same way, we need two things to get started with daily Bible reading: a private place and a Bible. And if we mean business, we may follow certain guidelines. For instance, we might:

- Read at the same time every day.
- Set aside the things in our lives that would distract.
- Open the Bible.
- Focus on reading the words without getting hung up on what weighs us down.

This simple system motivates us while helping us avoid discouragement that can come when we get bogged down. Reading God's Word takes time, but if we keep in mind that it's much like weighing ourselves every day, the discipline of it makes it achievable. Without having a program or a plan, it's easy to let Bible reading get lost in the shuffle of our busy days. And ultimately our spiritual health suffers as a result.

Someone once asked a great Shakespearean scholar, "How do you study Shakespeare?"

His response was very clear: "*Read* Shakespeare."

Studying the Bible is the same. You read it, and as you read, you become acquainted with its precepts, promises, power, and the Person of God the Father, his Son, and the Holy Spirit.

The Bible is the bedrock of truth, and in it are the words of life, so there are understandable reasons to read it daily. I hardly remember a day in my growing-up years when I didn't see my mother reading her Bible. Sitting in her bed, on the sofa, at the dining table, or on the front porch, she'd have her Bible open, reading it every single day. Rare were the times she told *me* to read it. But by modeling Bible reading, the message was perhaps stronger. It's a vivid picture in my mind.

Mother often copied verses on three-by-five cards and tucked them here and there around the house where she could see them and meditate on them throughout the day. She didn't want to miss what God said to her and what he wanted to do in her life. Those verses were both life giving and life changing. Nothing influenced the life of my siblings and me more than our mother's consistency in reading the Word of God.

I now have—and treasure—the Bible Mother loved and read daily until she died in 1971. It's filled with her markings and notes, and it's held together by tape. Right in front, in Mother's inimitable handwriting, are these words, written along with the verse I've quoted in this book's dedication. I don't know if they're her words or if they're something she heard and loved in her Bible class: "The Word of God reveals the righteousness of God and the sinfulness of man. It reveals the plan of God about salvation to unbelievers and the way of life for believers in any age."

Because Mother believed and lived out that truth on a consistent basis, she made me want to read the Bible daily as well. Frankly, I like it much better than stepping on those scales every morning.

{ ELEVEN }

Draw a Picture to Understand

Years ago, I had an art teacher who loved birds. She drew them every chance she got. During the time she was my professor, she found a dead duck and took it home to study. She especially wanted to know how the wings worked and made drawing after drawing as she tried to figure it out. She looked at all of the feathers under a blow dryer, studying how they might move in flight.

Don't you love that? She wanted to understand ducks, to satisfy her curiosity.

The key word in this secret is *understand*. Of course, in today's world with so many electronic gadgets, you may think you don't need to put pencil to paper and literally draw something to understand it.

But I believe making a drawing, even a rudimentary one, can help you get a more detailed picture of what you see. And you don't have to be a great artist.

This secret was reinforced for me in May 1999, when three friends and I went to Africa on safari. We each took a small walkie-talkie so we could talk about what we were seeing without yelling when we ended up in different groups. I wanted to make sure I would be able to use it easily and quickly, so I made a drawing in my travel journal with all the parts labeled: talk button, monitor control, microphone, on/off switch, volume control, antenna—the whole nine yards. Having done that, I became familiar with the device and comfortable using it at the drop of a hat. Because I understood how to work it, when two of my travel companions were on a "walking safari," the other two of us could enjoy their excited reports every ten or fifteen minutes, keeping us up-to-date on what was happening: "Baby giraffe, twelve o'clock," or "We're looking straight into the eyes of a bush buck," or "We're lying on the ground to avoid a swarm of bees."

Seeing the drawing of the walkie-talkie in my journal helps me even now, letting me enjoy that sweet memory to this day.

And then, there was the time I had an inner ear infection. In my desire to understand exactly what was going on in my sore ear (after the doctor had explained it to me), I looked it up in a medical book and made a drawing of it in my journal. Several years later, when I had the same kind of infection, I went to an ear-nose-throat doctor, who confirmed that I had correctly diagnosed my own problem because of that earlier drawing.

Actually, to draw is part of being me. I'm not the artist I'd like to be, but being able to sketch helps me understand various things in life that interest me. Not only do I draw to understand, but also for my own pleasure. It's my style.

During the early 1970s I spent many summer vacations in Greece with my friend Sophia, who lived in Athens. One year, instead of going to a Greek island, as we had done before, she suggested we go to Arachova, a little town on the mountainside of Parnassus that is famous for its beautiful woven items. Since I was doing a lot of weaving back then, I loved the idea. We rented a Volkswagen and started out. On the way, Sophia thought it'd be fun to ride donkeys up Mount Parnassus, just to see everything from another perspective. When we came to a place called Donkey Stop, we left the car there and each got on a donkey.

With a ballpoint pen, I drew on the leg of my blue jeans as we rode along, noting a little car, the donkey stop, various trees, and a stream we crossed. When we stopped to look at the scenery— houses picturesquely spilling down the mountainside—and take a few photos, we decided to have a little picnic right there. It was fun . . . until we got ready to leave and realized we were completely turned around and didn't know which way to go! Fortunately, by consulting my "leg map" we could look for a stream (the one we had crossed getting there) and then the trees and then the donkey stop and the little car, and we managed to retrace our steps back to our beginning spot, laughing all the way.

Drawing pictures not only satisfies my curiosity, it also helps me understand the things I use, the places I go—and the adventures (and sometimes the misadventures) I enjoy. Try it, and you'll see what I mean.

{ TWELVE }

Accept Events As They Happen

I don't panic. Ever. I'm exceedingly calm in a storm and have been that way all my life. I'm like my father. My mother was "a balloon on a string," but Daddy? Cool as a cucumber. Really.

It was amazing to watch. One of my oldest memories occurred when I was about seven and we lived in Fort Worth. Someone in the house (I say it was one of my brothers; they say it was me) had accidentally left the water running in the bathtub with the stopper in it and then joined the family to go visit our cousins. When we got home, water was all over the house. Mother was sick at heart and could hardly believe her eyes. She went into the kitchen and cried, but my brothers and I thought it was one of the coolest things we'd ever witnessed. Daddy, calm as could be, assigned us various rooms to mop up, and within an hour, we had moved furniture, dried the floor, wrung out a dozen soaked towels, and sat down to steaming cups of hot chocolate Mother had made for us while wading around in the kitchen. It was an adventure.

Like Daddy, I'm calm in emergencies. But don't talk to me about interruptions! Or delays. I hate those and could write a book about why they drive me nuts. Delayed flights, long waits at the doctor's office, and s-l-o-w drivers in the fast lane challenge me. I have to remind myself to breathe.

Accepting events as they happen—good or bad, hard or easy, horrific tragedies or mere inconveniences, our fault or not—is often very difficult to do. It requires the ability to get outside ourselves, look at the big picture, and rely on the sovereignty of God. In his second letter to his friend Timothy, the apostle Paul gave Timothy (and us) guidelines on how to do just that: "But you—keep your eye on what you're doing; accept the hard times along with the good; keep the Message alive; do a thorough job as God's servant" (2 Timothy 4:5).

Not long ago, a Florida friend and I decided that would be "our verse" for the year. We found it at the same time in our Bible reading, loved it, and chose it as a great verse for our lives. To me, the most difficult part of it is accepting the hard times along with the good because I know that, for me, "hard times" include interruptions and delays. If it's just inconveniences, I can manage, but to be detained . . . that's another story.

But I finally figured this out: to "accept the hard times along with the good," I need to apply the context of the rest of the verse. In order to "accept" I have to:

- Keep my eye on what I'm doing (no matter what).
- Keep God's Word alive in my heart and behavior.
- Keep being God's servant to other people.

When I do that and stay at it, I have a much easier time accepting events as they happen.

I had occasion to put that reasoning to the test recently when a friend called me while I was knee deep in writing. I desperately wanted to get on paper what I was thinking for the next paragraph before I forgot it, so I had little or no interest in listening.

I could feel myself losing patience, when all of a sudden "my verse" hit me. Under my breath, I asked the Lord to calm my spirit, to help me listen carefully to what was being said, and to remember I was here to serve my friend, not to finish my paragraph.

Meanwhile, he went on and on about the burdens he was facing and how sad they made him feel.

I listened.

Then, after a bit, he told me how much it helped him just to talk about what he was going through and how much he appreciated my time. His circumstance hadn't changed, but his spirit had.

When I hung up, I finished writing the paragraph and found myself feeling glad my friend had called and grateful that I was able to help him. Then I again stopped writing and thanked God for that verse and that reminder.

{ THIRTEEN }

Stay Proactive About Your Health

It's been said that the human body, with proper care, will last a lifetime. Makes one wonder what constitutes "proper care." I think of the body as a home. It's your home because you live in it. Because you live in it, you want to protect it from intruders. It's an important investment and provides you shelter. Consider this:

- Your bones are the two-by-fours that support the structure.
- Your frame of mind is what gives you joy and peace.
- Your eyes are the windows; your lungs provide ventilation.
- Your heart is the water main, and your brain is the food processor.

· Your hair is the lawn, and your weight is more often than not that stuff in the attic you want to get rid of. The better you know things about your home, the easier it is to maintain it, decorate it, and enjoy it.

Using that analogy, let's look at your body as something that needs, from time to time, the same maintenance and repairs as your home. If your toilet won't stop running, for example, you don't call a plumber first thing. No, you take the top off the tank and fool around with the floating ball until the problem corrects itself. If a lightbulb burns out, you don't call an electrician. Nor do you call the pest-control guy when a fly lands on your kitchen counter. You rely on yourself to maintain control over simple issues that need attention. In short, you are proactive about what has to be done.

Our goal in life should be to maintain our bodies in such a way that we avoid things that cause the most wear and tear and seek things that provide the most value. But do we do that? Realistically, I don't think so. But I have found, in my seven decades of living, that the best health care is moderation. We ourselves can control a lot when it comes to the maintenance of our own bodies. And in many ways, that maintenance controls the destiny of our health.

I'm no expert on this topic, although I've almost always enjoyed amazingly good health. And because I've studied art all my life, I've had a keen fascination with the human body. It is nothing short of miraculous, a dynamic reflection of the genius of our Creator.

A couple years ago I bought a book that has helped me enormously with this whole subject. It's *YOU: The Owner's Manual* by Michael F. Roizen and Mehmet C. Oz. It's a guide to feeling healthier and younger. Initially I bought it because I loved the title and the very clear, clever, descriptive drawings and lettering throughout. But as I began to read it, I found it had the answers to many of the questions I was asking about how my body works.

However, there's an even better book that teaches us to be proactive about good health. It's the Bible. Look at the apostle Paul's words in Colossians 2:19: "The source of life, Christ, who puts us together in one piece, whose very breath and blood flow through us. He is the Head and we are the body. We can grow up healthy in God only as he nourishes us."

Last week I was in the doctor's office for my annual physical, and I overheard an elderly woman say to the desk person as she was leaving, "Good health doesn't just take care of itself, and it's most often lost by those of us who assume it will." She's right! The better our health, the more energy we have to enjoy life to the fullest.

{ FOURTEEN }

Value the Things You Have

When I was nine, my parents bought me a bicycle. I had no idea how to ride it, but that didn't stop me from climbing on and heading out. Somehow, I expected the bike to automatically do what I wanted it to. I assumed it would "mind me." (After all, my other toys seemed to.)

Of course, it didn't. I spent a lot of time falling, getting up, crying, and throwing it against a tree in the front yard. The girl next door also had a bike, and she could ride like a house afire. That's what I wanted to do. We kept telling each other we'd race one day, but how could I do that if I couldn't even stay up on the thing? It never occurred to me to ask for help in learning to ride the bicycle.

I was much too independent (or maybe stubborn?) for that. So I tossed the bike aside and tried to ignore it. It was of no value to me.

One evening I overheard my parents talking about the money they had spent on my bike. They weren't complaining; they were just trying to figure out how to help me enjoy their investment. It made me feel awful. My dad had carefully looked through the Sears and Roebuck Catalog to choose just the perfect bicycle for me: right weight, correct height, perfect wheel balance, name-brand company.

After eavesdropping on their conversation, I went into the room where Mother and Daddy were talking and told them how bad I felt about throwing my bike against the tree.

Ever the encourager, my dad said something like, "We understand, honey. We know you want to ride, and your bike just won't behave long enough for you to stay on it. Let me show you all the things that make this bike a wonderful machine. Maybe it'll help you figure it out."

Then he opened the catalog to the section on bicycles. He pointed out the one they had bought me and talked about all its features that help people become good bike riders.

Once I saw what went into that little two-wheeled beauty, my whole attitude changed—toward it and toward the skill of riding. I respected the bicycle and wanted to learn how to ride. The next morning, I went to the garage and apologized to the bike for throwing it around. I know this sounds a little strange to those of you who don't have a history of talking to inanimate objects, but that's what I did. I talked to my bike and told it that I now realized what a good bike it was, and I promised to be nicer to it in the future. If my daddy believed in it, and if he chose it especially for me, I wanted to believe in it too.

In his typical way, my father, full of kindness, had helped me appreciate the value of his and Mother's purchase. Somehow, his high regard for its quality made me want to appreciate the bike's impressive features too. With my dad's encouragement and my new attitude—a new determination—I quickly learned to ride the bicycle. From that day forward, it was a trusted companion and dependable mode of childhood transportation for me.

Since the bicycle, I've been cautious about what I've bought, and I've treated my possessions with great care. My home is filled with things I've purchased and gifts I've been given through the years. Some of them are almost as old as I am. I take great delight in being surrounded with stuff that has meaning for me. My friends tease me, but it seems like even the pots and pans have their own story.

Of course, valuing the things we're blessed to own and living for our possessions are two separate things. They are, after all, only *things*, and we don't want them to distract us from what's really important: living a life that's pleasing to God. Instead, as we enjoy and value the things we own, we need to simultaneously value the life God has given us, thanking him for gifts of friends and experiences.

Looking at my possessions brings back memories of yesteryear, of friends of long ago, of places I've visited on God's beautiful earth. These are the treasures in my house that reflect who I am. Without ever speaking, they tell the story of my life.

FIFTEEN

Focus on What's Important *Now*

I woke up this morning, sneezing. Don't you hate it when that happens? Today had been set aside to write, and it's hard to concentrate when I have a cold. All morning I blew my nose, coughed, sneezed, and talked in the bass cleft. I felt lethargic, and the further I went into the day, the more lethargic I got. My phone rang, and when I answered, my neighbor said, "You don't sound like yourself."

"Oh, really?" I croaked. "I'm doing well to answer the phone, much less breathe. I think I have a cold."

She was very sympathetic and asked if she could take me to the doctor. That was the last thing I wanted to do. I shot back, "I don't have time for the doctor. I'm not going. I know this is just a little cold, and it'll pass."

"What's more important today than your health, Luci?" she asked.

When I told her I needed to work on chapter 15, she asked me the topic. I was hesitant to tell her it was "focus on what's important *now*," but when I did, she said, "Well, duh! Isn't your cold a perfect example of what you're writing? If you don't focus on getting rid of that cold, I'm afraid you're going to feel worse, and you won't be able to write at all this week. Think about it."

I did, and as I was thinking, I happened to remember back to my topic in chapter 13: "Stay Proactive About Your Health."

I decided to follow my friend's suggestion and go to the doctor. In fact, she drove me. Turns out I had a bronchial, upper respiratory infection that required a steroid shot and antibiotics to treat. My chest had a bit of congestion, and the doctor told me if I had put off treatment, I probably would have been very sick in a few days.

My neighbor had helped me focus on what was most important in that moment, and I was better off for her intervention.

It goes without saying that *God* is of utmost importance in my life 24/7. My faith underlies every breath I take. But given that foundation, I need to keep my earthly priorities properly aligned and at any moment focus on what is most important *now* in order to live the fulfilling, rewarding life I believe God wants his children to enjoy.

This morning, writing was a priority for me, but as the hours passed and health declined, something else became more important. Yet I was slow to acknowledge it until my friend called and made the obvious, well, obvious: I was sick and needed to go to the doctor to keep from getting sicker.

What is it that makes us put off doing something we know we need to do? For some reason, it often seems easier to think about other things rather than to focus on what's the most important thing *now*. Maybe that's because a most important thing can feel too needy and way too demanding in the present moment.

Focusing on what's important now means to live consciously. It means recognizing what's most important in this moment and not wanting to be anywhere else or do anything else with anybody else. I read once that when we "let go of wanting something else to happen in this moment, we take a profound step toward being able to encounter what is here now." Living consciously means we're simply mindful of focusing on this very moment in time, gratefully acknowledging the fact that we have it and are alive in it, and focusing on what is most important for *now*.

This morning I needed to drop the preconceived plan I had made—writing—and take care of the need at hand—my health. The whole thing boiled down to trusting God with and for this very moment and what was most important in it.

Being mindful of that relationship motivates us to face the important things in our lives with confidence, knowing God is in control. We may not understand what is happening or why, but we can have a trusting heart that God is in charge. And if we live from that center of focus, we will be consciously present every second of the day and mindful of what is important.

I'm reminded of the passage in Psalm 31:15 that says, "My times are in Your hand" (NKJV). As is so often the case, I'm asking the Lord to keep my eyes and heart open to whatever he wants me to do, moment by moment, trusting him to guide me in recognizing what is most important.

{ **SIXTEEN** }

Decide What Is Not Necessary

After I moved into my current house in Texas, it took me three years to get around to cleaning out my closet, the big one that's just off the master bathroom with all my clothes in it. Crowded, unsightly, and embarrassingly messy, that closet lowered my spirit every time I went in there. Being a neatnik, I kept asking myself why I was waiting so long to clean it up. It finally hit me that I didn't do it because I didn't know what to keep and what not to keep. I couldn't figure out where to start. There were times I even thought about blasting that closet off the end of the house so I wouldn't have to look at it anymore.

One vulnerable day, fortified by a pot of coffee and empowering

Scriptures like "With God all things are possible" (Matthew 19:26 NKJV), I decided to take matters in hand.

I started by laying out three little governing rules.

First: clean the closet in geographical sections, first the NE corner, then the NW corner to the SE corner, so I wouldn't be overwhelmed right off the bat with the magnitude of the mess. Little by little, I followed that course. Working steadily but not hurriedly, I covered the entire closet in sections, and as I saw progress along the way, it strengthened my determination to keep going. Some days I'd spend a couple of hours and then stop until I had more energy; other days I'd work four or five hours. When I was sick of looking at piles of stuff, I just didn't go in there.

Second: any personal or family one-of-a-kind thing is an automatic keeper. This rule let me celebrate along the way when I found treasures that had been tucked away and forgotten. Oh, my gosh, the treasures! In two old cedar chests there were letters I had won in high school back in the forties for basketball, swimming, volleyball, and modern dance. I ran across ticket stubs from my performances with the Dallas Opera in the fifties and sixties, which brought back many wonderful memories. There were notes and letters in my father's handwriting from the seventies, written after my mother's death. I found old photographs from foreign trips I'd taken in the eighties, bunched together with original artwork from friends given to me at my retirement party in 1987. I tried on clothes (some of which I'd bought in the nineties), chose what I wanted to keep, and put the rest in bags to give away. (I won't even mention the old, full laundry bag I ran across that I'd misplaced about six months earlier—but, interestingly enough, not missed.)

Third: on the spot, determine what's necessary and not necessary to keep. By having this rule to go by, I didn't wind up with things I really didn't want, and I didn't put off making decisions I needed to make.

The unnecessary stuff was given to Goodwill, passed on to one of my brothers (if either of them wanted it), or tossed in the trash. In a few days, the closet was straight, clean, and organized. For months after that, when I went in my closet I'd do a 360-degree turn and stare. Seeing my orderly belongings pleased my heart and lifted my spirit.

I finally figured out the real reason I couldn't clean out that closet earlier: I was concentrating on what was *not* necessary, and I really didn't know what that was until I dug into all those stacks. Once I looked carefully at the things in my closet, the things I had loved and treasured through the years were easily separated from the items with no meaning.

We can decide what is *not* necessary to keep by simply making up our minds about what *is*. Nothing in life is more important than knowing what is essential, unless it's knowing what isn't.

{ SEVENTEEN }

Write Down the Important Things

When I think back on my childhood, I don't remember anybody ever telling me to "write that down." Nevertheless, something in me always wanted to take notes. To this day, I go around with a pen in my pocket or a pencil in my hand so I can write down appointments, commitments, lists, whatever. You may prefer to make note of the important things in your life on your smartphone, computer, iPad, or I don't know what else!

I write down lists of books I want to read, music I want to hear, movies I intend to see. The truth is, I often write down not only what I plan to do but also what I'm actually doing . . . or what I did. My pals may think it's weird (except when they call me because they've forgotten some detail of their own lives they're hoping I've jotted down somewhere).

I come from a long line of letter writers, note takers, jotters, journal keepers, authors, and poets. My grandmother used to write poems on the back of used envelopes, and I never got a post-card from her that didn't have a message in its proper spot as well as all around the edges in a circle where the words got smaller and smaller as they neared the end of her greeting. I still have a note Grandmother wrote to her children when they were little that read, "Gone next door to borrow an egg." I love that note because it was my grandmother to a T. Letting her family know where she was, and for what reason, was important to her—even to the point of leaving them a note that she's out of the house borrowing an egg.

I'm one who writes dates on almost everything I own. When I finish reading a book, I print the date of completion and sign my name on the last page. When I pay a bill, I stamp the invoice PAID, date it, and write the check number on it with my initials at the bottom. I've done it for years. I have a collection of jour-nals that cover the past twenty-five years, literally crammed with words describing my whereabouts, feelings, concerns, names, addresses, maps, directions, finances, and drawings. All this is important to me. That's why I write it down. It's second nature.

One of the primary reasons to write something down is because we're apt to forget it. And the older we get, the more apt we become. If I tell somebody I'll call him or her and then can't remember his or her phone number, it bothers me; so I write it down. When I go to the grocery store and forget why I went, that bothers me; so I write down a grocery list. If I promise somebody dinner at my house on a particular night and later have no idea when that night is because I didn't make a note of it, that bothers me; so I write it down. You get the picture. I write down what I might forget, which could be just about everything.

I've also written down my basic beliefs: I call it a credo. It's the twelve most important things in my life, out of which flows my value system. Anything that defines me is important for me to know, and I love seeing it in print. Every five or six years I read it again . . . just to see if my life is still making sense to me. It's similar to the mission statements many businesses, churches, and families draw up so that everyone in that group knows and understands the values that guide their activities and purpose.

And what about goals? I firmly believe I was able to take early retirement from business in great part because I wrote down that goal three years before it ever came to fruition. And personal goals? Financial? Travel? Physical? Each of these is very important when it comes to growth. With my goals written down, I have something to aim toward. They help me organize my time, thoughts, schedule, belongings—my life.

The most important thing for me to remember is the nature and nurture of God. I don't know where I'd be had I not written down notes from various Bible teachers through the years. Those notes have saved my life. They've not only instructed me but also comforted me and led me through heartaches. It's through studying the Word of God that I learned to believe, trust, forgive, endure, accomplish, and enjoy my relationship with him. Those notes directed me to the proper Scriptures I needed at different times in my life, and they continue to do so.

I hope when I die, I'll have a pen and paper in my hand and my friends will bury me with them. Sometimes we want to do something, but it's too hard, too expensive, too time consuming. But writing it down is none of the above. It's easy. You should try it.

{ EIGHTEEN }

Allow Yourself to Be Sad

Although I was never an avid fan of the Beatles, there are a few of their songs I really love. One of them is "Let It Be." They named an album with that title to make a statement about leaving problems behind and moving on in life. Paul McCartney wrote the song about his mother, Mary, who died when he was fourteen. He dreamed she came to him at a time when he was sad and in trouble, "speaking words of wisdom." Because her words comforted him and brought him peace, he wrote this song, which also includes the lyrics, "There will be an answer. Let it be."

McCartney's beautiful lyrics were, in part, a way to express the sadness in his heart. Growing up in a family that strongly encouraged being happy all the time, I had to learn how to express sadness without trying to hide it. I didn't know it was all right to let my sadness show. When I became an adult, I told a dear friend about how troublesome that dichotomy was, and she encouraged me to "lean into" my sadness—to feel it completely, not try to make it into some sort of fake happiness.

As time went on, I learned the value of feeling the entire range of my emotions. And it was only then that I understood I was really alive because I was able to feel my feelings—all of them. Interestingly, I also learned that some of my finest moments occur when I'm feeling unhappy, unfulfilled, uncomfortable—because through these moments I'm more likely to get out of my rut and look for other ways to answer life's hardest questions, as well as let my creative nature express itself.

I learned every zenith has a nadir, every high has a low. To know how fully we are living life, we need a basis of comparison as a standard. For example, we can't really know how well we are unless we've experienced true sickness. Nor can we know genuine victory until we've known defeat. By the same token, how can we know happiness in its fullness unless we allow ourselves to feel sad? It's by this basis of comparison we're able to equate the fullness we feel with the emptiness at the other end of the spectrum. If we build a wall around us to keep out sadness, we'll inadvertently keep happiness out, too. Therefore, we must allow ourselves to feel both.

Let me encourage you, when sadness comes, to "let it be." As it finds a place in your heart and moves through your spirit, it awakens creative genes that are waiting to find expression. Who knows? You may become another Franz Schubert or Vincent van Gogh. Their best compositions were born of their deepest grief—but look at the joy they brought to the rest of the world.

{ NINETEEN }

Acknowledge Your Need for Help

Leaving the dentist's office several years ago, I heard someone call out in a faint cry, "Help. Help. Can you help me?" I looked around the parking lot but saw no one. Then the cry came again. "Help me. Please help me."

I hurriedly followed the sound, and there on the asphalt lay an elderly woman with her head resting against the tire of a van. She had apparently missed her step coming off a curb into the lot and had fallen; now she was unable to get up.

Kneeling down quickly so she could see and hear me, I gave her my name and told her to lie still while I called for help. She had hit her forehead, which was bleeding a bit, and she had scratches on both her elbow and knee. I felt so bad for her. She told me her name was Martha, and she was trying to get to her car when she fell.

Within a few minutes, an ambulance arrived. As Martha was being loaded into the ambulance, I assured her I'd follow in my car and see her very soon at the hospital, which was just up the street.

I didn't know what to do, but I knew I wanted to be available for this woman if I could help her further. My heart went out to her. Even though she was a total stranger, it was obvious she needed help, and except for the ambulance personnel, I was the only one at the moment who knew that.

Shortly after Martha had been admitted, examined, and assigned a room, I went to her bedside and asked how she felt. Without hesitation, she said to me, "Oh, Luci, thank you so much for coming with me. I'm so clumsy, and I fall easily. Please promise me you'll stay with me and won't tell my daughter I fell. Will you promise me that?"

I admit I was a little shocked she didn't want her daughter to know of her fall. If she had been my mother, I certainly would have wanted to know—and I told her so. Once again, she insisted I not tell her.

"I think my daughter's tired of my asking for help," she said. "I'm too old for her to handle; I think she gets sick and tired of my asking her to do things for me."

As the day wore on and turned into evening and then nightfall, Martha and I talked more and more about her accident and the need to tell her daughter. I finally convinced her it was important for her family to know where she was and that she was all right. I knew they'd be worried. About 8:00 p.m., the daughter came; I met her and she was as kind as could be. She was genuinely grateful I had called her to let her know about her mother's need. Of course she wanted to know.

Martha had suffered a broken collarbone and was in the hospital a week. I visited her a couple of times and was so glad I had been able to be of assistance to her. I've thought about her many times through the years, and it's become a reminder to me of how difficult it can be to ask for help or even let someone come to our aid, including our own loved ones. I'm amazed at how self-sufficient we think we are.

Psalm 3:8 says, "Real help comes from God," and more often than not, he uses a person to provide that help. We're not created to be self-sustaining, self-sufficient, or self-centered. We need each other. In several different verses, the Bible talks about our being the "body of Christ," with each part, each one of us, having his or her own place and purpose.

Acknowledging our need for family, friends, or a caregiver is vitally important when it comes to our health and well-being. You may start thinking they don't care, or, like Martha, you may fear you're a burden on them. Don't assume that. With everything, there are appropriate boundaries. But I can tell you from experience, it's much more of a burden for your loved ones *not* to know when you need them.

One of the great lessons in life is finding the right balance between giving and receiving help from our loved ones. Or from total strangers. Ask Martha.

{ TWENTY }

Find Contentment in Doing Without

I once read a definition of contentment that stuck with me, probably because it reminds me that contentment has nothing to do with money, yet the people who live this way are millionaires in their souls. It's truly one of the primary secrets to a happy life:

> Keep your heart free from hate, your mind from worry, live simply, expect little, give much, sing often, pray always, forget self, think of others and their feelings, fill your heart with love, and scatter laughter wherever you go. These are the links in the golden chain of contentment.

I don't know the source of the definition, but I liked it so much I jotted it down in my journal years ago, and I've never forgotten it. Learning to do without is almost an art form because it's the opposite of *more*, which is what most of us want—or think we want. The best way to be content is to count our blessings, not our cash.

In the early days of 1993, I was faced with a lot of financial challenges and knew it was going to be a hard year for me regarding money. I made a list of things to consider before I spent a penny. There were twelve considerations on the list, and the twelfth was, "Do without."

I stuck that list in the front of my '93 journal and asked the Lord to help me remember those twelve items and not gripe about anything having to do with money, spending, saving, tithing, and investing. And, just for fun, next to the list I stuck a note I had received from a friend. It said, "The more you complain, the longer God lets you live." I knew that joke would help me keep my mouth shut when I wanted to gripe about having no money.

What a year that turned out to be:

- Instead of going to movies, I wrote poetry and read books.
- Instead of eating out, I cooked meals at home and made up recipes.
- Instead of buying birthday gifts or greeting cards, I made them myself.
- Instead of buying fresh flowers, I resurrected discarded mums out of Dumpsters—seriously!
- Instead of buying new music CDs, I listened again and again to the ones I already owned.
- Instead of calling my friends long distance, I wrote them long letters.

- Instead of tossing or giving away what was broken, I repaired it myself.
- Instead of fretting over what I couldn't do, I rejoiced over what I could.

That same year I got a whopping federal income tax bill I was totally unable to pay, but instead of worrying about it, I asked the Lord to guide my thoughts and steps so I'd know what to do. I took back some stuff I had purchased and got refunds, and I completely stopped buying anything I didn't absolutely need.

As hard as it is to believe, it all turned out to be kind of fun! I tightened my belt every way I could and took money out of a few investments and paid the IRS. The Lord brought me through it and taught me some very important lessons about handling money and about trusting him. I knew he was with me every step of the way.

Here's what happens when we count our blessings instead of cash: we confront the issues of everyday living and examine our inner feelings. In so doing, we find new responses that better satisfy our needs and the needs of the people closest to us.

PART THREE

Achieving Balance

{ TWENTY-ONE }

Build Yourself
a Small Library

It occurred to me the other day that being reared in a home that had books and treasured them set me on a path that has had many wonderful rewards. One of them is that my two brothers love books as much as I. Just last month I mailed both of them a copy of the book I was reading so we could share its contents. This is second nature to the three of us, and it all started with a small, insignificant collection of books in our childhood.

Yet it was my friend Kurt, who lived down the street from me back in the 1960s, who first encouraged me to create something I could call a *library*. We became friends as I discovered that Kurt liked to read; I liked to read too. He loved books; I loved books. He had a little library; I didn't.

One Saturday morning when he was at my house we started talking about our mutual love of books. He said, "You know, Luci, you could build a library right here in your living room if you wanted to. You have lots of books. Let's figure out how to do it. Okay?"

My bookshelves were bricks and boards, but they served the purpose well. Together, Kurt and I started classifying books and had the time of our lives. Since book cataloging is more of an art form than a science, we were in heaven.

We organized everything according to topic: art, biography, gardening, history, music, novels, poetry, theology, travel, and so on. I printed out small labels, and Kurt stuck them on the shelves under each appropriate section. In a matter of minutes, I knew where everything was, and in short order, I had the beginnings of what would in time become the most beautiful room in my home.

Eventually, we had everything categorized so that my gathering of books looked like a very professional collection that made me nearly swoon every time I walked through the living room. That happened in 1965, and to this day, I'm still building a library. My two brothers have personal libraries in their homes too. We agree with Mark Twain, who reportedly said, "The man who does not read good books has no advantage over the man who cannot read them."

My books are my friends. Some I know like the back of my hand; they've been with me through trials, and I've read them three, four, and five times. Others are new friends with whom I'm just getting acquainted.

Since I was a senior in college, I've been a member of book clubs. I vividly remember the first "big" book I bought. It was *The Columbia Historical Portrait of New York*, printed by Doubleday & Co.

in 1953; it's a large hardback that cost me about $25—a fortune when I bought it back in 1955. But from that moment on, I couldn't get my fill of books. Many times I bought small, inexpensive volumes published by Modern Library, one of which is *Out of Africa* by Isak Dinesen. I bought it in 1970, and it's one of my closest friends, even now—magnificent writing and an incredible story. I've read it three times. (And if you've not read it, you should plan on starting it as soon as you finish *this* book.)

Unfortunately, people often think that to have a home library, you have to be an upper-class citizen with first edition antique books and lots of money. Let me clear that up right now. Granted, I do have some beautiful, leather-bound books and a few antiques, but I also have hundreds of paperbacks, as well as beat-up, old, and torn copies of books that I treasure as much (if not more) than those with beautiful leather bindings for which I paid a pretty penny. Finding a good book that's a bargain to boot is just icing on the cake. Those are the ones you find at Goodwill and Salvation Army thrift stores, yard sales, friends-of-the-library shops, and all sorts of other places where recycled items are sold.

I'll be eighty years old when this book is published, and there's nothing in my home I treasure more than the 450-square-foot library I designed when my house was built in 2004. The library might have started small, but now it's a treasure trove of books I've collected for sixty years on every topic you can imagine. Not only do I have the first book I ever bought but also the book I bought yesterday, and every one in between.

TWENTY-TWO

Establish Integrity in Your Life

When I was in the eighth grade, I was dashing out the door one morning so I could walk to school with my friends, when I remembered I needed notebook paper. I asked my mother for money to buy some after school.

That afternoon I stopped in the grocery store and bought the paper, and on the way out I spotted a package of macaroons and decided to get them too. I only had enough money for the paper, so I paid the cashier and stole the macaroons to eat on the way home. I was certainly not in the habit of stealing anything, but who was going to miss one little package of cookies?

Walking through a big field to get to my house, I ate the stolen macaroons as fast as possible, throwing away the packaging so there would be no evidence of my theft. By the time I got in the front door of the house, I was sick at my stomach from gorging—and from stealing.

My mother was peeling potatoes at the kitchen sink for dinner. Feeling exceedingly guilty, I went straight up to her and in one long run-on sentence said, "Mother-I-bought-the-notebook-paper-and-paid-the-man-and-on-the-way-out-the-door-I-stole-a-package-of-macaroons-and-ate-them-all-the-way-home-and-I'm-sick-at-my-stomach-and-I-think-I'm-gonna-die."

Long pause.

Mother put the knife down (a good sign), turned to me, and said very softly, "I beg your pardon?"

Oh, gosh. I've gotta repeat it? Once again I told her my dilemma.

Very calmly, she said, "Well, honey, you'll need to get your money because we're going back to that store now so you can pay the man for what you stole."

While she'd been willing to give me money for school supplies, I would be paying the restitution out of my own savings tucked away in my bedroom. I begged Mother not to make me go back to the store, but she wouldn't take no for an answer. She laid her apron aside, picked up the car keys, and said with all the self-restraint in the world, "Get your money and meet me in the car."

I was mortified. The last thing I wanted to do was find that guy and tell him I had ripped off a package of macaroons. But before long, we were backing out of the driveway.

On the way, I begged and pleaded with Mother to *please* not make me confess. "That guy thinks I'm a Christian, Mother. Don't make me go back in there and pay him for those cookies. I'm begging you," I said.

She kept her cool, driving on without saying a word. When we pulled up in front, she finally spoke: "Go in there. Find the man; introduce yourself and tell him what you've done. Then pay him for the cookies. I'll wait for you in the doorway."

Reluctantly, I walked in and looked for the manager. When I told him who I was and that I had stolen a package of macaroons, he did the strangest thing. He took the money for the cookies, looked straight into my eyes, and said, "Wow. We have a lot of kids who come in here and steal things, Lucille, but I've never ever had anyone come back and pay for what they stole. You must be a Christian."

When we got in the car, Mother thanked me for doing the right thing. "Now, let's go home and have dinner," she said. "You're probably hungry." Not once did she mention that episode again, and for many years, neither did I.

That incident made an indelible impression on me. I will never forget that day or the lesson I learned about being a person of integrity. I might not have known I needed to learn it, but my mother did, and she taught it to me by quietly standing her ground in doing what was right.

Integrity is demonstrated by how we behave when no one is looking. It starts inside us and grows into a lifelong collection of sound decisions based on discernment, good judgment, knowledge, and wisdom. As Shakespeare wrote, "This above all, to thine own self be true. And it must follow as the night the day, thou canst not then be false to any man."

{ TWENTY-THREE }

Engage People in Fun Conversation

One of the most enjoyable conversations I've ever had happened thirty-seven years ago when I was talking with a friend's daughter. Beth was eight at the time and as bright as a silver dollar: funny, astute, sweet, and exceedingly clever for a little girl her age. I loved our visit so much, I wrote about it in my journal.

When I asked Beth how she was doing, she told me she'd been chatting with Gertrude Sweatstein. Not knowing Gertrude, I inquired further.

"Oh, Luci, Gertrude is weird. She sleeps all day and night; she has ten children and is divorced. Her ex-husband is Dr. Bloodworth. He's a psy-chi-a-trist [pronounced with very deliberate speech] who found a lot of significance while picking through people's scalps."

I laughed heartily and stopped her right there. "Wait a second, honey. Who *are* these people? How did you meet them?"

Within the next few minutes Beth introduced me to a fascinating collection of characters who lived in her head. There was Mabel Chatican, a woman who cried all the time, talked through her tears, and had all the quirks of a strange bird right out of Charles Dickens. Two of the others were Mrs. Weatherworth, overwhelmed with life, and Colonel Stridesbaker, a tough army woman with a strong Texas accent.

After that initial conversation, Beth and I chatted many times about these people she had dreamed up. I loved them and loved talking with Beth about them because she could describe them perfectly.

As time went on, Beth and I left that group behind and enjoyed even more interesting visits. While chatting a couple of years later, Beth asked if she and I could have a philosophical conversation. "My mom told me she loves talking to you because the two of you have philosophical conversations. Can we have a conversation like that, Luci?"

"Of course."

Then she said, "What *is* a philosophical conversation? How do we do it?"

"Well, let's see . . ." I had to think for a few seconds. "It often starts with a *why* or *which* question."

"Like what?"

I thought for a minute and recalled that Beth had once told me she wished her piano teacher were a Christian. I asked if she remembered saying that. She did.

"Okay then, here's a philosophical question about that: *Why* do you wish she were a Christian?"

Beth looked at me lovingly and slowly said, "Maybe we shouldn't have a philosophical conversation." We both laughed heartily.

So many years have passed since those wonderfully fun verbal exchanges with little Beth; we've had a million philosophical conversations since then. She's in her midforties now with a master's degree in sociology and is married with children of her own. We can (and often do) talk about every subject under the sun, and it's just as fun and exciting today as it was in the early days of our friendship. Why? Because the root of fun conversation is *in* Beth.

If you want to have a blast conversing with friends, here are some suggestions for how to do it. They may sound simple, but I promise you, they're effective:

- **Be** warm and friendly to those around you.
- Listen carefully to what's being said.
- Ask fun, open questions.
- Smile when you talk.
- Think of interesting topics to discuss.

A few Sundays ago after church, a group of us had lunch with my brother Chuck Swindoll and his wife. In the course of visiting, I asked Chuck, "Which was harder—being a student at Dallas Theological Seminary or being president there, thirty-two years later?"

That question opened an hour of fun and very, very interesting dialogue, not only with Chuck, but also with everybody at the table. There was rapt attention, processing, laughter, other questions, comments, and enjoyment for all of us.

No one person was doing all the talking; everybody was totally engaged. Not only was it unforgettable, it had all of us wondering when we could meet again for lunch. Fun conversation always makes us hungry for more.

{ TWENTY-FOUR }

Remember to Notice Things Today

I once heard Diane Sawyer say, "The most important thing in life is to pay attention."

I *love* that phrase! There's so much to see, experience, watch, and enjoy in life. But many times we miss it simply because we're not *present*. Our minds are a million miles away. We're simply not paying attention.

It's been said that troubles and weeds thrive on lack of attention, so if we've got either in our lives, we need to stop and do a bit of uprooting. One of the Old Testament prophets emphasized that point when he wrote, "Use your eyes, use your ears, pay careful attention to everything" (Ezekiel 44:5).

About a year ago a friend gave me a book called *How to Be an Explorer of the World*, with the subtitle *Portable Life Museum*. Since I'm a nut for museums anyway, the idea of having a portable one really turns my crank. There are pages in the book for taking notes, making lists, drawing pictures, storing collections, recording data, and documenting objects. I mean, what's not to like? Obviously, this book was tailor-made for *me*.

So I put it to the test. I had an appointment with a doctor to check my left eye, in which I had undergone cataract surgery a couple of weeks earlier. On my way to the post-op examination, I decided to make it a point to look for things I'd never seen. In other words, I wanted to notice *everything*. I was on the lookout for findings I could record in my new portable-museum book. I even asked the Lord to make me conscious of hidden, unusual, or different objects, not only for my own enjoyment, but to be consciously aware of life around me.

Since the eye exam called for my "bad eye" to be dilated, a friend asked if she could drive me to the appointment. Hot dog! "Great idea," I said, knowing that plan would allow me to use my "good eye" for noticing things. Off we went, she watching the road, and I watching the countryside.

I saw several things I'd never noticed before and recorded them. But the clincher and winner, hands down, happened when we got to the doctor's office, which is on the second floor and has windows all around. Across the street there's a railway stop, and between that building and the doctor's office are telephone poles and high wires.

Of course I had seen the railway stop before and had watched people walking around over there, but I had never noticed the poles or high wires between the buildings, even though I'd been going to that doctor's office for several years. As I was noticing things that day, I realized that not only were the poles and wires new to me, but hanging on one of the high wires was a pair of tennis shoes somebody had thrown up there after tying the laces together. There they were, swinging in the breeze.

I was thrilled to death. What a find!

I asked three or four people who worked there how long the tennis shoes had been blowing around up there, and not one person had even noticed them. Every employee I asked said something like, "Oh, my gosh. Would you look at that? Wonder how long those have been there?"

Not only did I write about that in my book, I also wrote a little note of helpful criticism to myself: "STOP, Luci! Take note more often."

How frequently do we go through the day without any awareness of what's in front of us? We don't mean to be oblivious to the world around us, and it's not that we don't care. We just don't pay attention.

I challenge you to keep your eyes peeled and your heart open to God's unique, colorful, and sometimes humorous surprises in your life. It'll make your day brighter and a whole lot more fun. Try it. You'll like it. Write it down.

And while you're at it, write this down too. It's good advice: "You made me so happy, God. I saw your work and I shouted for joy. How magnificent your work, God! How profound your thoughts! Dullards never notice what you do; fools never do get it" (Psalm 92:4–6).

TWENTY-FIVE

Disregard What Isn't Your Business

When I worked in California many years ago, an engineer came into the drafting room one day where six or eight of us were working at our tables. We all knew him and could tell something was wrong. The guy (let's call him Fred) was furious. Another engineer, younger than he and with less seniority, had been promoted to a leadership position, and Fred was livid. He took off his hard hat, threw it across the room, and started telling us what happened and how mad he was at management. (In short order, it was easy to see why he didn't get the promotion.)

Those of us at the drafting tables just looked at him with a blank stare, trying to figure out what he wanted, and then we went back to work. Nobody said a thing—it was none of our business—so he eventually stalked out, madder than a wet hen.

A little later, Fred was fired from his job, and for the rest of us, life went on as usual.

There are times when stuff happens that's none of our business. We might want to say something, but if we're wise, we know better. We keep our mouths shut, turn away, and disregard the fact that it ever happened.

Knowing when to pay full attention, my topic in the previous chapter, and when to pay *no* attention, the focus of this chapter, is a matter of discernment. And, dare I say, discernment is a gift of years. Discerning when to pay no attention may be the harder choice.

Being by nature averse to conflict, it's easy for me not to get involved in situations like the one described above. I don't like confrontation, and if people argue in my presence, I often get a stomachache. It's always my first choice not to get involved in issues that have nothing to do with me.

Each of us needs to maintain an imaginary line in our thinking that we won't cross when something isn't our business. If somebody is verbally fighting at the next table in a restaurant, for instance, keep out of it. It's none of your business, or mine. If furious Fred bounces into your office, wanting you to choose up sides and tell off the management, keep out of that too.

I love 1 Thessalonians 4:11, the little verse that says, "Stay calm; mind your own business; do your own job." That *so* works for me.

Let me hasten to acknowledge, however, that there are times we do need to get involved, whether or not we want to. Maybe the word *disregard* in this chapter's title should be *discern*, because discernment is perception that comes through one of the senses or the intellect, and that's what I'm really talking about here.

I was with a dear friend a number of years ago on a road trip, and the two of us stopped at a crowded outdoor short-order shack of a place for ice cream cones. While we were there, a busload of Cub Scouts also stopped, and the little boys were running around, having a good time, while the Scout leader, a woman, was getting their ice cream and calling each of them to come pick it up. Little Ronnie didn't come when he was called, which made the woman mad. When he finally arrived, she was so upset, she yelled, "You brat. You come when I call you. Do you hear me?"

She slapped him on the head and knocked him to the ground.

I just stared and nearly dropped my teeth. But my friend? She stood up tall and very firmly said to the woman, "You're the brat. And if you hit him again, you'll have to deal with me."

I'm telling you, I could have crawled under a rock, I was so embarrassed. While I was coming to my senses, every person in the area (except for the Scout leader and me) was applauding my friend. She was simply not going to put up with child abuse, and that day I learned that neither should I—no matter how humiliated or embarrassed I might have been.

We all have to decide for ourselves what is none of our business. We have to set our own limits. Some limits are very clear, and others involve weighing options, making judgments, discerning truth, drawing boundaries, and considering all that's involved. I can't answer for you—and you can't answer for me. But God can answer for both of us, and we can ask him to guide us.

{ TWENTY-SIX }

Think Before You Say It

Wisdom is a virtue. A wise person thinks before she speaks. Talking too much usually reflects thinking too little. Recently I found these fantastic verses in Ecclesiastes 5:2–3 and was surprised to see how the Bible states this advice so clearly: "Don't shoot off your mouth, or speak before you think. Don't be too quick to tell God what you think he wants to hear. God's in charge, not you—the less you speak, the better."

That passage leaves no room for doubt, does it? Have you ever noticed how impossible it is to retrieve your words once they fall out of your mouth? I've known a few people who need a rewind button close to their lips so they can surreptitiously roll back words, sentences, or paragraphs that should never have been uttered in the first place. One of them is a very dear friend to whom I am devoted for life. I love her company, admire her enormously, and would lay down my life for her, but there is one thing I would love to change about her, and she knows it. In her enthusiasm about almost everything, she often blurts out something she wishes she hadn't said—or I wish she hadn't. She simply doesn't stop to think before she speaks.

For example, it's not unusual for her to be so enthusiastic about a piece of good news I've told her privately that she eagerly blurts it out publicly because she wants to share it with the world. The second she remembers it wasn't hers to tell, she quickly apologizes to me and wants to punch her little rewind button—but there isn't one. Oops! Through the years the two of us have often laughed at this quirkiness in her because she absolutely means no harm; it's just that her enthusiasm gets the best of her.

Many years ago, when we hadn't known each other very long, the two of us planned a little weekend trip over a holiday that we had decided to celebrate together. In talking with an acquaintance of hers, my friend offhandedly said to her, "Hey, you can come with us if you want," never thinking her friend would accept. But she did.

Later, when she was confessing that there would be three of us instead of two on the trip, she said it had never occurred to her that she should have asked me first, even though the plans were initially for just the two of us. So the three of us went on the trip, which was fine; but when I think back on it, the incident seems like an example of enthusiasm run amok, if there is such a thing.

Proverbs 27:6 says the wounds inflicted by a friend are more precious than the flattery of an enemy. Since I believe this (and so does my friend), I've asked her many times through the years to please talk to me before she commits me to do something or go somewhere or before she represents me in any way. I've said, "Think before you say it."

She's been very teachable, and while she doesn't have what I would call a perfect record, she's doing much better these days. She always means well, but unfortunately her enthusiasm still occasionally causes regret—both in her and in others.

How many times have you or I reacted negatively or thoughtlessly to a friend (or even a total stranger) with words we wish we could retract? I've seen women say unkind things to their husbands in social settings and felt uncomfortable for how it must have made the husband feel. I've watched total strangers yell obnoxiously at store clerks and airport workers. I've witnessed kids being rude to their parents and parents harshly scolding their children. And it could all be different, if we just stopped and used our brains before we opened our mouths.

Jesus put it best: "It's your heart, not the dictionary, that gives meaning to your words. . . . Words are powerful; take them seriously" (Matthew 12:34).

{ TWENTY-SEVEN }

List Your Thoughts and Dreams

Did you know the first word Picasso ever said was *pencil*? I have a feeling it was my first word too. I've loved pencils all my life, and if pencil and paper are close at hand, I'm a happy girl. So it stands to reason that I love lists. I make them constantly: what I do, what I want to do, what I've done. Laugh if you will, but I believe making lists is one of the most important secrets to a happy life. And best of all, it's simple; it requires no money, no skill, no education, no schedule. No kidding! Just write it down, and there you go.

My proclivity for list making began when I was about the age of twelve and people started asking me what I wanted to be when I grew up. Believe it or not, I knew! I'd made a list—written down what I wanted for my life: I knew I wanted to go to college and work in an office. I wanted to sing on a stage and learn other languages. I wanted to travel all over the world and meet people from other countries. I wanted to read lots of books and maybe even write a book one day. I had no idea how I'd manage to do all I wanted to do, but that didn't matter. What mattered was that I had written it down on my to-do list.

God also has a to-do list for us. He creates us uniquely and has dreams and plans for our lives. As we take one baby step at a time, he opens doors and in his still, small voice whispers, "This is the way, walk in it" (Isaiah 30:21 NKJV). The joy of my entire life has come from my dependence on him as he has both fulfilled my desires and changed them. I've learned to trust God because I'm very intentional about and cognizant of his leadership.

Let me tell you what he did. In May 1959, there was a small article in the *Dallas Morning News* that reached out to me. The opening sentence read, "Dallas Civic Opera will hold chorus Auditions May 29 and 30 at Maple Theater for its 1959 season at State Fair Music Hall."

The piece went on to say what operas would be performed and on what dates. I'd learned an aria in college, so with that under my belt, I auditioned. And folks, the rest is history! I was accepted into the chorus and sang with the Dallas Opera for fifteen years, from 1959 through 1973, when I moved to Southern California.

What happened as a result of that audition proves the truth of Ephesians 3:20–21: "God can do anything, you know—far more than you could ever imagine or guess or request in your wildest dreams! He does it not by pushing us around but by working within us, his Spirit deeply and gently within us."

By my being an opera chorister, the door opened for me to work onstage with many interesting people, including opera stars Dame Joan Southerland, Placido Domingo, and Maria Callas.

Many wonderful things resulted from my desire to sing on-stage that were never even on my to-do list. I took lessons in Italian and traveled abroad. I met people from other countries and visited in their homes. Through that one dream, God gave me much more than I could have asked for or even imagined. I doubt I would be doing what I am today, in fact, if my life had not taken the path it has.

Truthfully, we have no idea what God is going to do in and through the life he's given us. Scripture says he can do anything. *Anything.* Within the confines of our hearts, he is doing things this very minute about which we know nothing. He's opening doors, putting out fires, rearranging schedules, making crooked places straight. He's gently molding and making us into what he wants us to become while opening pathways to get us there, whispering, "This is the way; walk in it."

Making a list of thoughts and dreams has been an amazing experience for me. Not because God takes his cues from my to-do list but because it serves as the map I can look at to see how far he's brought me.

I strongly urge you to make a list of your heart's desires, no matter your age. Someday you can actually trace how those dreams deeply and gently came to fruition by God's Spirit.

{ TWENTY-EIGHT }

Rise to the Occasion Often

I read something interesting the other day about aging. For the first time in history the number of people under the age of seventeen and those over sixty-five will be almost equal by the year 2030. That means Americans are living well into old age.

Scientists say that while we older people may not be as sharp on the computer as those who are younger, we think as well as the young . . . but differently. (Good to know!) We in the older generation think with more reflection, depth, and awareness. We may not be as fast at processing data as our younger friends, but instead of manipulating it, we reduce it to concepts and live out of those concepts.

The reason this is valuable to know is that some of you who are reading this are as old as I am (seventy-nine) or older, but you may be thinking it's time to give up, drop out of life, and let somebody else be responsible for whatever challenges come down the pike. Yet, believe it or not, now is the time *we* need to be the sages of the world. We're the ones who must evaluate, intercede, bring experience to bear, and rise to the occasion when need be. By virtue of age, we're the mentors for those who follow in our footsteps. We need to do the things that need to be done.

My maternal grandmother was a perfect example of one who rose to the occasion often. I was a teenager when she was well into her sixties, and I grew up understanding she was sharp as a tack. She taught piano, sang in the church choir, entertained guests in her home right and left, made gifts for her friends, and was personally acquainted with practically everybody in her little Texas town. We kids called her Momo, although her real name was Jessie Lundy. My grandfather, Orville, was an insurance salesman, but when money was tight, Momo rose to the occasion and found ways to bring in income too. She sold boxes of greeting cards. And since she knew almost everybody in town, she made a killin', as we say in Texas. Some months we laughed because she brought in more revenue than Granddaddy.

Momo's greatest gift, though, was throwing parties. She thrived on getting folks together and finding ways for everybody to be entertained. If they were lonely or blue or feeling left out, they'd be invited to Momo's for dinner and an evening of laughter and fun. I well remember, as a young girl in the 1940s, our family going to Momo's home in El Campo for the weekend. On Saturday night she invited all her neighbors and church friends over for a party. My brothers and I performed in the living room: one brother playing piano, one quoting poetry, and I mimicking Danny Kaye in patter songs from his movies. We all laughed, sang, danced, and carried on, meeting new people and enjoying old friends. Momo was in her element, bringing joy to everybody she knew.

Even when my grandmother began showing her age and wasn't feeling her best, she managed to get on a bus, come visit us in our home in Houston, and encourage us to see the bright side of life. She used to say, "A day is wasted unless we fall over in a heap laughing." What a spirit she had for life. Not only was she loved, but needed. She helped us see the rainbow instead of the clouds. Her very presence gave us purpose in life. She loved the Lord with all her heart and showed it in a thousand ways. By stepping up to the plate as long as she lived, she delivered a home run every time.

My emphasis so far in this chapter has been on older folks who rise to the occasion, but all of us, no matter what age we are, need to be ready to do what needs to be done in whatever circumstances surround us. Think how inspiring it is to see teenagers stepping up to mow an elderly neighbor's lawn—or volunteering for mission trips to impoverished areas of the world. Consider what an impression a busy young mother makes when she steps in to help care for the children of a military spouse in her church or neighborhood so he or she can deal with an emergency—or just take a break—while the husband or wife is serving abroad. A friend told me how amazed she was one Christmastime to be hurrying into a discount store and realize the guy standing out in the cold alone, ringing the bell over the Salvation Army collection kettle, was a top administrator at the state university in that town. That bell needed to be rung, and volunteers were in short supply; sure, the college administrator was busy, but he saw the need, put on his coat, and stepped up to serve. We see people rise to the occasion often, and we're inspired to follow their example.

I believe it's our duty to rise to the occasion as often as possible.

Life is a spiritual responsibility, a moral force around us with challenging tests. It's not some private enterprise we live unto ourselves. As Christians, we have a calling to live Christlike lives even in tough times. The first chapter of James gives a clear picture of that calling: "Consider it a sheer gift, friends, when tests and challenges come at you from all sides. You know that under pressure, your faith-life is forced into the open and shows its true colors. . . . Anyone who meets a testing challenge head-on and manages to stick it out is mighty fortunate. For such persons loyally in love with God, the reward is life and more life" (vv. 2–3, 12).

{ TWENTY-NINE }

Thank Others for Their Efforts

Isn't it interesting what the two words *thank you* can do? It's been said that gratitude is the most exquisite form of courtesy.

As I write this, it's Sunday afternoon, and this morning in church, the message was on the value of saying thank you to those around us who often go unnoticed or ignored.

There was a reference to people in uniform—military, postal service letter carriers, police officers, and firefighters—as well as to those who perform thankless jobs, such as garbage collectors and street sweepers. What about the person who checks you out at the grocery store or the woman on the phone who makes your flight reservations?

It might be easy to remember to thank family members or coworkers for gifts and favors: passing the mashed potatoes, giving us a ride home when our car's in the shop, surprising us with a birthday present. But what about the big-picture things our family members do for us?

I asked a friend who has a young son about seven years old, what is the hardest thing about motherhood? She thought for a minute, then gave me a wonderful answer: "Everything is critical." I loved that! I'm sure it's true. Wouldn't it be nice when her little boy grows up to say to his mother as a grown man, "Thank you for the years you did things for me. Not only did you pick up my clothes, do my laundry, help me with my homework, see that I got places on time, teach me how to be nice and get along on the playground, but you also got me where I am today because you knew *everything* mattered. I just want to thank you for that, Mom."

Most women would probably faint if their grown kids said that. Yet what a wonderful thing it would be.

When I was in high school, I played the cello. Primarily I'm a singer, but everybody in my family played an instrument, so I wanted to play one too. Just for fun and at bonfire parties, I played the ukulele, but when I was offered an opportunity to play cello in orchestra class, I said yes. I've always loved the sounds that come from the cello, but I had no idea how difficult it was to play. Nevertheless, I was determined to learn. Little by little I improved, but I never was what one would call good. However, my high school music teacher, Mr. Seastrand, who could play every instrument beautifully, encouraged me to keep at it. I was even given a little solo part in one of the pieces our orchestra played. I was scared to death I'd botch it, so I practiced hours on end to do it well. When the performance was over, Mr. Seastrand said to me, "Lucille, you played beautifully tonight. You really made that solo part *sing*. Every note was on pitch. Just think, one day you might be a famous cellist. You never know. Thank you for a job well done."

I couldn't wait to tell my parents and write that in my diary. It was one of the nicest, sincerest compliments I've ever gotten—and coming from him, it was unbelievable. You can tell it meant a lot because that was sixty-five years ago, and I've never forgotten it. Here's what really made that compliment stand out: Mr. Seastrand didn't just say the usual, "Good job," that so many of us toss off to performers we know or encounter. He said *thank you*, acknowledging the hard work I'd done to prepare for my solo.

A cellist played the offertory in church this morning just before the message on thankfulness. The two parts of the service made me think of Mr. Seastrand's words, which reminded me of the deep value of gratitude. It costs us nothing to thank someone else, but to the person receiving our thanks, our words may be priceless—and unforgettable.

{ THIRTY }

Acquire a Brand-New Skill

My friend Scott is paraplegic. When he was seventeen he was in a motocross accident, and his spinal cord was severed in two places. Hospitalized for twenty-eight days, Scott was told by one of his doctors he should get used to the fact he would no longer have a normal life. It was doubtful he'd ever have a job, a home, or a family of his own. In an effort to prepare Scott for the worst, the doctor told Scott to resign himself to being confined to a wheelchair the rest of his life—and all that meant.

In contrast, Scott's mother looked at his circumstances very differently. She told Scott that while it was true he would be in a wheelchair, the only thing he couldn't do was walk. Everything else was up to him, and with the right spirit he could do anything he wanted.

Tremendously motivated, he started dreaming about what he could do and stopped limiting himself by dwelling on what he couldn't.

Scott is now forty-three and happily married with a nine-year-old son, Garrett. Having giant-sized willpower, Scott does more than most men who are able-bodied. He is strong and physically fit. He drives a car, mows the grass, cleans the house, plays on a tennis team, and skis on both water and snow. He's built a barn and a fence on the acreage around his home. He delights in coaching Garrett's basketball team and riding four-wheelers with him. He takes his family camping and jet skiing.

Scott is a wonder. Truly, he can do everything but walk. And even now, he's learning new skills. Because of his innate verve and a mother who encouraged him to be courageous, he's learned how to do things that defied that doctor's grim prediction all those years ago.

Learning new skills can be challenging, but it can also lead us to the most enjoyable, rewarding activities in life. Yet some of us are very hesitant. We worry, *Am I good enough? Strong enough? Fit enough? Brave enough? Do I have enough money or training?* Or maybe, as adults, we learn new skills out of necessity and figure, why should we tackle any more than we have to?

If this is your attitude, here's a suggestion: learn something *fun*. Instead of sitting for hours in front of a TV or computer or electronic game killing time, consider learning how to . . .

- **Knit**: It can be fun—and rewarding—to learn how to create something from "nothing." I had a friend who became so good at this skill she knitted a pair of gloves while watching a movie.

- *Juggle*: Picture the day you throw three balls in the air and can actually keep them there.
- *Yo-yo*: I once met the world champion, who was so good he made the yo-yo land in his pocket.
- *Play the harmonica*: My harmonica-playing dad was in high demand at parties.
- *Sketch*: For me, time flies when I draw pictures of the people, places, or things around me.
- *Build something*: One of my former coworkers and his wife built a boat and lived on it.

When you're learning a fun new skill, you're not trying to impress somebody; you're just enjoying one of the secrets to a happy life. Your pursuit of a new interest or your learning of a new skill can even help you make new friends. And if none of these physical skills appeals to you, dream up your own. Set goals, start small, invite friends to join you, and have the time of your life.

But if you don't want to do something physical, how about working on a few mental skills? We all need improvement in those. Here's a list for starters, but feel free to make your own:

- Coping with life
- Staying calm
- Enjoying solitude
- Managing your time
- Laughing at yourself
- Practicing your faith

As long as we're alive, we have the ability to learn. When you hear a voice in your head whispering that you can't do something, think about Scott or others you know who have overcome challenges and learned a new skill.

Life's too short to wait until everything is perfect or until you can walk on water before acquiring a new skill. That day will never come. Start right here, right now. Start with what you have without worrying about what you don't.

{ PART FOUR }

Living a Good Life

{ THIRTY-ONE }

Get Doctrine Under Your Belt

The year I graduated from college, I moved home to Houston to live with my parents for a couple of years. During that time my mom and dad, younger brother, and I went to a sound, Bible-teaching church. (My older brother had married and was living elsewhere.) The Bible classes we attended were held four nights a week, and I can't remember ever missing a single one. I *lived* to go to that Bible class, and each week I took copious notes. I couldn't seem to absorb enough teaching about God, his Word, and his ways. I was a sponge that fell in the ocean and drank it dry. For example, even though I had read 2 Timothy 3:16–17 many times with my family, when we studied it in that class, I really understood, for the first time, what it meant: "Every part of Scripture is God-breathed and useful one way or another—showing us truth, exposing our rebellion, correcting our mistakes, training us to live God's way. Through the Word we are put together and shaped up for the tasks God has for us."

Doctrinal teaching instructed me how to live the Christian life. I learned doctrines that clarified the Bible and God the Father, Son, and Holy Spirit. I studied doctrines regarding humanity, sin, salvation, the church, and the end times that will come one day. A world of data and information was opened up to me and set me on a new path.

I learned the Ten Commandments were written under the law of God and—*most importantly*—I now live under the wonderful grace of God. And living under grace, I learned that the culture, my past, peers, fears, even my feelings could no longer dictate my way of life. I learned that walking by faith I could please God, know him, and enjoy a lifetime in his presence.

For a good part of my young life, my feelings had ruled my behavior. And when those feelings fluctuated, so did my actions. But once I got a solid foundation of doctrine under my belt, I understood that *no matter how I felt*, God still loved me and his Spirit would be with me—guiding, forgiving, leading, caring, encouraging me regardless of my feelings, because biblical doctrine doesn't fluctuate. It's as solid as a rock. Through faith, I trusted God and his Word.

To embrace doctrinal teaching and make it one's own, three factors are essential: accepting the fact that all Scripture is God-breathed, understanding the structure of how Scriptures are written, and having a clear interpretation of scriptural truths. Doctrine is a system of teachings that relate to a particular subject. In this case, when I talk about biblical Christian doctrine,

I mean revelations in the Bible about God and humanity. It's as simple as that—and as difficult as that.

As a young girl, I placed my faith in Jesus Christ and invited him into my heart, but back then the only thing I knew for sure about the Bible was the gospel: Christ died for my sins and rose from the dead, and by trusting him as my Savior, I was forgiven of my sins, had an eternal home in heaven when I died, was assured that God loved me completely and that I could do nothing to lose my salvation. By virtue of my redemption, I was to share this good news with everybody I met. I believed that, and I lived solely out of that belief.

While all those truths are absolutely wonderful, and certainly life changing, and although I'd been an active church member forever, I knew little or nothing about the deep truths that help a person *grow* in faith. My sweet parents and brothers didn't have that foundation, either, until we all began attending the wonderful Bible class that changed *everything*.

So, in my opinion, a working knowledge of biblical doctrine may just be the most important factor to having a happy life because it puts and keeps everything in one's life in proper perspective. *Selah*.

{ THIRTY-TWO }

Look for Ways to Help

It was a long time before I knew the Bible talked about something many call the "gift of helps." I was acquainted with more prominent spiritual gifts like evangelism, teaching, prophesying, healing, and so forth. But a *gift* of *helping others*? I hadn't a clue. The idea comes from 1 Corinthians 12:27–28, which makes reference to those of us in the universal church having various parts to play. Those parts are defined by one's spiritual gifts being used to keep things going.

In retrospect, I can tell you for sure my mother had the gift of helps. She seemed to sense the needs of others and meet those needs without effort. It was second nature for her to take food to neighbors who were sick or recovering from surgery, bring groceries to folks who had no car, invite people to join us when they were alone. I loved that trait in her. I love it in anyone.

The spiritual gift of helping others is generally manifested in a servant attitude. Being responsive to the needs of others, the helper does whatever it takes to get the task accomplished. Interestingly, the Greek word in Scripture for *helps* means "to take instead of." It's doing the work of another. A beautiful word picture!

I have two friends who share a home together in my neighborhood, and they both have this wonderful spiritual gift of helps. They're forever looking for opportunities to be of assistance. It's not that they actually have *time* to help; they just *think* to help. It's a gift. More often than not, when either of them goes to the mall, the discount store, the grocery market, the cleaners, or anywhere else, they ask if they can run an errand for me while they're out. And even if I say no thank you, they will very likely show up on my doorstep later with a little surprise. A love gift!

When the home in which I now live was being built, one of them (who had overseen the work of building her own home nearby) worked every day with my builder whenever I was away on trips or speaking engagements, just to be sure things were done to my liking. And the minute I moved in, the other one volunteered to help me set up shop—putting books on shelves, arranging my kitchen, hanging clothes, unpacking boxes. As she engaged others to join in, it all became more like a party than a chore. My friend's attention to every detail never stopped. While she and her housemate are very different in terms of their gifts, they both serve and help friends all over the neighborhood. I'm beginning to think the gift of helping might be contagious!

Last spring their washing machine broke right in the middle of a huge load of laundry and water went *everywhere*. When they called to ask if they could bring their wet clothes to my house to wash them, I was thrilled to death. While one contacted a plumber, the other walked into my garage dragging behind her a huge black trash bag crammed with wet clothes. Together we hoisted it up into the utility sink and put the clothes in the washing machine. She was so apologetic I could hardly get out my words of gratitude. As I was waxing eloquent about how thrilled I was to help them with this problem, my friend smiled and said, "Luci, this isn't all. I've got six more bags full of wet towels in the trunk of my car. We used every towel in the house to mop up water. May I leave you those to wash?" I can't even tell you what it meant to me to be able to say, "Oh, my gosh! Yes!" to these friends who had done so much for me. And I meant every word of it. I washed, dried, and folded clothes and towels for the next six hours, listening to music as the work got done. I loved helping with this unexpected problem.

Trust me, you don't have to have the "gift of helps" to say to a friend, "May I do that for you?" Even if it's a person you have never seen before in your life, when you extend a helping hand it creates joy in both you and the recipient of your help. There's something about finding happiness in helping others that's indescribable.

I love serving those who need a lift. Maybe it's verbal encouragement. Maybe it's a ride when their car breaks down. Maybe it's a letter, an e-mail, or a visit because they're lonely. Maybe it's a meal together—and picking up the tab. Maybe it's just doing the laundry for friends whose washer breaks down. God gives us opportunities for all these things, and much more, when we simply reach out with a helping hand.

Second Corinthians 1:6–7 says it quite well: "If we are treated well, given a helping hand and encouraging word, that also works to your benefit, spurring you on, face forward, unflinching. Your hard times are also our hard times. When we see that you're just as willing to endure the hard times as to enjoy the good times, we know you're going to make it, no doubt about it."

{ THIRTY-THREE }

Tell It Like It Is

In 1989 I wrote a book called *Quite Honestly: A Journal of Thoughts and Activities for Daily Living*. My friend Carla helped me create the artwork, and together we provided the reader an opportunity to say what he or she honestly felt during fifty-two weeks in any given year. It was a place for the reader to "tell it like it is" day after day. Being one who loves journaling, I wanted to encourage people to be open, honest, real, and unafraid.

I've kept journals many years of my life and have recorded my thoughts and activities. Of the forty-six journals I've filled, there's not one that isn't precious to me. And when asked the question, "If your house were on fire, what would you grab first?" I can answer without hesitation, "My journals." That would be an armload, I know, but it's the truth. These journals chronicle my life. They contain my joys, sorrows, changes, fears, goals, dreams, desires, regrets, concerns, and imaginations.

When he was about my age, E. B. White wrote, "Even now, this late in the day, a blank sheet of paper holds the greatest excitement there is for me—more promising than a silver cloud, and prettier than a red wagon." I totally agree.

Look at a few ways journaling helps us enjoy happy lives:

- *Knowing ourselves.* When we take time to write in a journal, we open our hearts honestly but privately. We cry, laugh, fret, worry, cheer, feel, and process everything as deeply as we like without anyone criticizing or caring—or knowing. Being autobiographical is an excellent medium for revealing the truth about ourselves.
- *Gathering facts.* Think of the people whose legacy is found in their journals: Eugene Delacroix, Leo Tolstoy, Queen Victoria, and Anne Frank, to name a few. Because of gathered facts that were written in their diaries and journals, stories were saved that would have otherwise been lost.
- *Enjoying solitude.* While alone, we might feel lonely or aimless. But having a journal gives us the feeling there's a friend in the room who knows and accepts us. Telling the journal how things are going is like talking with a loved one.
- *Referencing memories.* When we can't remember dates, facts, and resolutions, it's quite likely they're somewhere in our journals. With a little time, we can go back through them and find what we're racking our brains to remember.
- *Feeling nostalgic.* Oh, the times I've reread entries about parties, reunions, and journeys with family members

or friends who are dear to me. There they are in my handwriting for me to rediscover in the stories that took place many years ago.

· *Asking questions*. The best conversationalists I know are those who ask good questions, and a journal is a perfect place to ask them of yourself first. This creates an environment to figure out what you want to say and how to word it.

· *Writing books*. For an author, journals are invaluable; they keep facts available forever. You can't imagine how often I've looked up activities that happened way back when, just to get my information straight. And it's right there in front of me, accurate, because I wrote it down when it happened.

When we see or feel something, more often than not we want to verbalize it. How frequently have we said, "I need to write that down so I won't forget it"? A journal is the place to do it. By telling how our life was lived, we leave a trace of who we really are. Or were.

I love Oscar Wilde's statement about his own journal, and I feel the same way about mine. "I never travel without my diary," he said. "One should always have something sensational to read in the train."

THIRTY-FOUR

Know for Sure
You're Insured

I was hospitalized in 2003 for a troublesome condition called atrial fibrillation. It was first thought to be a heart attack, but after a few days of medical care and attention, the doctors determined my heart was simply out of sinus rhythm. It righted itself on the third day, and I was dismissed. All of that was an interesting episode to me, but the most astounding thing happened when I got the bill. It was $33,000! Also amazing was the amount I actually owed on that invoice: $420. That's it! I still have the canceled check to remind myself of the importance of having health insurance.

Ironically, about that same time a dear friend who had no health insurance was hospitalized for surgery. She is a few years younger than I and didn't believe in having health insurance. Much later she told me when her costs were added up and sent to her, she owed somewhere between $75,000 and $100,000. She looked me straight in the face and said, "Luci, what was I thinking when I decided not to get health insurance? I must've been crazy. I had to take out a huge loan to pay that bill, and now I'm struggling to pay it off. I have the feeling I won't ever get out of debt."

A young girl from Oxford, Ohio, died in 2009 a few days shy of her twenty-third birthday. At an urgent care unit she was diagnosed with swine flu and pneumonia, but her condition got worse when she refused to go to the hospital for proper treatment because she had no health insurance. Of course, she might have died anyway, whether or not she had gone to the hospital. My point is that she felt she had no choice simply because she wasn't insured.

I recently read an alarming statistic that said 30 percent of nineteen- to twenty-four-year-olds refuse to get health insurance so they can have more spending money. Sadly, there are many older adults who apparently feel the same.

As you can see, I'm a firm believer in having insurance. My father was an insurance salesman when I was young, and our family was "insurance poor," as they say. I have no idea how much Daddy spent annually on insurance, but he was very conscientious about insuring everything he could: life, health, automobile, and home. Even though the policies were rarely used, they were in place if needed. My dad was a living example of what Suze Orman teaches: "Hope for the best, prepare for the worst."

There are lots of reasons why people need to be insured, but the main reason is protection. And part of being protected is knowing what your policy says. Again, I follow my father's example and do as he did. I'm aware of what my policy covers in the event of a problem. I suppose there's a lot of jargon that people don't read, or don't understand when they do. Nonetheless, it's important to spend time figuring out what you have.

I want to say this with all the love in the world, but very seriously: if you don't have insurance, get it. To those of you who say you trust the Lord to take care of you, I would also say very seriously: God gave you a brain. Use it! Until we move on to heaven, we live in an imperfect world where bad things happen. Insuring the resources and gifts God has given you in this life is good stewardship.

Even if you have to cut out something else, don't try to live without insurance. I consider it mandatory to having a happy life. I can tell you from experience, overwhelming debt that rules your life will eat you up alive. My friend is living proof that debt can result when one isn't properly insured. Part of being happy is knowing how to manage money, and some of that money must go into insurance policies, otherwise you'll spend it paying off the debt you incurred because you didn't think you needed it. It's as simple as that. I ain't eighty for nuthin'!

{ THIRTY-FIVE }

Batten Down All the Hatches

Much of my childhood was spent at Carancahua Bay, a small inlet along the southern coast of Texas, not far from Palacios. My grandfather owned a cabin there, where our family went on vacation. It was a place where we could swim, fish, sleep outdoors, meet relatives for family reunions, and have a high ole time inexpensively. We loved it.

My dad's favorite pastime was fishing, so to him these vacations were sheer bliss. The only one in the family who didn't give a hoot about fishing was my older brother, Orville. Nevertheless, because we were too young to be left in the cabin by ourselves, Orv had to go with us. Instead of fishing, he'd sit on the bow of the boat working miracles with his chemistry set while the rest of us caught the evening's meal. I always had a fear he'd blow our ship out of the water, but thank goodness we were spared.

Often while fishing we saw clouds gathering on the distant horizon, indicating a storm was coming. Drops of rain would begin to fall and the wind would pick up. If we ignored those signs and stayed out too long, a waterspout whirlwind might form in the shape of a tornado. Then a progressive gyrating mass of air would erupt into a violent and sudden downpour. I remember these occasions well, because my dad's instruction was always the same, "Batten down the hatches—now!"

Oh, brother! That's all it took: we hurriedly pulled in our fishing lines, tied the "catch bucket" to one of the seats, threw the rest of the bait overboard, and held on to our hats while Daddy started the motor and took off for safety. We'd go top speed back to the boathouse. I can still hear Orv saying, "Daddy, don't go so fast! My beaker's gonna blow away."

But Daddy wouldn't slow down. Danger was lurking, and he felt responsible to get us out of it. We all held on tightly and zoomed to the shoreline.

"Batten down the hatches" is a nautical term meaning to close the doors or openings on a boat before a storm hits. It's become an American idiom meaning to prepare and protect yourself in every way possible for whatever life storm is coming. Since my preteen years, I've used that phrase to remind myself to start getting ready for trouble whenever I sense it lurking on the horizon. And that trouble can come in different forms: anxiety, fear, poor health, aging, lack of money, and letting go of something, to name a few.

We don't have to be rocket scientists to know we should prepare for what *might* happen when these circumstances occur. For example, we might have to make a difficult decision that will determine the quality of life for our remaining years. We might have to forfeit well-laid plans. We might need to forgive an enemy. We might have to look into asking, or even hiring, others to help us instead of tackling our problems alone. Whatever it is, we must consciously decide what is best for ourselves and then *do* it. Battening down all the hatches is *not* a time to do nothing.

By sharing this step to a happy life, I'm encouraging all of us to confront the storms of life with acceptance, fortitude, and grace. Scripture provides a perfect guideline for the best way to face these problems. It's found in Mark 14:38, which says, "Stay alert, be in prayer, so you don't enter the danger zone without even knowing it. Don't be naive."

When we know danger is up ahead, preparation, prayer, and patience will get us through.

The last time I was with my father in a boat, a squall came up that scared me. As a young teenager, I kept thinking we'd never make it to shore because the waves were so high and strong. While Daddy was busy working the motor, I said nothing. I simply tried to keep my mind focused on getting home safely. And now that I've lived all these years and my heavenly Father has seen me through many a storm, I know he's able to take me all the way home if I just trust him. And when I enter a danger zone, I'm not naive.

THIRTY-SIX

Figure It Out for Yourself

One of the most sterling examples of someone who figured out life for himself is George Washington Carver. Born into poverty and slavery, his childhood was virtually unbearable. Nevertheless, he left us a legacy of gifts that are, by their sheer magnitude, almost unbelievable.

When George was a week old, slave night raiders kidnapped him. His owner hired someone to find him and get him back. In doing so, he was traded for a horse. George was taught to read and write by an unknown woman named "Aunt Susan" who imprinted into his memory this phrase: "You must learn all you can. Then go back out into the world and give your learning back to the people."

That's exactly what he did. Driven to get an education, he went to school through great hardship and learned all he could about every subject that came his way, winding up with a master's degree in agriculture and several honorary doctorates.

As if that were not enough, he was the recipient of awards of merit, and in 1952 *Popular Mechanics* selected him as one of fifty outstanding Americans. Coins and stamps were printed with his likeness. Museums were named after him. A movie was made in his honor, and he was inducted into the National Inventors Hall of Fame. My favorite recognition of George Washington Carver happened in 1941 when *Time* magazine dubbed him the "Black Leonardo" in reference to the great Renaissance inventor and artist Leonardo da Vinci.

His humility, humanitarianism, frugality, and good nature enabled the rest of us today to enjoy and benefit from his accomplishments in the fields of agricultural education, improvement in racial relations, mentoring children, painting, and writing poetry—one of which is entitled "Figure It Out for Yourself."

George Washington Carver didn't leave a stone unturned. In his seventy-nine years on earth as a slave, scientist, botanist, educator, inventor, and Christian (he invited Jesus Christ into his heart when he was ten), he's left a legacy of figuring out life in such a way that we find ourselves wanting to emulate his rejection of materialism and embrace his love of learning. Carver died in 1943, and on his tombstone are these words: "He could have added fortune to fame, but caring for neither, he found happiness and honor in being helpful to the world."

Figuring it out for oneself requires discipline. It asks us to observe a few simple, personal guidelines, such as having character matter more than reputation, knowing what we can control and what we can't, learning that the good life is a life of inner seren-ity, never suppressing generosity. It means living wisely. To figure something out, we have to examine how things fit together. We all come equipped with the same set of tools: a brain, a conscience, a will, and a heart. With these tools, we look within our own souls in order to understand what lies within the souls of others. And our goal is to figure out what constitutes who we really are. We try to establish common sense, to understand others and what they're saying, to accept ourselves, and to figure out why we carry grudges or make judgments. We learn from our mistakes. It may not be easy, especially at first, but this is the most courageous way to live.

Because George Washington Carver was as interested in his students' character development as he was in their intellectual development, he lived by a list of eight virtues and taught them in his classes. I'll leave you with those. As you think through them, try to apply them in the days, months, and years ahead.

- Be clean both inside and out.
- Neither look up to the rich nor down on the poor.
- Lose, if need be, without squealing.
- Win without bragging.
- Always be considerate of women, children, and older people.
- Be too brave to lie.
- Be too generous to cheat.
- Take your share of the world and let others take theirs.

Remember this: as you figure out life for yourself, start doing common things in an uncommon way. When you do, you'll com-mand the attention of the world.

THIRTY-SEVEN

Discover What
Makes People Tick

People fascinate me. I could sit on a park bench all day and strike up a conversation with anyone about anything: rich or poor, young or old, male or female. I'm not as interested in externals (Where'd you get that purse? Where are you flying today?) as I am in discovering what makes people tick. For me, discovering what powers someone's inner workings has been the pursuit of a lifetime.

It's equally fascinating to discover who we are, ourselves. Perhaps others define us as someone's sibling, wife, mother, grandmother, friend, neighbor, or employee, but who are we inside, walls down, roofs off? What makes us tick?

Proverbs 22:6 says, "Start children off on the way they should go, and even when they are old they will not turn from it" (NIV). That means children reared in the nurture and admonition of the Lord will be trained to follow him as they grow older. It doesn't mean they absolutely *will* follow him, but they've been trained to do so. It also means if they seek to live within the confines of their giftedness, or "bent," they'll more than likely *tick* in that direction.

Let's look at it this way: I have two very close friends who know each other well but are as different as daylight and dark regarding their individual inclinations. One is almost clairvoyant when it comes to the physical needs of others. She seems to know when to offer help, even when there's no request beforehand from the needy person. More often than not, my friend takes care of the need before it manifests itself. She can sense what should be done, and does it. Meeting the physical needs of others is basically what makes her tick.

The second friend has the ability to determine what action should be taken when it comes to psychological needs. She's a born counselor and was that way as a young girl. When she was a high school student all her girlfriends discussed problems with her regarding themselves, boyfriends, parents, neighbors—because she innately knew how to help them. It's as though she could have been a counselor at the age of fifteen. That innate ability was her bent. It made her tick.

I've spent many years getting to know what makes *me* tick. I've found it true what Viktor Frankl said: "The creation of personal meaning is central to a satisfying life." Discovering what makes me tick has helped me see and understand the inclinations that make others tick as well.

I suggest you get to know what makes *you* tick by asking yourself a few simple questions:

- *What is important to me?* Write down a list of essential and meaningful attributes or activities in your life in the order of value. I did this a few years ago, and I look at it now and then to see if these same things still matter. They do.
- *Do I lead with my head or my heart?* Take time to analyze how decisions are made, and once they're made, determine what is to be done next. Keep a good balance between what needs to be done and how you feel about it after it's done.
- *How do I treat other people?* This is a very important question. On your answer hinges your belief system, behavior, and reputation. There's no substitute for kindness and grace in daily living. It says volumes about who you are.
- *Do my actions harmonize with my way of life?* This is not so much what you do but how you do it. When you understand this and live by this principle, inner peace will be possible even if hard times come. Don't make up your own rules. Seek harmony.
- *Who is the person I want to be?* Determine your goals and ideals. Determine who you admire and why. Don't be vague. Learn to define who you are with only yourself in the definition.

I encourage you to spend time by yourself, getting to know yourself. It's been said that people who celebrate solitude make the most contributions to humankind. Solitude gives clarity and enlightenment, and those two attributes help you discover who you are and who others are as well.

THIRTY-EIGHT

Fight Resentment Before It Festers

For years I held a grudge against a friend. It was a long time ago, but I well remember the feelings of that pain. I carried the grudge with me wherever I went, and it was a slow-eating cancer in my soul.

After much conviction and many tears, I finally poured out my broken, self-centered heart to God and asked him to forgive me and help me clean up the cesspool of resentment I had carried around too long. And he did. It was slow and tedious at first because of my stubborn will, but I can say without a shadow of a doubt that God healed me. When I stopped wanting to get revenge and reached out for God's forgiveness, everything changed, and I learned some of life's most important lessons.

The Greek philosopher Epictetus once said, "One of the signs of the dawning of moral progress is the gradual extinguishing of blame." I believe it. The minute I started taking my eyes off my own rotten attitude and turned them to a forgiving God, the blame game stopped. There was no resentment left.

I've asked myself a thousand times why I didn't fight that resentment before it became a festering pool in my spirit. I was a fool to wait. I was immature. I wanted the other person to suffer because of the grudge I carried. I really believe it's as simple as that.

Have you ever found yourself in that boat? You probably have. Rare is the individual who can go through life without feeling resentment, harboring a grudge, or blaming somebody else for an offense. And seemingly the only way for that not to happen is to fight resentment before it has time to fester and become a boil on the surface of a relationship. This is what it takes to win that FIGHT:

- Figure out what went wrong and determine to seek resolution.
- Initiate a conversation with the person who has offended you.
- Get feedback, then give your interpretation of what that means.
- Hear ideas for discussion without being stubborn.
- Together, seek clarity, understanding, and forgiveness.

Nobody knows better than I do that this is not easy. One of the hardest things in the world is to forgive somebody who has wronged us. But there are countless Scriptures on the value of forgiveness, and God makes doing it possible. I can tell you from experience, if we put it off because we fear confrontation or deny the offense ever happened, it will get bigger and bigger. It will fester.

I hate confrontation and will do almost anything in the world to avoid it, but I've learned from the school of hard knocks, if we gently confront someone about an issue that separates us, it pays off in the end. Once the rift is healed, there is peace, calm, and gratitude like you've never felt before.

After the situation got better between my friend and me I remember reading in Matthew 5:22–24 these convicting words from Jesus: "This is how I want you to conduct yourself in these matters. If you enter your place of worship and, about to make an offering, you suddenly remember a grudge a friend has against you, abandon your offering, leave immediately, go to this friend and make things right. Then and only then, come back and work things out with God."

I also believe this verse applies to the one holding the grudge, not just the one against whom the grudge is held. As I read it, I was reminded again of how we can undermine ourselves when we allow something this detrimental to decay in our spirits. But when we ask for forgiveness and *mean* it, we open ourselves up to the God of the universe, who not only forgives but also teaches us how to forgive others.

Matthew 6:14–15 says, "In prayer there is a connection between what God does and what you do. You can't get forgiveness from God, for instance, without also forgiving others. If you refuse to do your part, you cut yourself off from God's part."

THIRTY-NINE

Cook Something Special for Yourself

Half my life has been lived in small, rented apartments when money was tight. I learned to make do with what was at hand. I had to be creative about clothes, furnishings, gifts, and meals. And certainly about travel—when I was able to go anywhere, that is.

Now that I look back on those years from the vantage point of a debt-free homeowner, I have to say those were some of the best and most enjoyable years of my life. There's something about being in a small space, with little to work with, that makes one's creative juices flow. Truly, necessity is the mother of invention.

One of the ways I enjoyed those years was spending time in the kitchen. My mother was a fantastic cook, and she taught me some of the tricks of the trade. Because so much of my life has been spent alone, I learned to cook special things just for myself and build a whole evening around the meal.

For example, every December I would set aside a night that was just for my out-of-town friends and me. Of course, none of them could be there in person, but they might as well have been because the entire evening was devoted to being with them. We exchanged gifts, by mail, and I opened their gifts under the Christmas tree and then called each one after his or her gift was unwrapped. We talked, laughed, caught up on each other's lives, and had a wonderful visit about the gift I'd been given. I called that annual celebration "my very own Christmas party," and one of its highlights was the meal. I would cook most of the day in preparation for the evening, making some delectable dish for myself.

One year I made a recipe from the "centerfold" of *Gourmet* magazine. Of course, I had lots of leftovers, which I enjoyed for days to come. I still laugh about it because a little part of the kitchen caught on fire when the recipe got out of hand. But I managed to put out the flame almost as fast as it started. Now it's a laughable moment in my memory bank.

Unfortunately, lots of people simply don't want to cook if they don't have others eating with them. They open a can and throw some unappetizing concoction together just to get through the grind of having to fix a meal. They ask themselves, *Who needs the mess? Why dirty the pots and pans and do all this work just for me?*

If you do that, you're missing the joy of cooking something special for yourself, as well as the possibility of having a creative adventure in the kitchen. On the other hand, when you're willing to step out on the edge a little, you might find recipes that will not only please your palate and your pocketbook but also provide you with a fun story for your memory bank (in case you set *your* kitchen on fire).

I had a delicious meal at an Italian restaurant in Los Angeles one night and wanted to repeat that pasta recipe for myself. So I called the restaurant and asked to speak to the chef. Not only did he come to the phone, but he gladly told me the ingredients and exactly how to cook the pasta. I was absolutely *thrilled*. As he walked me through the whole thing step by step, I made the recipe. Now and then he excused himself from the phone to answer various questions from his waiters. Not only did I have a wonderful pasta dish for dinner that night, but I've also cooked that recipe dozens of times since then, and it's become a favorite of friends who've eaten around my table.

"Cooking is my *kinderspiel*," said Wolfgang Puck, "my child's play. You can make it yours too. And while you're cooking, don't forget to share and laugh. Laugh a great deal, and with much love— it enhances the flavor of the food."

Don't hold back from cooking something time-consuming or difficult for yourself simply because you feel like it's too much work for one person or that people might wonder why you go to the trouble. Sing while you cook. Rehearse your Bible verses. Pray. Talk to the food. Have fun, and write about it in your journal when the meal's over. There'll always be people who don't understand why you do what you do. But quite honestly, if you knew the truth, they might be wishing they were more like you.

{ FORTY }

Celebrate the Life You're Given

Not long ago, I read Eric Metaxas's biography of Dietrich Bonhoeffer, and I don't know when I've appreciated a book more. Everything about Bonhoeffer's life had meaning and purpose, from his childhood till the day of his martyrdom at the hand of Nazi officers in 1945. In every sense of the word, he celebrated the life he was given. He loved his family, friends, work, ministry, art, music, literature, theater, travel, learning, teaching, and studying different cultures from all over the world.

Bonhoeffer gave his life away to encourage and bless others, no matter the cost. He was a gentleman to the core and a dedicated Christian. Even during his years of imprisonment, he didn't complain; he loved his enemies and prayed for them daily. His confidence was not in his circumstances but in the Lord Jesus Christ.

One of the many inspiring things Bonhoeffer wrote was this remarkable thought: "The right to live is a matter of essence, not values. In the sight of God there is no life that is not worth living. . . . The fact that God is the Creator, Preserver, and Redeemer of life makes even the most wretched life worth living before God."

The words "the right to live is a matter of essence, not values" caught my attention, and I've continued to think about them since I first read them. Bonhoeffer believed that each of us lives and has our being, and that's what enables us to celebrate. He was saying the value of our lives is not predicated on who we are or when and where we were born. The worth or value of one's life is inherent in every human being—it's in the fact that we are simply alive in the first place. Being alive is enough in itself to give us reason to celebrate.

But sometimes it doesn't seem so. It's easy for us to think our lives and even our worth can be measured by the number of degrees behind our name, the money in our bank account, the languages we speak, and the heads that turn when we enter a room. We can easily bypass the reality that life itself is the gift God gives us. It matters. We matter. And, quite honestly, *that's* what matters. Think about it.

What is more important than the fact that you have breath in your lungs? Is accomplishment more important? While that's both satisfying and profitable, is it more important? Is accumulation? The people we know? Where we go? What we think of ourselves? What others think of us? Or is the value of your life in the "essence" of you, as Bonhoeffer wrote?

As I read this perspective of Bonhoeffer's, I thought of my own father, who had a stroke when he was in his late eighties. It almost killed him and left him very frail and faltering. His level of activity, speech, and lifestyle changed, but the "essence" of him didn't change. Who he was remained the same before and after the stroke. He remained exceedingly generous, giving away what he had.

The day before Daddy died in a nursing home, I went to see him (not knowing, of course, that would be our last visit). I took him a Hershey bar, his favorite treat. He asked me to unwrap it for him, which I did. Then, without hesitation, he offered it to me and then to the man with whom he shared a room. Next he offered it to the nurse, to the doctor, and to passers-by in the hall. By the time the bar got back to Daddy, there were only two little squares left.

"I only wanted a taste," he said. Then he looked at me and said, "Thank you, honey. Just having you with me is sweeter than this candy bar anyway. I so appreciate your coming. You look beautiful."

Bonhoeffer was right. God's value, as well as yours and mine, is in our essence—that which is inside us, that which God has redeemed and will live forever.

{ PART FIVE }

Staying Connected

{ FORTY-ONE }

Listen with Your Whole Heart

I come from a verbal family. More often than not, everybody talked at once. If I were to step back into that childhood scene, knowing what I know now, I'm sure I'd be surprised at all the noise. We three kids were certainly made to obey our parents, but I don't remember anything being said about the importance of listening. It seemed everybody was eager to be heard, but nobody was eager to listen. Maybe your home was like that too.

I remember reading somewhere that there are two kinds of bores: those who talk too much and those who listen too little. That was our family in a nutshell. It wasn't until I was grown that I realized I'd probably been boring people into a coma for years.

Now that I've lived a long time and changed some of my bad habits into good ones, I've learned how to listen, and now I realize it's an art form. Generally speaking, these days I prefer listening to talking. When a few rules are followed, anybody can become a good listener, and when those rules are kept, one can easily practice it.

Listening with your whole heart takes concentration and focus. Here's what works for me: look directly at the person talking and don't interrupt. If you're afraid you're going to forget something important you want to say, jot down a quick word so you can refer to it later. Keep an open mind to the facts being shared without judging actions or behavior.

Along the road of life, I was blessed to have friends who cared enough about me to model these rules and pass along helpful pointers. But maybe my best listening teacher has been Proverbs 20:5. That verse has helped me immensely, both in listening to others and in having them listen to me. I like to see how it's presented in two different versions of the Bible, first in the New King James Version, and then in *The Message*:

Counsel in the heart of man is like deep water, but a man of understanding will draw it out.

Knowing what is right is like deep water in the heart; a wise person draws from the well within.

Picture two people talking. One is the person with the counsel in his or her heart and the other is the person of understanding. As the first person talks, the second one listens. But where is the counsel? It's in the heart of the first person, not in the one who is listening.

So often when we're the listener, we feel like we have to give our counsel, our opinion, our judgment in response to what's being said. But all that counsel lies in the heart of the one talking. The listener just draws it out. He extends an empty bucket of kindness and questions down into that heart and gently draws out what the other person needs to know that is already there. As the listener, it's not our job to point out what should be done. It's our job to receive, encourage, occasionally ask pertinent questions, and simply listen. As the talker processes his or her thoughts aloud and the listener receives those thoughts, the counsel will come from inside the one talking. And if the "man of understanding" doesn't listen, no progress will be made.

Undoubtedly, the thing we all want when somebody listens to us is to be understood and valued. We shut up the minute we're judged. Remember this: we're only open to the degree we are received. We want to be heard by one who cares about us and listens to what we have to say. Are you that person? Am I? That's the question we need to ask ourselves.

The golden rule of friendship is to listen to others—as you would have them listen to you.

{ FORTY-TWO }

Communicate Often with Loved Ones

The first time I met the members of Hawk Nelson, a Christian rock band from Canada, I loved them immediately. Not only are they talented musicians, but they're also warm and friendly. Even though they're decades younger than I, they're welcoming and thoughtful in every respect. But the most impressive thing to me was when lead vocalist Jason Dunn told me how much he loved his mother and called her every day.

I was *stunned*. Here he is in his twenties, and he knows what it means to a mother to hear from her son often. So he calls her every day.

How cool is that? When I see him from time to time now at

conferences, my standard question is, "Have you called your mother today?"

Sometimes before I even open my mouth, he greets me with a big smile and says, "Yes, Luci. I've called her."

Some people might think it's way too much for a twenty-something young man who's married to put in a daily call to his mom. They'd view that as being a "momma's boy," but I can tell you he's anything but. He's simply thoughtful to someone he loves.

One of the nicest things we can do for our loved ones is to call them or contact them in some other personal way. Most people live busy lives, and that busyness keeps them from reaching out to their loved ones. But it doesn't have to be that way. There are lots of avenues, especially in today's world, to communicate with those we care about. It's almost mind-boggling the number of ways we can keep in contact with people now.

Personally, I loved the days of letter writing, and I was good at it. Anybody remember those days? That's when you actually took a piece of stationery and composed a letter to somebody by hand, put a stamp on the envelope, and took it to the mailbox. Of course, being a packrat, I have most of the letters I ever received—boxes and boxes of them. In fact, when a friend of mine died about twelve years ago, her family gave me back the 107 postcards I'd written her during our friendship. She had saved them all, and her loved ones saw to it that I got them. I'm sure they knew I'd treasure them as much as she had. I *love* postcards and have collected them from friends all over the world. It's a quick and loving way to touch base.

I have to admit, though, perhaps my most prized possessions in terms of communication are the forty-seven letters from my brother, Chuck Swindoll, that he wrote me during his time in the Marine Corps in the 1950s (especially when he was stationed on the island of Okinawa). To me, those letters are pure gold. Many of them refer to his relationship with the Lord and his desire to go into public Christian ministry. They're part of his foundational thoughts for where he is today, which is right here in the Dallas area, where he works as a pastor, head of Insight for Living radio ministry, and chancellor of Dallas Theological Seminary.

I love looking back on all the years we've stayed in touch through letters, phone calls, reunions, ministry, birthdays, family gatherings, texts, and now e-mails. I know people who don't even know where their siblings are, and here I am with one of my sweet brothers living just a few blocks from me. We were pals when we tossed the football in the backyard of our little Swindoll house in Houston, and we've laughed together on fishing trips with Mother and Daddy. I sang in his wedding more than fifty years ago and said good-bye to him at the airport when he went off to military duty. I witnessed his graduation from DTS and his becoming president at that same school thirty-two years later. And now, every Sunday I'm home and not at a conference somewhere, I hear him preach at Stonebriar Community Church in Frisco and often have lunch with him after the service.

Did I know we would wind up as neighbors, spending our final years together in rich fellowship? Of course not. Neither of us planned this, but we've stayed close all our lives because we love each other. Being neighbors now is one of those surprising gifts of God's grace.

If you've lost contact with family members or friends, don't put off getting in touch with them. You never know how your life will be enriched by reestablishing those relationships. Job 5:8 says God is "famous for great and unexpected acts; there's no end to his surprises." Staying in communication with your loved ones—or reconnecting with them—pays off, folks. Don't miss those surprises God has in store for you. Pay attention to the little things God does, especially those for which you've never asked. Then thank him and tell somebody you love what he's done for you.

FORTY-THREE

Set the Table for Company

The French gastronome A. Brillat-Savarin once said, "To invite a person into your house is to take charge of his happiness for as long as he is under your roof." That was my mother's philosophy. In spite of our family's small quarters, she rolled out the red carpet for guests: courtesy was extended at the door, soft music came from the radio, the best chair in the house was offered, a meal was prepared, and the table was set to perfection. Unless we were having a picnic, I can't even remember a time when our little dining table was not set for a family meal. We had no television, so nobody ate off a TV tray. Everybody came to the table when called, and a blessing was said before we ate. Long after my mother had passed away, a friend said to me one day, "Your mother was so civilized." Indeed she was.

To my mother, setting a beautiful table often expressed more love to the family and guests than the food we were about to eat. It showed thoughtfulness, care, and attention to details. Mother, in her simple way, was a lot like Brillat-Savarin. In his book *The Physiology of Taste* (first published in 1825 and still in print today), he tells us that even the simplest meal pleased him if it was executed with artistry.

In many ways, I've inherited Mother's love of beauty and the value of artistry when setting a table for company. She put a great deal of emphasis on the dishes and silverware being in the right spot, napkins folded just so, and the guest or guests seated at a place of honor. Today I do the same.

When I was a senior in college in 1955, my mother began painting a set of china for my graduation gift. I still have that sixty-piece set with orange blossoms painted all over the cups, saucers, plates, and bowls. Even as I sit here writing this chapter, those dishes are displayed in a china cabinet about twenty feet away that I designed and had especially built to show off Mother's gorgeous gift. She signed and dated each piece. When I look at those dishes now, I'm reminded again of the time and love it took to complete that project. Mother died forty years ago, so I treasure this gift more with each passing year.

From time to time, I throw a dinner party. With the care I inherited from Mother, I set my long table in the library. Not only do I use my best dishes and the silver utensils she gave me, but I also make place cards for every guest and have a flower arrangement as the centerpiece. In my spare time, I work on that table for days on end, starting early with the place cards that are representative of the season or the reason for the party. I've made cards from beads, balls, birds, baskets, and balloons. I've copied quotations or Scriptures to fit each person, drawn pictures of animals and children, and cut apart maps and folded paper to make model airplanes, toys, hats, and bracelets. We've had treasure hunts at the table, and at times I've handed out sheet music so we could all sing together in harmony. I always enjoy making these efforts because I want the guests around my table to remember a meal that's fun and different.

Does this take time? Of course. Does it require going the extra mile? Yes. Have I ever said I'll never do this again? Just the opposite!

Next time you throw a dinner party or invite guests to share a holiday meal or even when you prepare a weekday family meal, do something out of the ordinary. Use the best of what you have and set the table for company. Not that you have to have expensive china or silver. You don't even have to have a dining room. Just make the kitchen table look special with some kind of attractive centerpiece. Serve a delicious meal. Talk and laugh a lot. Take pictures. Make a memory. Then, if you've invited guests, say good-bye with love and kisses and God's blessings on those who have to leave. You won't regret a single moment you spent making the occasion special. Brillat-Savarin also said, "The pleasure of the table belongs to all ages, to all countries, and to all areas; it mingles with all other pleasures, and remains at last to console us for their departure."

I predict that you'll find you don't have to spend a lot of money on the extra details that go into setting the table for company. It's the love and care for your guests that your gesture shows.

FORTY-FOUR

Trust Friends for the Truth

Some of my closest friends are shrinks. Or they've had therapy with one. Personally, I love people who've had therapy and think like therapists. The way they reason interests me, and their viewpoint of mental and emotional challenges helps me look at life through another lens.

One of the things I value most about these therapeutic friends is that I can count on them to tell me the truth, which in my view, is exceedingly important in friendship. If my friends won't be honest with me, who will? And since I've been single all my life, some of my friends are as close to me as members of my family. In some ways they know more about me than the people I grew up with because we've been together on a daily basis for most of my adult years.

Sometimes I don't really like the truth they tell me, but even when I don't, I almost always come around and eventually accept what they say. Here's why: they know *how* to say it.

You see, there's a catch to the value of truth telling: it's all in how it's told. Of course we need to know the truth about ourselves, but remember this from chapter 41: We have to be really willing to *listen* and *receive* the truth that's being shared with us. If the truth hurts us, we're inclined to back away. As the prophet wrote in Amos 5:10, "Raw truth is never popular."

Instead of feeding something "raw" to the hearer, why not cook it a bit on the back burner of our hearts before offering it to someone else? Couch what you have to say in gentleness. I'm not saying you should beat around the bush; simply be mindful that what you're saying could be hurtful. Make sure it doesn't sound angry or accusatory.

And if you're the one hearing the truth, receive it as something that probably took courage to say, and appreciate your friend's honesty. It might be that he or she felt brave enough to speak the truth to you only because your relationship is strong enough to allow it.

In my close circle of friends, we have a somewhat unspoken rule that we'll be up front with each other. Because our community is a "sisterhood" and we all live near one another geographically, we try very hard to stay current and sensitive when it comes to each other's feelings. Sometimes it can be painful to hear the truth we need to know. But in our circle—and I imagine in yours too—truth has to be told to keep communication open. Not being truthful causes more harm than good.

Eight years ago, when I was building my home, a neighbor helped me make decisions regarding the tile, brick, and trim I wanted to use. Together we went to the design center to select the right colors and textures, but, as I mentioned earlier, because I had to travel so much during those days and she didn't, she volunteered to oversee a lot of the construction when I couldn't be on the premises.

One day while I was out of town she and I had a little disagreement on the phone. She discovered the workmen were putting the wrong color on the window trim, and she wanted to represent me in telling them to change the color to what I had initially chosen. Knowing that would delay the process, after a few exchanges back and forth, I told her we'd just stay with the color they were using. "After all, it's my house," I said curtly.

I was perfectly willing to let it go, thinking it didn't matter that much in the end, but she was not. She kept saying it wouldn't be that hard to change and I would like it better when all was said and done.

I grew frustrated because I felt she was trying to "run my business." Oh, brother! I knew at some point we would have to talk about the issue. Hating confrontation, I dreaded that encounter.

When I got home, my friend kindly asked if we could look at the problem together. Reluctantly, I said yes. She carefully and truthfully spelled out her side of the story. Appreciating her gentle manner and her desire to make it right, I confessed my stubbornness and my bad attitude when I had talked with her on the phone. I asked her to forgive me. At the end of our conversation, she suggested we pray together. In that prayer she thanked the Lord for helping us both to be transparent.

Because of my friend's kindness and her genuine effort to get to the truth of the matter, I was reminded again of Proverbs 24:26: "An honest answer is like a warm hug."

I love the way my brother Chuck put it when he said, "Honesty has a beautiful and refreshing simplicity about it. No ulterior motives. No hidden meanings. An absence of hypocrisy, duplicity, political games, and verbal superficiality. As honesty and real integrity characterize our lives, there will be no need to manipulate others."

FORTY-FIVE

Forgive Others Over and Over

Several years ago I frequented a particular flower shop owned by a horticulturalist. He told me that when his grandfather died, he left him a plot of land in his will so the boy could grow plants and have a nursery. He also said the grandfather had done the same thing for my friend's older brother. The older brother, however, was given a greater portion of the land than he. After three years of disagreement between them, their mother sided with the younger son and the father with the older. Ultimately, what was to have been a gift became such a point of contention that the two sides wouldn't speak to each other. It was a full-fledged family feud.

When I first heard this story, I have to say my response was disbelief. One day while at the flower shop I was talking with the owner, and I said to him, "Do you ever think about sitting down with your brother and making amends? Might you ever forgive one another? What was meant to be a gift has become such a burden; forgiveness might make you both feel better."

"Forgive?" he asked, looking inquisitively. "I will never forgive him. Forgiveness is a myth, and it doesn't work. I'd rather carry a grudge than forgive him. I want what's mine, and I plan to get it."

I decided to drop the issue and ultimately stopped going to the shop. Frankly, the presence of that spirit made me uncomfortable. There were other places to buy flowers, and I simply found myself choosing to go elsewhere. Lack of forgiveness for his brother was destroying this man, and every time I was in his presence, I could feel it more and more.

The Bible tells us to "forgive one another as quickly and thoroughly as God in Christ forgave you" (Ephesians 4:32). Of course, that's much easier said than done. When we've been offended, something in us wants to get even. Some of us have a veritable mineshaft of grudges and offenses we've carried for years, and nothing is going to stop us from retaliating.

I've now lived long enough to tell you from experience that this kind of bitterness and rancor will eat you alive. If you let it happen, your heart will harden, and without an open heart, there will be no way for the Holy Spirit to do his work of healing because the one who's been wounded will lick, feed, and nurture that wound. As a result, the hardness intensifies until it is far beyond the hard-heartedness of the one who caused the offense; it reaches a stage where a simple apology would never do. It's too late for that.

Yet even in that situation, the only solution is to forgive. Forgiveness wipes the slate clean. Instead of rubbing it in when we've been hurt, we must learn to rub it out. Forgiveness is much more important to the one who does the forgiving than to the one who is being forgiven. Healing starts when we forgive. An open heart heals much more easily. God can work in a heart that's open.

We have all failed. Made mistakes. Said and done stupid things. Be that as it may, life goes on, and we must go with it. Those who give and forgive are the richest people in the world. They've accepted their inadequacies and shortcomings and have learned to forgive others over and over. And in so doing, they can forgive themselves.

I have no idea what finally became of the two brothers. But when I think of them, I'm reminded of these lines from Alfred Lord Tennyson:

> *Two aged men, that had been foes for life,*
> *Met by a grave, and wept—And in those tears*
> *They washed away the memory of their strife:*
> *Then wept again the loss of all those years.*

Perhaps this is what happened with the two brothers whose relationship was broken by a gift.

FORTY-SIX

Invite People to Your Home

One of my close friends comes from a family of eight children. When she was growing up, it was the custom in her family to invite school chums over for meals, to spend the night or, on occasion, the weekend. Their mother thought nothing of it if there were ten or twelve kids at the dinner table instead of the usual eight. On the other hand, because there were so many in the family, they were never invited out, so their mother had an open-door policy for friends. It was the norm. She never objected; she was such a gracious and hospitable woman, she made it a point to see that nobody known by her family was left out if he or she needed a meal, a bed to sleep in, or a place to stay.

I was amused when my friend told me she was attending the funeral of her older sister many years later, and in the crowd of those who had gathered, there was a gentleman she knew but couldn't quite place in her mind. She asked him to refresh her memory.

"I was your brother Phil's friend. He was wonderful to me. In fact, I don't know if you remember this or not, but I lived with your family for a year. I had no place to stay, so Phil asked me to live there. I'm not sure your mother ever knew it. I just sort of joined the crowd and was considered part of the family. I loved it."

When I was told that story, I laughed out loud. Not so much because it's humorous, but because of the joy it must have been for that young man to live in a home like that, where no questions were asked about how many were at the table, sleeping over, having fun with the kids. Perhaps without knowing it, this woman has been practicing what the apostle Paul encourages us to do in Romans 12:13: "Be inventive in hospitality."

Hospitality is a state of mind. It's having a spirit of giving and caring. We're told throughout Scripture to be hospitable, but unfortunately, it's rapidly becoming a lost art. Nobody has time anymore—or takes time. Life goes too fast. Inviting people to one's home is a luxury—and who takes time for luxury these days?

When I talk about hospitality, I always think of my older brother, Orville, and his wife, Erma Jean. They are classic examples of those who have invited people to their home all their married lives. And they still do it now, even though they're in their eighties.

Orville and E. J. spent the majority of their lives as missionaries in Argentina. But no matter where they live, there has rarely been a time they didn't have someone else living with them or spending a week or so with them. Their friends have left luggage or belongings there while doing mission work in the area. I so commend them for their extensive outreach of hospitality. It speaks volumes of love and grace. The welcome mat is always out.

They now live in Miami, but they seldom have a weekend when someone isn't visiting, having a meal with them, holding a meeting in their home, or sharing an evening together with them. Their friends are all over the world, and those friends know full well when they come to (or through) Miami, they're welcome at the Swindoll home—day or night, breakfast or dinner, alone or with family members. They model 3 John 1:5: "When you extend hospitality to Christian brothers and sisters, even when they are strangers, you make the faith visible."

Neither of these families, my friend's or Orville's, waited until everything was perfect to practice hospitality. They started the minute they had a home, as simple and unassuming as it might have been. People often think they'll have guests over when they get new flooring in the kitchen. Then it's when they get new carpet, then a new sofa, and then a bigger patio. It never ends. Don't let life pass you by because the placemats don't match. Reach out. Share stories. Laugh together. Create memories. Make your faith visible.

{ FORTY-SEVEN }

Share the Bread of Life

For more than sixteen years, I've been a speaker with Women of Faith. Every year I travel to about fifteen cities and speak to about two hundred thousand women. The irony is that I've never wanted to be in ministry. I didn't like the word. To "do ministry" meant I had to dress up, go somewhere, talk to somebody about sin in her life, and then set her straight with the gospel. (Or at least, that was my thinking.) I felt like people who engaged in ministry were called to preach. Or teach. All I wanted to do was enjoy life. Besides, I have two brothers who have been in public Christian ministry since their twenties. *That's enough for one family*, I thought.

I was reared in a Christian home where studying the Bible was emphasized, prayer was encouraged, forgiveness was practiced, and reverence for all things spiritual was taught. And I believed it.

At the age of ten, during Vacation Bible School at our little church down the road from our house, I accepted Jesus Christ as my Savior. My grandmother was my VBS teacher and explained how to pray a prayer of faith, and having done that, I became a Christian. That was enough for me.

But when I grew up, started going to Bible classes, and learned about the depth, width, and breadth of God's Word, I was truly amazed, and my life changed in every way. I realized I could live a grace-filled life as opposed to one controlled by legalism. I was introduced to theological doctrine that counseled and taught me the truth about the Trinity: God the Father, God the Son, and God the Holy Spirit. I learned to look at life from God's viewpoint rather than my own. I learned Jesus Christ loves me just as I am.

In short, I learned about the Bread of Life, and I wanted to share that knowledge with everybody by the way I lived, loved, learned—and enjoyed life. Jesus says in John 6:35–38:

> I am the Bread of Life. The person who aligns with me hungers no more and thirsts no more, ever. I have told you this explicitly because even though you have seen me in action, you don't really believe me. Every person the Father gives me eventually comes running to me. And once that person is with me, I hold on and don't let go. I came down from heaven not to follow my own whim but to accomplish the will of the One who sent me.

When I became acquainted with that verse, I ran to Jesus Christ, and he's never let me go; I've found constant nourishment in this Bread.

And when I finally figured out the importance of doctrine, I saw that God was basically in the business of two things: bringing those who don't know him as their Savior to knowledge of himself, and bringing those who know him to maturity in their faith.

When we believe we have sinned and come short of the glory of God and invite Jesus Christ into our hearts, he comes in, lives there, and fills us with his Spirit. That action of belief is when God declares us righteous, while we are still in our sinning state. We don't deserve it; nevertheless, by grace he gives us forgiveness, peace, purpose, and redemption in a moment of time. That is called *justification*. It happens once and for all time; once it happens, we are justified forever and ever. That will never change.

Becoming mature in Christ is very different. It will take the rest of our lives. It involves tests, challenges, growth, setbacks, waiting, trusting, disappointments, and so forth. All the things we go through to grow up as a human being. That is called *sanctification*. It will go on until we are taken in death, to live in eternity with God.

They are complicated-sounding words, but they're easy to understand. Look at it this way:

- What we are in Christ never changes: *justification*.
- Who we are in Christ never stops changing: *sanctification*.

Knowing and believing this truth is by far the greatest gift you can give yourself—and then give to others. It's a matter of faith, and once it's inside you, it becomes your ministry—whether you want it to be or not! You are carrying around the Bread of Life, and how you live *your* life has the capacity to feed people who are starving to death and don't even know it.

Enjoy life—and live generously!

{ FORTY-EIGHT }

Support Your Community with Love

In all the years I've lived on this earth, all the communities I've shared with friends, all the neighbors who have showered me with love and help, one of the best examples I know of is a guy named Pat. My friends and I call him Pat the Handyman. And that title really fits him.

There seems to be nothing he can't do. We call him day or night, rain or shine, sick or well, and his response is always the same: "Piece o' cake. I'll be right there." And he means it. Even though he's married with a family and lives a few miles away, within a short time, his car rounds the corner, and he's on the front porch, ready to take care of the problem or meet the need. I'm convinced this guy can do everything but walk on water, and frankly, I've wondered if he does that, too, behind closed doors.

For example, he's come to my house and hung pictures, polished silver, brought groceries, cleaned my garage, repaired a broken chair, rewired a lamp, and fixed my garage door. At my friends' home, he's taken down Christmas decorations, caulked sinks, carried boxes to the attic, turned mattresses, driven them to the airport or the doctor, planted trees, worked on cars, cleaned patios, swept off porches, repaired toilets, unstopped sinks, and fed the dog.

But here's my favorite thing about Pat: he never complains. Never. Nothing is ever *too much* or takes *too long*. It's his spirit. He's even called my friends and me out of the blue to ask if we need something lifted, painted, lugged, mowed, started, or stopped. And there has never been a time he's asked for a penny. More often than not, he tries to refuse payment by saying, "Hey, I was down the street anyway. You don't need to pay me for this."

A couple of weeks ago I asked if he could pick up my mail when I had a five-day out-of-town commitment.

"Piece o' cake."

When I got home, the mail was all sorted in a bag and placed in a basket awaiting my return. I had to actually track the man down to pay him for that service. Oh, my gosh! Why don't we have more people like Pat? He's the kind of person you want as a neighbor, a helper, a friend, a companion, and an employee. When I'm around him, Pat makes me want to be a better person and a better Christian. I find myself wanting to help everybody on my street and in my neighborhood. He models what the apostle Paul says in Galatians 5:13: "Use your freedom to serve one another in love." (And I just know somewhere in the Greek Paul must have added, "with no strings attached.")

If we were all supportive of one another like this, I'd bet my bottom dollar there would be fewer conflicts and hurt feelings. And a lot less one-upmanship. Kindness breeds kindness, and teamwork breeds teamwork. If somebody on your block needs a helping hand, why don't you be the first one to volunteer out of sheer love for life and for what God has done for you? Have fun with it and make it memorable by not asking for pay. Just smile and say it was a "piece o' cake."

{ FORTY-NINE }

Give Your Time, Energy, Money

When I got up this morning, I took a shower, washed my hair, threw on my sweats, rode my stationary bike, had breakfast, and then sat down at my desk to write a check for the electric bill. A few minutes later it hit me: within a couple of hours, I had spent every commodity I have in my power: time, energy, and money.

Have you ever stopped to think about how you spend *your* resources? All day long, right and left, we spend—rarely stopping to consider what's being spent. We're just trying to live our lives in a way that'll keep us going and not wear us out or break the bank. More often than not, we live our lives in all-about-*me* mode: all the duties I have to accomplish, all the meetings I have to attend, every inch of Dietrich Bonhoeffer's life. The three of us read it at the same time and compared notes. The minute each brother finished, he wrote me a thank you note, telling me what he loved about the book and why it meant so much to him. I put their notes in my copy of the book and will keep them forever.

There is something about hearing the words *thank you* that can make all the difference in how we feel, how we act, how we look at life. There's no way to prove this, but I wouldn't be surprised if I have every thank you note that was ever written to me. They are scattered throughout my journal pages, and I often read them again, years later. I also love hearing the words *thank you* in any language.

Just thanking someone for his or her support says volumes. It starts in childhood. Remember that little rhyme? "If I can count on you, and you can count on me, just think what a wonderful world this will be."

Someday, when my life is over, I'd like to be remembered for three things, that I was gracious, generous, and grateful. If I can achieve that, I'll feel like I've lived a life of meaning and richness. Golda Meir once said, "Create the kind of self that you will be happy to live with all your life." That's what I've tried to do. We can have money, fame, comfort, belongings, titles, and all that comes with each of those, but if we are not grateful or generous, we've missed the mark of being happy. And if we don't treat other people graciously, we'll never have friends. Max Lucado puts it beautifully: "The people who make a difference are not the ones with the credentials, but the ones with the concern." Preach it, Max! Let's not ever forget, authentic happiness is independent of external conditions. It's based on who we are inside.

My favorite holiday every year is Thanksgiving. That's been the case as far back as I can remember because Thanksgiving requires nothing but grateful hearts. All we do to celebrate this wonderful day is think of the things for which we are grateful—all the things that make us happy to be alive. Oh, we *can* decorate and fix a big meal for friends or relatives—or go to *their* house for dinner—but the commemoration is in the attitude of gratitude, a spirit of happiness not based on external conditions.

My prayer is that everyone reading this chapter (and this book, for that matter) will experience a rich life, filled with thanksgiving and love. The best way to describe my hope for you has already been written in Romans 12:3, so I close my last simple secret with that:

> I'm speaking to you out of deep gratitude for all that God has given me, and especially as I have responsibilities in relation to you. Living then, as every one of you does, in pure grace, it's important that you not misinterpret yourselves as people who are bringing this goodness to God. No, God brings it all to you. The only accurate way to understand ourselves is by what God is and by what he does for us, not by what we are and what we do for him.

May the Lord give you a long and happy life filled to the brim with grace and gratitude.

About the Author

No one enjoys herself more than Luci Swindoll. She's full of antic-ipation, fun, and a sense of adventure that just won't quit. Her exuberant love for life has seen her through a career as a corpo-rate executive at Mobil Oil (long before it became ExxonMobil), fifteen years as a chorister with the Dallas Opera, and a stint as vice president of public relations at her brother Chuck Swindoll's ministry, Insight for Living.

One of Women of Faith's original speakers, Luci has been inspiring women in conference audiences across North America for sixteen years. She has traveled to fifty-three countries on every continent and (in her words), "speaks just enough Italian and German to chat with friends and order lunch." She is the author of more than a dozen books and curriculum studies.

Luci lives in Texas in a home she designed that's part art gal-lery, part library, part studio, and all Luci.

Other Books by Luci Swindoll

Doing Life Differently

Free Inside and Out (with Marilyn Meberg)

The Best Devotions of Luci Swindoll

Life! Celebrate It: Listen, Learn, Laugh, Love

*Notes to a Working Woman:
Finding Balance, Passion, and Fulfillment in Your Life*

I Married Adventure

I Married Adventure Journal

You Bring the Confetti, God Brings the Joy

Celebrating Life: Catching the Thieves Who Steal Your Joy

*After You're Dressed for Success:
A Guide to Developing Character as Well as a Career*

*The Alchemy of the Heart:
Life's Refining Process to Free Us from Ourselves*

Wide My World, Narrow My Bed

Also available from
LUCI SWINDOLL

"Adventure is an attitude, not a behavi

raising
low-fat
kⁱds

in a high-fat world

JUDITH SHAW

Foreword by
Peter O. Kwiterovich, Jr., M.D.
The Johns Hopkins School of Medicine

CHRONICLE BOOKS
SAN FRANCISCO

Library of Congress Cataloging-in-Publication Data:
Shaw, Judith B., 1935–
    Raising low-fat kids in a high-fat world / Judith Shaw.
        p. cm.
       Includes index.
       ISBN 0-8118-1441-6 (pbk.)
        1. Children—Nutrition. 2. Low-fat diet. I. Title.
RJ206.S553 1996
613.2'083—dc20   96-5717
                                         CIP

Printed in the United States.

Cover design by Sarah Bolles
Book design by Julie N. Long
Composition by Cat Arnes

Distributed in Canada by
Raincoast Books
8680 Cambie Street
Vancouver, B.C. V6P 6M9

10 9 8 7 6 5 4 3 2 1

Chronicle Books
85 Second Street
San Francisco, CA 94105

Web Site: www.chronbooks.com

To Bob

and

For John, Charles, Sarah, Lizzy, and Michael

[PEOPLE] OCCASIONALLY STUMBLE ACROSS THE TRUTH, BUT MOST OF THEM
PICK THEMSELVES UP AND HURRY OFF AS IF NOTHING HAD HAPPENED.

—WINSTON CHURCHILL

CONTENTS

STEP FOUR: Feeding Your Lower-Fat Family

foreword

Cardiovascular disease is the number one cause of death and disability in America; cancer is number two. The issue is no longer whether Americans should decrease the amount of total fat, saturated fat, and cholesterol in their diet, but how can we accomplish this task, which promises to decrease the incidence of both cardiovascular disease and some cancers.

A number of books have been written advocating the benefits of lowering dietary fat for adults and children. There remains much confusion in the minds of parents, however, about what to eat ourselves and what to feed our children. Part of this confusion relates to the difficulty in deciphering how much fat is in supermarket packaged foods, in the foods served by restaurants, and offered in school lunches. This book offers the clearest explanation to date on how to easily calculate the amount of fat in packaged foods, how to eliminate some of the fat from restaurant meals, and how to make instant at-home changes in the family diet, including the food in your children's lunch boxes.

It is clear that knowledge alone is not translated into behavior change. This is in part due to the constant temptations of high-fat foods and their convenience. Judith Shaw has three decades of experience in helping her own family successfully eat a healthy, low-fat diet; she provides valuable information on how to make dietary changes without making your life impossible and without causing your children to feel deprived or different from their peers; and she is extraordinarily skillful at anticipating how a dietary shift such as this can affect a family. Besides being an expert at low-fat family cooking, Ms. Shaw, the director of the Family Institute of Berkeley, is a nationally known family therapist and former consultant to the Residency Training Program in Family Medicine at the University of California, San Francisco.

This book is overflowing with many practical examples of delicious and easy-to-prepare low-fat foods. Recipes for a "milk shake," "French fries," and "mayonnaise" catch your imagination and help you realize how easy it can be to make some changes. You may wish to make general changes in the diet of your family with only a little effort; or you may wish to really become an expert, conversant with all the subtleties of such changes. In either case, you will find this book indispensable, very helpful, and easy to read.

Your family may have members with a known cholesterol problem or a history of heart disease. If your physician has prescribed a low-saturated-fat, low-cholesterol diet, this book will be particularly valuable in assisting you and your family in achieving your dietary goals thoroughly and completely.

Read this book. Make it part of your library. Your cupboards will never be the same, and you and your children will lead healthier lives. Enjoy, and have a wonderful "low-fat" sojourn through a high-fat world.

—Peter O. Kwiterovich, Jr., M.D.
Professor of Pediatrics and Chief, Lipid Research Unit,
The Johns Hopkins School of Medicine

author's note

This is a book for parents with a concern in common: Raising low-fat kids in a high-fat world. In response to that concern I wrote this book to help demystify and simplify this concern for you *and* your children as well as to explain how you can make some important, healthful changes to your children's diet without creating havoc in your own life and theirs. As you know, many books and articles have been written about lower-fat eating for adults who want to stay healthy, but I don't know of any book that has your child as a primary focus while also considering you and *your* life. I know personally that contemplating feeding one's children lower-fat foods can evoke images of spending the rest of your life shopping, steaming vegetables, baking tofu loaves, and confronting dissatisfied family members. Even the thought of this task can be overwhelming!

I wrote this book because as you know, we are ultimately responsible for our children's diet. No one else takes the same care—not their schools, not your friendly local marketplace, not restaurants, not packaged foods with their ambiguous labels, and certainly not the food moguls who manufacture edibles with harmful fats and sell them to you and your children every single day. I wrote this book because I have some solutions that will fit into your busy lives, and can eventually make your children devotees, and perhaps even advocates, of eating well.

Studies show that premature heart attacks and certain kinds of cancer claim more than one-half million Americans each year. Countless books, newspaper and magazine articles, and medical journals have shown that this epidemic is in considerable part the result of a lifetime of eating diets high in certain fats. In other words, the problem begins in childhood. These grim statistics don't just point to the future health risks for someone else's children. The statistics are a prediction of the vulnerability of *your* children. The American Academy of Pediatrics (AAP) has also noted that vulnerability and in 1992 issued a position paper urging that the diets of *all* healthy children over the age of two years be limited to no more than 30 percent total fat, with no more than 10 percent saturated fat. Do you know that despite that recommendation, American children eat a diet of between 37 percent and 50 percent fat daily? Do you also know that a dangerously large percentage of those fats are the most unhealthy of all fats?

What I want to share with you in the area of lower-fat eating is the result of more than thirty years of experience with my own family—my husband, Bob, and myself, and our four children, Lizzy, Sarah, Charles, and John, who are now adults. Also, through a chain of serendipitous connections evolving out of my past experience as a researcher for *Time* magazine, I have had special access to major figures in the scientific and medical community. Not least of all, I am a family therapist and have had the privilege of working with hundreds of families. In this work, in private practice, as Director of The Family Institute of Berkeley, and as a lecturer and consultant to the Medical School at the University of California, San Francisco, many parents and their children have sat in conference with me. I have listened not only to their concerns about communication, respect, and partnership, but also questions about food preferences, diet, and exercise. It is my hope that I can nudge you in the direction of understanding better the issues that confront you and your family as you begin the journey that I call The Lower-Fat Kids Plan. With this unique plan in hand, you can begin to implement solutions toward a healthier diet for your children. Most importantly, the Lower-Fat Kids Plan allows you to follow your own inclinations about what's best for your family.

Let me tell you how this all began. In the early sixties in the first years of our marriage, my husband's mother died of a heart attack at age sixty-eight. Seven years before that my husband's dad had died, yes, of a heart attack. There were other instances of cardiovascular disease in my husband's extended family. In addition, the relatively young parents of several of our friends were also dying. The severity of what was happening around us alerted us to the possibility of our children being at risk. Back then, evidence was beginning to accumulate that high serum cholesterol (along with hypertension and cigarette smoking) was an indicator of the possibility for serious heart disease. My husband, Bob, was and is still a voracious and curious reader. Not only that, he is always quick to see the good sense of a hypothesis. Thirty years ago doctors did not advocate "prevention," nor was the idea of "reversal" of atherosclerosis even a consideration. But based on emerging scientific and epidemiological research suggesting that diets lower in saturated fat resulted in less coronary artery disease—and better health in general—Bob was convinced that we should begin to reconsider our usual food choices. His concern was not only for himself, but for our children who might have a predisposition to heart disease.

So, in 1964, in an America where medical schools had still not taught medical students about nutrition and diet (as though they were irrelevant to good health), in an America that endorsed high saturated-fat diets, and in an America in the midst of embracing traditional French cooking, we found ourselves opting for the uncharted domain of lower-fat eating.

Without a supportive press or markets stocked with nonfat or lower-fat foods, we began to do what we could to invent a new style of eating and cooking for our family. We were unique then; one small group trying to survive in a world of butterfat and eggs. In those early days we had to make our own nonfat yogurt and sometimes even our own nonfat (skim) milk. Bob took to making simple bread. He used rennet and nonfat milk to make cheese. Friends were tolerant but not actually supportive in the beginning. I think they saw me as excessively preoccupied with what looked like the annihilation of one of life's sublime treats. Did people hide their butter and cartons of sour cream and frozen cheesecake when they saw me rounding the aisle of the supermarket, or was it my imagination? In the beginning dinner did look less than wonderful and sometimes tasted that way too. From the film *Five Easy Pieces,* we learned to order Jack Nicholson style: Two fried eggs, hold the butter, hold the yolks! We laughed a lot, but in many ways it was not an easy time.

Now, thirty years after we began to first modify our family diet, lower-fat is sanctioned and supported. In fact, it has actually become fashionable. And unfortunately, thirty years later, there is more and more evidence suggesting the connection between lung and colon cancer and high intakes of certain dietary fat and the relative absence of fruits and vegetables in the diet. And, thirty years later, heart disease remains the number one cause of death and disability in this country, hardly a satisfactory outcome of years of investigation and research. Sophisticated surgical procedures, high-tech drugs, and adults paying closer attention to diet are all making an impact and reducing the death toll from heart disease. But now after many years of epidemiological research, notably the long-range Children's Heart Study of Bogalusa, Louisiana, we know that heart disease begins silently in childhood—the manifestations appear in adulthood. Why should your children grow into young adulthood compromised in any way by the potentially lethal result of a diet high in unhealthy fats? Your physicians know, the epidemiologists know, and the science writers know which fats are beneficial to your children and which fats aren't. Why shouldn't you?

If you're like most parents, especially if your children are young, a full night's sleep or a quiet afternoon is probably high up on your wish list. You are likely to shudder at the thought of even the tiniest alteration to a system you already have in place for shopping or preparing food. The thought of complicating your life by adding another time-consuming chore may seem daunting, if not impossible. It doesn't have to be. The Lower-Fat Kids Plan can coexist peacefully with your real life without turning you into a full-time chef and shopper. The Lower-Fat Kids Plan is self-tailored: You pace yourself and your family. You decide just how much you want to take on. The Lower-Fat Kids Plan is meant to serve as a guide to help you develop and embrace a diet philosophy that you can adapt to your family's needs. Adopting even one or two or three of the simple changes you read about in this book will lower the unhealthy fat in the food your children eat.

By reading this book and adopting The Lower-Fat Kids Plan you will discover a community of people, more than you think, who, like you, care deeply about their children's health and, like you, have recognized the important role parents have in that future. No one else will take the same interest in your children's welfare as you; no one else has that much at risk. Thousands of parents are reorganizing their kitchens. Join them. Teach yourself and your children about healthy nutrition. Don't hand down a legacy of ignorance— or a legacy of disease.

raising
low-fat
kids

in a high-fat world

1

getting started

As a parent today you are literally surrounded by new food products and ideas about healthy eating, the result of many people crusading over many years to lower the fat in the American diet. As you clearly see when you shop, your supermarket is a showplace of emerging (and frequently confusing) innovation. Many new food products claim to be better for you than others, and there are so many of each kind to choose from. How do you know which claims are true, which products have the least of what's not good for your children? Do you feel like a compass without a "north" sometimes? I'm sure you do. I know the abundance of "healthier" foods can create chaos if you don't know what you are looking for. You want to feed your children "right," but how? Paradoxically, with consciousness regarding lowering fat in food at an all-time high, more children are eating more high-fat food. What happened?

In our concern as parents that our children get sufficient nutrients to grow, we tend to feed them foods that are calcium rich and full of protein (meat, chicken, cheese, dairy products). These foods are also usually full of saturated fat, one of the most dangerous fats. Parents also tend to feed their children convenience foods that come in familiar packages, all foods that children have grown to love. But these foods also have something else—hydrogenated oils, which produce trans fatty acids. Trans fatty acids and saturated fat are the two sinister dietary fats—the killer fats you will learn about as you read on. They are the fats associated with the elevation of serum cholesterol that leads to heart disease and they are also associated with the development of various forms of cancer. Saturated fat and hydrogenated oils have become staple ingredients in the foods children of all ages love most—cookies, crackers, chips, dips, instant dinners, frozen pizza, hamburgers, fries, shakes, fried chicken, and whole milk dairy products and ice cream. These are the foods children have become habituated to and beg for. Perhaps they are major players in your children's daily diet as well. They are the foods that require no thinking to set upon the table and stuff into lunch boxes. So what do I feed them instead? you ask. Is there anything left? Can I survive without these familiar foods? Will I be spending all day in the market? All day at the stove? Will my children have to live a hamburgerless childhood? And who will handle the massive food dissatisfactions my children will express while I am handling other important issues, like remembering that the shredded Hard Rock T-shirt on the floor under the toilet really isn't intended for the trash?

I had to consider these same questions for my own family and over the years came up with real-life answers. I needed answers so that our family life would work. Yes, in the beginning there may be times when your children will do their wickedest best to undermine you, go on a hunger strike only when you are looking, or just plain sulk. But I want to reassure you that The Lower-Fat Kids Plan will help you find answers to all your concerns about providing healthier meals and snacks for your family—without completely upsetting your lives. When I realized I could do this thing called lower-fat eating without being an embarrassment or a trial to my children, husband, and friends, that I could easily enroll all the children in the idea and encourage them to help find solutions to our high-fat problems, and that I could relinquish rigidity in favor of flexibility, the Lower-Fat Kids Plan came into being in its most complete and practical sense.

This book does not know *your* specific child. This book is addressed to the generally healthy, average child whose parent knows that a high-fat diet can cause disease later in life. "Diet" in this book does not mean weight-loss but is synonymous with food—what is eaten during the day. A healthy diet for the average child must contain adequate amounts of protein, carbohydrates, calcium and other minerals, vitamins, and fiber. The Lower-Fat Kids Plan urges you to provide these nutrients by offering your children as wide a variety of foods as possible, while keeping unhealthy fats to a minimum. Remember that you must always consult with your pediatrician or family physician about the suitability of any eating program for your children. If your child is at risk due to family medical history or a congenital disorder, use this book ONLY with the supervision of your physician. This book is not intended to replace your child's medical care in any instance, but to inform you about current medically accepted nutritional recommendations for the average, healthy child.

If your child is a vegetarian, or especially if they are on a macrobiotic diet, you must also discuss your child's diet with your doctor to verify your dietary decisions. If your child is overweight or underweight, and even if serious health reasons have been eliminated as a cause, do not use the ideas in this book to put your child on a weight-loss program. You must bring your concerns to your physician to arrive at a plan that will best support your child's emotional and physical well-being. Specifically, The Lower-Fat Kids Plan advocates the recommendation of the American Association of Pediatrics (AAP) that children under the age of two years not be put on a lower-fat regimen.

THE LOWER-FAT KIDS PLAN

The Lower-Fat Kids Plan is designed to guide you easily, food by food, to a lower-fat food plan for your children. You don't have to learn any new recipes to succeed (although you will find recipes scattered throughout the book and a recipe section at the back of the book): you don't have to prepare foods with strange-sounding names, and you don't have to find new markets to shop in. The Plan not only takes your needs into account, it teaches you to consider your children's (and your partner's) needs as well. It includes *real* hamburgers, real beef or chicken stew, healthy burritos, "fried" potatoes made without harmful fats, delicious soups, pizza, and colorful—not gray—food. And, of course, peanut butter. In addition, The Lower-Fat Kids Plan emphasizes incorporating into your meals many plant foods—beans, grains, vegetables, fruit—foods that add healthful calories to help reduce the amount of fatty foods your children will need to eat to fill their hungry stomachs. Foods such as grains, beans, and vegetables also add a much needed nutrient to children's diets—fiber. Research continues to demonstrate that high-fiber foods are essential for digestive and overall health.

I am not suggesting that the food you purchase and the dishes you prepare will produce exact replicas of high-fat ones, nor am I suggesting that you and your children will lose your taste for high-fat foods and will yearn only for carrot and celery sticks. The foods that my family and I crave—cheese soufflés, custards, fried chicken, special pastries and cakes, certain casseroles and gratins and sauces that would taste uninteresting and bland without the fat—those are the foods I don't tamper with. If I did, they would sadly mimic the original and give lower-fat cooking a bad name. I save these foods as treats, to indulge my own urges as well as my family's. These are the luxuries food dreams are made of; they should always have a place at our tables.

However, The Lower-Fat Kids Plan will take you step-by-step through the transition from everyday high-fat cooking and shopping to a new and intelligent way to feed your family. In four steps outlined below, simply stated here as Educate, Shop, Restock, and Cook, The Lower-Fat Kids Plan will help you lower all the fat in the food you feed your children. This easy-to-understand plan will alert you to the fats that are essential and healthy, as well as to the "bad" fats, saturated fat and trans fatty acids from hydrogenated oils, that you want your children to avoid as much as possible. Here is a brief description of the four steps. They will be discussed in detail in the following chapters.

STEP I: EDUCATING PARENTS AND CHILDREN

The Lower-Fat Kids Plan first introduces you to the concept that the roles of caretaker of your family's health and teacher go hand in hand. The Plan begins with a focus on education—education about fat, the kinds of fat, where fat is found, and what fats do to little bodies—and also to big ones. Step one also stresses the importance of involving your older children in issues of health in general and in specific decisions about their own health. This ongoing discussion will broaden the base of your family's commitment to this project and to each other, which is essential for success. Step one also demonstrates that beginning to feed your younger children (over two years old) a lower-fat diet will put healthier habits in place even before your child can understand them.

STEP II: FOOD SHOPPING FOR HEALTH

Hereafter, you will never trick yourself into thinking you are buying healthy, lower-fat food for your family when you're not. This next step of The Lower-Fat Kids Plan shows you a simple, quick formula to calculate the *real* fat content of packaged foods. It then takes you on an eye-opening tour of your supermarket. Knowing which foods contain which fats and just how much of each will allow you to purchase foods with less fat, and foods without harmful fats. This will relieve you of the chore of spying on your children as they eat—a goal of all parents concerned about their children's well-being.

STEP III: RESTOCKING YOUR KITCHEN

Next, The Lower-Fat Kids Plan moves to your kitchen for a tour of your cabinets, your refrigerator, and your freezer. This crucial step will alert you, and perhaps also shock you, as to what foods you typically stock for meals and snacks. Designed to follow your supermarket trip, now you can begin to re-provision your kitchen with a wide assortment of good-tasting, lower-fat foods and condiments. Your new choices will guarantee you simpler preparation, provide a broad repertoire of seasonings and condiments for creative cooking, and most of all, assure a fully restocked lower-fat kitchen.

STEP IV: FEEDING YOUR LOWER-FAT FAMILY

Mention low-fat cooking and most people say, "But it must be so hard to cook without fat!" The final step of The Lower-Fat Kids Plan proves that it is just as easy to prepare healthy and delicious leaner meals as it is to cook with lots of unhealthy fat. Using all you have learned about choosing lower-fat foods and restocking your kitchen with healthier ingredients, you will learn the art of simple innovation to prepare wholesome versions of your family's familiar and favorite dinners. With simplicity and ease, these fat-cutting techniques will work for main course dishes as well as for breakfast, lunch, and snack recipes. Festive holiday eating and birthday parties can still include your family's important traditional celebration foods, along with new additions that are lower in fat.

AS YOU BEGIN

As with any change in behavior, altering your high-fat shopping and cooking habits will bring some new problems. Perfect solutions are rare in human endeavors, and all solutions bring with them a cost, sometimes tiny, sometimes larger. Resist overnight changes in your family's eating habits or your shopping habits. The revolution has already happened; your job is to gracefully incorporate The Lower-Fat Kids Plan into your life. Buying one new food, or modifying one recipe, or changing one lunch box item can eventually be more productive than moving at a pace faster than is comfortable for your family.

People and families make attitudinal and practical shifts at different speeds. Always respect that in yourself, your partner, and your children.

In addition to fat, many parents have concerns about sugar and salt in their children's diets, especially if they consume processed foods frequently. When food processors remove fat from a product, they often add either sugar or salt to compensate for the loss in flavor or texture. In this book I focus on the reduction of fat in your family's diet. The Lower-Fat Kids Plan makes no special recommendations about sugar or salt intake for kids, other than to advise you to discuss with your physician whether you need to place any restrictions on your child's consumption of these items.

DOING THIS TOGETHER

Teaching your children that lowering saturated fat, hydrogenated oils, and fat in general is a good thing to do will raise their expectations of *you*; they will look to see if you are taking your own advice. Throughout the implementation of this plan, ask your children for their opinions and about their reluctance regarding lower-fat eating. Also, share *your* concerns with them. This project can't be just for the children—it must result in a family way of life.

EXPLORING USING LOWER-FAT INGREDIENTS

As you continue to read this book, you will notice there can be amazing reductions of fat with only small modifications. And as you read you will see clearly that there is no attempt made to eliminate all fat or even favorite foods high in fat. Many fats are essential to proper growth. Throughout the book I will indicate which fats are healthy fats and perfect foods in moderate portions and which fats you want to more emphatically minimize. While The Lower-Fat Kids Plan stresses the importance of reducing unhealthy fat, it does not overlook the importance of keeping all fat to a healthy minimum. These two crucial health principles will still allow for sufficient fat to keep your children's meals and snacks appealing and satisfying. As well, I will teach you how you can include a high-saturated fat food such as hamburger, and serve it with very low- and non-fat delicious food, making that meal a generally lower-fat one. Chapter by chapter you will begin to see that total elimination of some favorite foods, snacks for instance, is not necessary and that "moderation" is the most useful adjective in this book!

CHILDREN AND THEIR EATING HABITS

In my work I have come to know many parents who express concern about their children's eating habits. Children who don't eat, children who won't eat, children who won't eat at the table, children who throw food on the floor, children who, it seems, never eat enough, and children who eat too much. While this book is about lowering fat in your child's food and not about parenting, dieting, or children's eating habits, I do want to say just a few things that I have learned both as a mom and as a family therapist that you may find useful.

The successful feeding/eating relationship between parents and children develops out of trust as opposed to control and rigidity. It can be a relationship that flowers or it can be one that is a constant source of negativity, distrust, and one-upmanship—with your child usually winning. Well-adjusted childhood eaters are either hungry or not and benefit from knowing it is alright with their parent either way. With a "cool" parent there is no struggle. Eating problems *usually* result from parents' fears of their child eating too much or too little and from a lack of respect for their children's right to respond to their *own* signals for hunger and food preferences, not their parent's. You know from experience that your healthy newborn eats until it is full or won't eat if it is not hungry. If your newborn was content, you trusted that all was well. If you trust that your young and older children are as wise about their appetites as when they were newborns, most of your problems regarding how much or how little they eat will disappear. What you will clearly see is that you are responsible for planning healthy meals, bringing the food home, and establishing regular eating times and friendly family conversation. Children must be given the right to decide which and how much of that healthy food they need, just like the infant they once were. Young, healthy children gravitate toward an adequate diet; if they don't eat one day, typically they will the next, or in some unusual instances, the next. When they are small, your children need you to offer appropriate food at appropriate times and to organize a regular sitting down place for them to eat, with an environment that encourages pleasant communication. When children are older they also need you to stock appropriate foods and continue the traditions you have established for regular meal times, family sociability, and nurturance.

chapter 1

Despite all these efforts, a very real part of your child's job in life, no matter what age, is to test or sabotage you, to play mind games at increasingly more sophisticated levels, and if they can, to find ways to reduce you to an infantile rage. They are, after all, trying to grow up, get smarter (by outsmarting you), and exert their power, however it occurs to them.

Some children never confront you directly and are only successful at sneaking and hiding; you will never know how they outsmart you unless they are caught. Some children are willing to be up front and confront you—eye to eye. These are the children who stay in communication with you, and who are willing to challenge you, tough it out, engage with you to test their strength.

If you don't already know it, another job of yours is to know that just when you think things are under control, just when life with your children seems perfect, *your* angelic four year old will bring forth a challenge you couldn't even have imagined. Knowing in advance that this is inevitable, perhaps you won't be as mystified by these sudden reaches for power. You will know that one day, angel that she is, your daughter will say of a meal she has loved for at least a year, "I hate this food, I *will* not eat it." Here she is, ready to take you on. With an uncanny ability, she has ferreted out your weakness. These are the times you must remember you are the adult and not fall into her trap. Begging, imploring her to eat is playing *her* game—not yours. Your job is to remind yourself, after you have recovered from the shock, that it doesn't matter if she eats the food, what matters is that she doesn't see that she has upset your world. In a situation like this you might suggest she keep you company at the table or perhaps choose a dry cereal instead. Don't punish your child for being direct, expressing her heart, and being willing to assert her developing self.

EXERCISE AS A PART OF A HEALTHY BODY PLAN

Nothing exists in isolation and exercise in addition to a lower-fat food plan is essential to healthy bodies. Recently released figures show that obesity in children more than doubled in the last decade. Researchers estimate that more than 4.5 million children ages six through seventeen are severely overweight. Exercise is a crucial support to children's physical, intellectual, and emotional development. In our world of computers, computer games, and television, however, exercise is sometimes forgotten or put on hold as technology competes for our childrens' attention. These activities encourage sedentary lifestyles and exposure to an endless stream of unhealthy food advertising. With so many mothers working full- and part-time, many children do not have an opportunity for after-school physical activity, or before-school physical activity. If it is difficult for you to organize "action" activities for your children, or they are reluctant to take part in school sports, why not incorporate exercise into routines that can become part of family activities: Walk to the movies and play word games on the way; skate or speed walk and *then* go out to dinner; buy a Frisbee to keep in the car for impromptu games; race-walk around a local track or a bit more slowly around a local mall; pack a sandwich and walk to do close-by shopping. Yes, all these activities take more time than by car, time you are short of. But if your children sit for more hours than not, you must reconsider schedules, both theirs and yours. Exercise must be part of their day.

You are now ready to begin to use The Lower-Fat Kids Plan to guide your family toward healthier eating, to a commitment to a wholesome diet that can have a positive impact on your children's health for the rest of their lives. I feel a kinship with you as I recall the early days of my own hit-or-miss lower-fat experiments and my family's mostly good-natured cooperation and patience with my blunders. I think of my children now, healthy young adults living lives I am proud of and taking responsibility for their overall health in ways I had never known to consider when I was their age. As well, each of them has made a choice to continue a lower-fat style of eating, now freely advocating a healthy diet. I am grateful for who my children are. I am grateful, too, for their successes and for ours with them. I wish you that same success and joy with your own children. It is just about the best!

chapter 1

about fat

Where did the high-fat habit come from? Well, from your parents, your relatives, your friends, and advertising. In other words, our particular local culture influences our food choices. We associate good taste and good mouth feel with fat because, in our experience, good taste always had fat (or sugar). Most of us grew up eating eggs and bacon for breakfast, sandwiches with mayonnaise and meat and cheese for lunch. We paired butter with bread, and chocolate sauce with ice cream. Our mouths loved the feel and taste of crackers, cookies, imported cheeses, frankfurters, pot roast, corned beef, fried chicken, pizza, hamburgers, bacon, pasta with cream sauces, and French-fried anything. Mayonnaise "made" the chicken salad—gave it its particular taste—otherwise it was just chopped chicken. The richness of high-fat milk was sumptuous, and who would have thought of eating baked potatoes without butter or sour cream? High-fat foods meant comfort and indulgence, and the food moguls saw to it that that particular comfort was constantly appeased; they are the "pushers" of the high-fat habit. They know our weakness—and our children's—for the taste of fat, and they have successfully nurtured that weakness.

Your children, very likely, are very much like you. Their tastes became theirs the way yours became yours; they have you for a parent, your folks as grandparents, seductive television advertising, peers whose parents are like you, and the belief from the culture we live in that fat equals good taste.

We stay with the high-fat habit because we haven't had the opportunity to discover that fat and taste can be separate: Your children can have good taste with fat and good taste without fat. However, in trying to achieve a lower-fat diet, many people are tempted to eliminate all added fat. Do not do this to your children—or to yourselves. (It would be impossible anyway, and dangerous to your children's growth and development.) While mounting scientific evidence is demonstrating the downside of high-saturated-fat diets, no one is advocating the elimination of every kind of fat—or the elimination of any naturally occurring fat—for healthy children. All children need a variety of healthful fats for proper growth. What children do not need is the excess saturated, unsaturated, and artificially manufactured fats we feed them.

We are all well aware in our own lives that unnecessary extra fat adds pounds, and in addition unnecessary unhealthy fat compromises children's well-being in other ways, and puts in place another generation of high-fat consumers with a precarious health prognosis. The Lower-Fat Kids Plan recommends moderate portions of foods containing fats, such as oils, nuts, seeds, dairy products, fish, chicken, and lean meat. At the same time, this regimen supports an all-out attempt to incorporate a large proportion of complex carbohydrates (fruits, vegetables, grains, and beans) into your children's daily diet.

While the Lower-Fat Kids Plan follows the recommendations of the American Academy of Pediatrics for a diet that limits saturated fat to 10 percent of the daily caloric consumption and total fat to 30 percent, hardly any of us will have the inclination to keep pen and paper at hand each day, marking down every morsel our children eat and counting fat grams. Nor would it be, in my opinion, an achievement to aim for. What could be worse than being a fat monitor? The Lower-Fat Kids Plan will show you an easy method for choosing lower-fat healthier foods that your children and family will love.

As you read in Chapter One, all fats are not created equal. In the next section, I will sort out the differences between saturated fat, unsaturated fat, cholesterol, and partially hydrogenated oils, the food industry's Trojan horse.

chapter 2

SATURATED FAT. WHAT IS IT? AND WHERE IS IT FOUND?

Saturated fat is the fat that, in the amounts most children eat in foods such as whole milk, ice cream, cheese, and hamburgers, can be harmful to growing bodies. High saturated-fat diets can cause damage in children's arteries that can lead to heart disease later in life.

Saturated fat is primarily found in animal foods. It is easily recognized because it is solid at room temperature, such as butter and beef fat. Plant foods (except for avocados, olives, nuts, coconuts, and seeds) have very *little fat* of any kind, including saturated fat. Coconut and coconut oil, and palm and palm kernel oil, often referred to as tropical oils, contain significant amounts of saturated fat.

Animal foods (with the exception of nonfat dairy products) are high in saturated fat. Saturated fat is found in all meats, including chicken; in butter, lard, cream, and eggs; and in *all* whole milk *and* low-fat dairy products, such as whole milk and low-fat milk, whole milk and low-fat ice cream, and whole milk and low-fat frozen yogurt. Saturated fat is found as well in all foods prepared from whole milk dairy products, such as pastries (butter, eggs), mayonnaise (eggs), quiches (eggs, cheese, butter), and pizza (cheese). The good news is that you do not have to eliminate all saturated fat from your children's diet, just wisely reduce it.

WHAT ARE HYDROGENATED OILS?

Hydrogenated oils are fats that have the same capacity to do harm as saturated fats, and that are found in almost every high-fat processed food you bring home from the supermarket: soups, cookies, crackers, mixes of all kinds, pastries, chips, imitation cheese, frozen foods such as pizza and pot pies, solid or semi-soft margarine, and even some cereals. Partially (or fully) hydrogenated oils are shown in the ingredient listing on packaged food as *partially hydrogenated vegetable oil (soybean, cottonseed, corn, palm, canola, etc.).* In addition, processed foods made with hydrogenated oils pose another health hazard: trans fatty acids.

WHAT ARE TRANS FATTY ACIDS?

After hydrogenation (a heating process that alters once-benign vegetable oils), oils no longer have the essential properties of untouched oils. In fact, the molecular structure of their essential and important fatty acids is now so disturbed that they are jokingly termed "molecular misfits" and scientifically called trans fatty acids. But it is no joke! According to Mary Enig, Ph.D., a research associate in the Department of Chemistry and Biochemistry at the University of Maryland, the trans fatty acids produced by the hydrogenation process are so different in structure from what they once were that they cannot be legally designated as monounsaturated or polyunsaturated for purposes of labeling. Be aware that these harmful trans fatty acids are hidden fats in every product that lists hydrogenated or partially hydrogenated oils on the label. Researchers need to pay closer attention to the long-term effects of these substances on children, but what we do know now is that these harmful trans fatty acids contribute significantly to raising LDL levels (the "bad" cholesterol) and lowering HDL levels (the "good" cholesterol) in children who eat a diet high in these fats. As Harold McGee states in *On Food and Cooking* (New York: MacMillan & Co., 1984), these oils are "artificially saturated," or converted in the process of hydrogenation to saturated-like fats.

In addition, the ongoing Harvard University Nurses Study has reported that women who consumed large amounts of these harmful fats in margarine, cookies, pastries, and French fries negated the benefits gained from reducing their saturated fat intake. Harmful effects such as low birth weight and diminished quality of breast milk appear to be related to consuming large amounts of trans fatty acids.

How much of these trans fatty acids do your children eat? Only you can answer that. How often do your children eat fast foods and processed foods?

HOW TO RECOGNIZE SATURATED FATS AND HYDROGENATED OILS

Pure saturated fat or hydrogenated fat is solid or semi-solid at room temperature. Some of this fat is easy to recognize in your kitchen and can clearly be seen for what it is:

- the hard, white fat of beef and lamb chops (saturated fat)
- the yellowish fat under the skin and just inside the cavity of chickens (saturated fat)
- the chilled, white, waxy mass of lamb, beef, or pork fat, or yellow semi-hard dense mass of poultry fat on soups (saturated fat)

- a stick of butter (saturated fat)
- thick white lard (saturated fat)
- hard and semi-soft margarine (hydrogenated oil)
- vegetable shortenings (hydrogenated oil)

Fat as part of foods is more difficult to see:

- MILK: The highly saturated fat of all milk (except nonfat, or skim) and cream is concealed by the process of homogenization, which disperses the fat globules throughout the milk. Before milk was homogenized, these fat globules quickly separated out from the liquid and congregated at the top of the milk in the form of heavy cream, leaving lower-fat milk below it.
- SOUPS AND STEWS: If you eat meat stews and meat soups that have not been chilled and defatted, the fat will mix with other ingredients (liquids and solids) and become mostly invisible except for a thin film of fat globules on the surface. That film of fat often means the soup or gravy is a 50- to 75-percent-fat liquid.
- PACKAGED FOOD: If the ingredient label reads "partially hydrogenated," the saturated-like hydrogenated fat is there, albeit unseen, mixed with the other ingredients. When you order deep-fried foods such as donuts, French fries, fish, or chicken, ask if these harmful fats are used. Avoid them as well as margarines and packaged foods that list hydrogenated oils as ingredients.

Consuming hidden saturated fats in the form of gravies, soups, or whole-fat and low-fat dairy products allows you to fool yourself or remain ignorant of the quantities of unhealthy fat your children eat. For example, the percent of fat calories in a 4-ounce serving of unskimmed, non-defatted beef stew is somewhere between 40 to 50 percent of the total calories. Trimming the meat well and skimming the chilled gravy cuts the percent of calories from fat in half!

The chilling process, as you have learned from your own cooking experience, forces the fat molecules out of the liquid and to the surface of soups, butter sauces, and gravies. When we see this waxy, whitish fat, most of us instinctively spoon it into the trash. The decision to throw away chicken fat, if you have cooked with it and know its pleasures intimately, may be harder to make. But chicken fat—whether used for cooking other foods, or eaten in the form of chicken skin or unskimmed chicken soup—is, along with beef fat, one of the highest-saturated-fat foods you can feed your child. Chicken soup as a comfort food soothes because of its fragrance and warmth; both qualities can exist without the fat.

When children's diets are very high in the saturated fats and hydrogenated oils of most packaged foods, other foods such as fresh and dried fruits, vegetables, grains, beans, and potatoes are largely ignored and tend to make up only tiny portions of your children's diet. When diets are altered to include more vegetables and fruits, grains and beans, and complex carbohydrates such as pasta and potatoes, then—without even trying—the amount of high-saturated-fat foods your children eat is automatically reduced. When the only choices after school are frozen pizzas and tacos, full-fat ice cream, chocolate cookies, and whole milk, children have no choice.

WHAT IS CHOLESTEROL?

Cholesterol is a word most everyone is familiar with and one many people have come to fear. Cholesterol is manufactured in the body by the liver and is carried in the blood by lipoproteins. Every body needs cholesterol and *every* healthy body produces the amount of cholesterol that is essential for the manufacture of hormones and the maintenance of cell walls. Cholesterol is one of the fats always present in the blood.

IF CHOLESTEROL IS MANUFACTURED IN THE BODY, HOW CAN IT BE BAD?

A certain kind of cholesterol is harmful; it is called low-density lipo-protein, or LDL, cholesterol, and is known familiarly as the "bad" cholesterol. When your children eat a diet that is lavish with saturated fat and partially hydrogenated oils, the usual command stations in the liver do not function as they should. When these command stations malfunction, more LDLs are produced by the liver because the signal to stop production cannot be received; hence the elevation of LDL (or "bad") cholesterol.

Another fraction of cholesterol is high-density lipoprotein (HDL) cholesterol. This part of the total cholesterol in your children's blood is known as the "good" cholesterol because it carries bad cholesterol *out* of the body.

The more there are of these HDLs, the better the task is handled of ridding the body of excess cholesterol. Diets high in saturated fats such as butter, dairy products, and partially hydrogenated oils *lower* the number of HDLs and raise the number of LDLs—just the opposite of what we want to happen.

MORE ON DIETARY FAT AND ITS EFFECTS ON YOUR CHILD'S CORONARY ARTERIES

Eating high-saturated-fat dairy products, processed foods, baked goods, and fast foods prepared with large amounts of partially hydrogenated oils, increases the levels of LDL cholesterol in the bloodstream. Researchers used to think that controlling one's intake of cholesterol—limiting foods that are high sources of cholesterol, such as meats, eggs, whole-fat dairy products, fish eggs such as caviar, organ meats such as liver and brains, chicken and turkey with the skin—lowered the risk of heart disease. Now it is clear that saturated fats and trans fatty acids produced from hydrogenated oils are the major dietary causes of elevations in cholesterol; reducing the fats that cause these elevations is the key to healthier bodies.

To better understand the effects of the American high-fat diet, consider the fact that the body has no way of storing the excess LDL cholesterol that results from eating too much saturated fat and hydrogenated oils. This excess cholesterol is carried in the blood and collects along the walls of the artery in deposits known as plaque.

These deposits begin to be laid down in childhood and continue through adulthood, as has been demonstrated by the research of the ongoing Children's Heart Study of Bogalusa, Louisiana. Known as plaque, these deposits not only narrow arteries but harden the arterial walls as well. Together this produces what is known as atherosclerosis. Forevermore, this growing patch sticks like Velcro to the arterial wall. Reducing your family's intake of unhealthy fats automatically reduces unnecessary cholesterol production, halting atherosclerosis and minimizing the progression of heart disease.

Now we know (thanks to the genius of Michael Brown and Joseph Goldstein, the 1985 Nobel Prize winners, and other illustrious scientists, epidemiologists, and physicians such as Bang, Dyerberg, Enig, Mensink, Katan, Ornish, Dietschy, Grundy, Kwiterovich, Althschule, and Willett) that saturated fat and hydrogenated oils are the dietary culprits of heart disease and some cancers. An all-out personal campaign to insure the best diet for your children requires a minimization of these fats.

A COMPARISON OF A DAY'S MEALS

To give you an immediate sense of how simple it can be to reduce saturated fat while nominally changing the actual foods served, look at the following comparison of a day of high-saturated- and lower-saturated-fat meals. Note that the lower-fat meals are not *no* fat—they are just simple reductions and simple additions, resulting in a far healthier diet for your child and yourself. Note, too, that you don't need nutritional analyses to see where saturated fat can be replaced easily.

BREAKFAST

HIGH-SATURATED-FAT BREAKFAST
- Juice
- Cereal with 2 percent or whole milk
- Toast and butter (or margarine)
- Perhaps another glass of milk

In this menu the saturated fat is in the milk and the butter and hydrogenated fat is in the margarine. Notice what happens in the menu below when you make a few small changes.

LOWER-SATURATED-FAT BREAKFAST
- Juice
- Cereal with a lower-fat milk than is usual in your home, such as nonfat, 1 percent or 2 percent
- Toast with jam or fresh fruit slices
- A glass of lower-fat milk

By reducing the fat in the milk you serve and substituting jam or fruit for butter in this menu you have dramatically reduced the amount of saturated fat.

chapter 2

LUNCH

HIGH-SATURATED-FAT LUNCH

- American cheese sandwich or tuna salad sandwich with mayonnaise
- Potato chips
- Two percent or whole milk
- Cookies or cake, and low-fat yogurt

This typical American lunch includes saturated fat in every food: cheese, mayonnaise, chips, milk, and dessert.

LOWER-SATURATED-FAT LUNCH

- Tuna salad sandwich made with Our Nonfat "Mayonnaise" (page 161) or lemon juice and a drop of real mayonnaise
- Sliced carrot, cucumber, celery, onion, or bell pepper, on the sandwich or wrapped separately
- Nonfat yogurt with a cookie and raisins to crumble into it
- Lower-fat milk
- Extra raisins

Doesn't this lower-fat lunch appeal to you as a lunch for your children? For this menu we substituted nonfat mayonnaise for whole mayonnaise, vegetables for potato chips, and a lower-fat milk and yogurt.

DINNER

HIGH-SATURATED-FAT DINNER

- Tomato juice with high-fat crackers
- Roasted, broiled, baked, or stewed chicken, with skin
- Potatoes roasted with the chicken
- Frozen green peas in butter sauce
- Salad with high-fat dressing
- Garlic bread with butter
- Two percent or whole milk
- Ice cream and cookies

Here again we have high saturated fat in chicken skin, butter, high-fat dressing, milk, and dessert, and hydrogenated oil in the crackers.

about fat

LOWER-SATURATED FAT DINNER

- Tomato juice with cucumber sticks
- Roasted, broiled, baked, or stewed skinless chicken
- Potatoes baked or roasted separately
- Any vegetable with lemon
- Salad with lower-fat dressing
- Garlic bread with olive oil
- Fruit or nonfat frozen dessert
- Lower-fat milk than you usually serve

Baking chicken without the skin, cooking the potatoes separately from the chicken (even chicken without the skin has fat that drips into the pan and disappears into potatoes), eliminating butter, and choosing a lower-fat dessert and milk significantly lowers the amount of saturated fat in this meal without sacrificing taste. None of these changes require much thought once you have considered them; as you begin to reduce fat this way it will eventually seem simple and matter-of-fact.

WHAT IS THE RIGHT AMOUNT OF FAT FOR YOUR FAMILY?

A goal of The Lower-Fat Kids Plan is to reduce saturated fat and hydrogenated oils as much as possible. Each child lives with a parent or parents who have widely varying notions of what constitutes lowering fat. Parents view their successes from many different vantage points: Is this project a success for my children? How much fat can I eliminate and still keep peace in the family? How is my food shopping affected? My time? Am I a real partner in this project? Are *they?*

Allow yourself the comfort of arriving at a "right" or "perfect" diet for you and your family. Using your new knowledge and your food preferences, you can determine when and how to take fat out.

REPLACING FAT CALORIES WITH HEALTHIER CALORIES

Like adults, children need different amounts of calories at different moments depending on their expenditure of energy. But children, unlike fully grown adults, use calories or energy in one particular way—to grow. Growing means making longer bones, developing muscle, and in general, stretching out. Even though this usually happens around certain ages, each child has a unique growth pattern, a very personal time schedule for spurts, starts, and stops. Growing children consume many calories, less when they are 3 or 4 years old and as you have seen, enormous amounts of calories when they are teenagers. Fats typically provide the most calories in our children's meals and snacks. Reducing the amount of fat your family eats, especially saturated fats and foods with hydrogenated oils, will bring along with it several noticeable differences: A significant change will be the volumes of food your child will eat to replace calories from fat if your child's diet was one high in fat. Reducing high-fat foods makes it necessary to substitute many more vegetables, grains, fruits, and snack type foods you hadn't thought about before.

During a time of stringent vegetarianism among our children, I recall one very early morning in our kitchen watching as our son Charles packed his lunch before he left for crew practice. He began by holding a large supermarket brown bag in front of the open door of the refrigerator and proceeded to toss yogurt containers (4), carrots (a bunch, unwashed and unscraped), apples and oranges (at least 6) and from the freezer a whole loaf of bread, into the bag—all without a napkin! First I thought it was a lot of food. But then I realized he would have practically used up almost all the calories by the time crew practice was over at 8:30! It was then I started to make large bowls of chili and buy many more loaves of bread for afternoon snacks—along with the usual fruit, pretzels, bagels, and milk. I could barely keep up with our son's need for calories during that time.

During these spurt times, serving cheese and hamburgers along with grains and potatoes when you know your children need more calories is exactly perfect. That is the beauty of The Lower-Fat Kids Plan. It teaches you how to rely on *your* acuity to know what your children need, and to rely on your good sense to know how much cooking you can take on to produce well-fed, satisfied kids, and satisfied, not depleted, parents. Cheese and hamburgers become bad foods only when they are constant daily choices and when the foods served with them are high fat as well.

THE LIE THAT IS MARGARINE

Did you know that the substitute for butter you always thought was good for you isn't? Regular margarine, like butter, is an essentially all-fat food. As well as being primarily fat, most margarines are manufactured from partially hydrogenated oil, which acts in your child's body as though it were saturated fat, and worse.

Margarine is made from vegetable oils (corn, soybean, safflower, canola, cottonseed) that are partially hydrogenated; hydrogenation (partial or full) makes the oils solid like butter. Yes, these are plant oils and plant fats are supposed to be good for you, but not when they have been heated and pressure-processed. As you learned earlier, hydrogenating oils produces the injurious trans fatty acids.

If you must have a fatty spread for bread, try just the barest amount of olive oil on toast; if you crave the delicious, creamy taste that only butter offers, use it sparingly and/or infrequently. What you want to avoid is the daily use of foods that can become bad habits, and that is possible both with margarine as well as butter.

UNSATURATED FATS

Unsaturated fats are the major fats of plants. Although most plants contain very little fat, every food that grows in the ground has some fat, even when you cannot see it or taste it—including lettuce! Of course, the amount of fat in lettuce is extremely small. The plant foods that have the largest quantities of fat are olives, avocados, nuts (except chestnuts, which are very low in fat), peanuts, and seeds such as sesame, pumpkin, and sunflower. But this doesn't mean your children should not eat these foods at all. Fat that is natural to a plant food is generally healthy. The key is moderation.

Unsaturated fats fall into two categories, polyunsaturated and mono-unsaturated. All plant foods will have both these unsaturated fats as well as some saturated fat, usually in tiny amounts. To eat the proper amounts of these foods, *you do not have to count or add;* just feed your family an assortment of vegetables, grains, beans, nuts, and fruits, all high-fiber complex carbohydrate foods.

MONOUNSATURATED OILS FOR COOKING

Because of components in olive oil that seem to be responsible for miracles, most scientists and clinical researchers (while not necessarily believers in miracles themselves!) recommend using extra-virgin olive oil for cooking and for adding to food. Healthy and delicious extra-virgin olive oil, a mostly monounsaturated oil, has a panoply of attributes that make it the perfect choice for all your recipes. Specialty oils such as walnut, almond, and hazelnut are high in healthy mono-unsaturates and are good choices to add variety to your cooking.

WHY IS OLIVE OIL GOOD FOR YOUR CHILDREN?

- Olive oil has the highest percentage of monounsaturated fatty acids of any common kitchen oil.
- Monounsaturates reduce the level of LDL cholesterol in your child's blood.
- The antioxidizing agents in the form of vitamin E (contained in all oils) help keep cell membranes healthier and alive longer.
- Olive oil has been, and is, used exclusively by people who live in the lands of olive trees: Greece, Italy, Spain, France, North Africa, and other areas along the eastern coast of the Mediterranean. Well-documented epidemiological research seems to indicate that the diet of these populations cannot be overlooked as one key to their longevity. These populations traditionally consumed oil made from olives, ate meat rarely, and used dairy products minimally. Now, in urban communities in these countries, children (and adults) are eating the "international diet" of hamburgers, French fries, and packaged foods made with partially hydrogenated oils. As a result there is more childhood obesity and evidence of arterial lesions in young people.

Extra-virgin olive oil comes from the first "cold" pressing of the olive fruit and is unrefined, meaning no chemicals are used in the refining process. "Cold" pressing means that the oil is extracted from the olives at fairly low temperatures rather than with high heat. Many people think that the absence of high heat in the pressing process produces a better-tasting oil.

Some of the recipes in this book use heated olive oil; most often, however, you will find cooking works just as well with water or stock. Food to be grilled or broiled can be marinated in herbs and spices, and nothing needs to be browned in fat. You can use olive oil right out of the bottle as a flavoring on toast, in salads, to toss with just-cooked steamed or roasted vegetables, and to flavor hot soups and casseroles and pastas. Extra-virgin oil does cost more, but I think it is worth the extra cost for the extra taste—and of course the health benefits it provides for your family. Always buy olive oil that is bottled where it is grown; oil that is shipped and bottled later is exposed to air longer and becomes rancid more quickly. Oils that are bottled somewhere other than where they are processed will indicate the bottling location on the container.

To prevent rancidity, buy pint-sized bottles of oil and keep them in dark cupboards, not exposed to light. Or, pour half the bottle into a tightly covered glass container and store it in the fridge until the first half is used up. Olive oil becomes thick and gray when chilled, so it is not convenient to use directly from the refrigerator; it needs to come to room temperature to return to its familiar state.

chapter 2

making the shift: helping your family break the high-fat habit

Now that you understand the kinds of fat in your children's diet, and the types of changes you want to begin to make in your family's food habits, Step One continues by helping you educate your family about the changes you have in mind. Children, like most adults, generally do not like change. Even when the change might be "fun," children often disguise their anxiety with curiosity: How high are the waves in *this* ocean? Where will we eat? Do we sleep alone? Do they have a dog? They also try to find reassurance in constancy: Will I be in the same bunk this year? Will Anthony be there too? Do you think Mrs. Marcus will let us pick the yellow flowers again?

Changing food habits is no different. It can also elicit responses of confusion and resistance from your children—"How will these new foods taste?"—especially if you leave them out of the planning.

Trying to change your children's high-fat habit by eliminating all high-fat foods won't work. Your children's "essential" foods—the foods without which life might not seem worth living—are truly essential to their food addictions, their lunch box trades, and to your convenience. But you can begin to alter the fat content of some meals gently and almost imperceptibly. When you're trying to break the high-fat habit, any reduction of fat is a victory for you and your family.

Once you've decided to embark on The Lower-Fat Kids Plan, your biggest task will be to involve the children and your partner in the idea so that it becomes their plan as well as yours. To me, this is the most crucial step in The Lower-Fat Kids Plan because it paves the way for future success. Living in a family, whether large or small, requires that you include all members of the group in any process that involves family change. Depending, of course, on the ages of your children, their curiosity and participation will vary. Instead of prejudging, why not see what level of participation your children are capable of?

Children thrive on purpose and partnership. As a lower-fat diet becomes more of an institution in the family, their alliance in the project will be more evident if you have offered partnership. Skepticism or sarcasm will diminish; suggestions and questions will begin to come from them. Eventually, food will begin to look "right," rather than "odd" and "nerdy." With careful leadership, with respect for young minds working on large problems, and with patience, most change can result in acceptance.

TACKLING YOUR FAMILY'S RESISTANCE TO CHANGE

Your family may be reluctant to move as quickly as you would like. Remember, you have had time to consider The Lower-Fat Kids Plan, but they are hearing about it for the first time. By the time you raise your concerns about fat to your family, you have made plans for instituting change; your mind has argued and relented, has juggled the pros and cons and, finally, has agreed to this adventure. Your family will need the same amount of time to adjust.

No matter what your child's age, no matter how favorably inclined you think the children are toward this regimen, you heighten the risk of turning the children off if you indulge in too much meddling too soon or the total banishment of familiar favorites. You may be the boss but bosses must know the limitations of the people they supervise. Unless it is the children's initiative encouraging you to move more quickly, practice restraint. Erma Bombeck called kids "suspicious diners"; they are frequently looking to see what new adventure you cooked for them to rebel against. Given that stance, your belief in this plan, not your urgency, is what will ultimately communicate the common sense of it; your self esteem is no less important in generating respect in this area of childrearing than in any other.

Children will have to confront some differences in taste and appearance in the foods they will begin to eat, and they will also have to deal with peer pressure. Will their lunch box be full of cold veggies so that they'll have nothing to trade? Will their friends think they are weird? Will their parents turn into the kind of embarrassing parents who watch what everyone is eating and who keep talking about diet all the time?

These are serious considerations for most children. At different ages, of course, their concerns are different. As very young children, ages two and three, their food habits are more easily changed. Some older children will move quickly toward these ideas; others will need more discussion and positive experiences to overcome their resistance or opposition. You must be cognizant of their hesitation.

If your family—or even one family member—seems particularly reluctant to participate with you, perhaps you have demanded that they do so, rather than introducing this idea as a suggestion and a concern. Demanding that your family join you—telling them the solution—only gets followers. In the worst scenario, you'll enlist angry followers. In the *very* worst scenario, your family will withdraw completely. Followers don't know why they are following: The spirit of the endeavor escapes them; they only know that they are captives.

RELINQUISHING POWER: ALLOWING YOUR CHILDREN TO CHOOSE

Even though our children were educated to be aware of unhealthy fat, my husband and I always let them know that away from home the choice of what to eat or drink was theirs. We felt that giving our children this permission was critical; away from home, the environment is different. Allowing children control in this instance is not only realistic, it's crucial. It relieves them of the need to lie if they eat a high-fat food, and most important, it allows them choice.

Food and eating is clearly an area in which children hold a great deal of power. They have the power to upset us by eating too much or too little, or eating "wrong." As parents, we have the opportunity to love and teach our children, and to motivate them toward a spirit of cooperation regarding food (or anything else, for that matter). We *must* consider their concerns and be practical and straightforward with them. The way that we, as parents, cultivate our relationship with our children—the confidence they develop in our judgment, the respect they feel from us toward them—contributes to a well-being that derives its strength from an alliance with us, not an opposition to us.

HOW YOUR CHILD CAN BE
PART OF THE PLAN

- Begin with a thoughtful introduction. Don't suddenly announce to your family that the household is going on a lower-fat diet; that declaration can only create alarm and rebellion. Instead, you might begin by saying something like this: "Know what I found out today? I was actually shocked to learn that the milk we are drinking has twice as much fat as this other kind. I was thinking of trying the lower-fat one because it is so much better for all of us. I'd like to try it." Or, "I bought some new frozen yogurts that have less fat than the ones we have been eating. Let's try them tonight and have a taste test." Putting yourself and your family into the discovery process offers up a partnership rather than a dictatorship.
- Take on the plan yourself. Feeding your children lower-fat foods and extolling their merits while you eat donuts or Brie will never work. Remember: You are not eliminating donuts and Brie forever—but they will no longer be daily choices.
- Involve your family in the planning. Nurturing the idea of the plan may take one day or thirty days, depending on how receptive your family is and how well you have prepared them. This is *your* task. Keep reminding yourself that you've had time to assimilate this idea. Give your family the same opportunity.

And what if they *all* say no? If you've expressed caution and reflection and presented the idea as something you have been thinking about, rather than a decision you have made by yourself, it is less likely that they will say "no." Children respond to thoughtfulness and suggestions that invite them to participate in family decisions. They are dying to be part of family discussions (which is not always possible but certainly can be here) rather than the recipients of ultimate decrees. Your children can generate ideas beneficial to the entire family if you let them. Giving them a vote along with asking for their thoughts allows them to be constructively involved. Grab this opportunity to include your children; it will elevate their sense of family and provide an opportunity for partnership with you.

Ask your children which foods they feel are essential: which foods they would die without. Discuss with your children and your partner the fact that any decision to delete a food is reversible. Share your own apprehensions about giving up specific foods. Ask your children for suggestions about your own diet: What do they see you eating that is high in fat?

MAKING SOME CHANGES RIGHT NOW

During this planning stage, you might look for one lower-fat or nonfat snack food item that tastes good and would make a good substitute for the high-fat snacks the family has been eating. (For some ideas, see the list of lower-fat snacks on page 78.)

- Make some invisible changes. Try minimizing the saturated fat (meat, cheese, butter, cream, eggs) in a traditional family recipe (see Chapter 12 for ideas and suggestions).

You can make a number of almost imperceptible changes in the way you cook; this is the prerogative of all family cooks. For example, you can cook with olive oil instead of butter or margarine (which lowers the saturated fat immediately); you can reduce the amount of meat in a stew—another saturated fat reduction; you can cut away most of the chicken skin.

Do it again. If that worked, minimize the fat in another family recipe. But be cautious: If the family thinks the lower-fat differences are bad, and feels short-changed or manipulated by your changes, the changes are more drastic than moderate. You have gone beyond your prerogative as the family cook.

- Make some other changes, such as substituting nonfat crackers or pretzels for crackers, chips, or pretzels made with hydrogenated oils.
- Keep including your children in the process. Talk to them about the changes in their diet. Ask them what they like, what they don't like, what they think might be good to try: foods they have heard about. They'll surprise and delight you with their energy and creativity—

for encouragement, see my son John's recipe for spaghetti sauce (page 171).

- If you live with another adult, talk to your partner about the changes you want to make. Your partner may have very strong feelings about your plan. He or she may not see the wisdom or practicality of a change in diet, or may see you as making a major decision that will dramatically alter a source of his or her pleasure. Go slowly. As I'm sure you have learned, adults sometimes need more time to adjust to new ideas than children do. Just because you live together or are the parents of the same children does not, as you've noticed, guarantee instantaneous agreement!

how much fat is in the food
i feed my children?
how to read nutrition labels

Before you begin to actually lower the fat in your family's diet, you need to know how much fat is in the foods you eat now and how to decode food labels.

Can you lower some of the fat in your family's diet without having to learn the decoding secret? Of course you can. You can eat less-fatty meat, buy nonfat frozen desserts and a lower-fat milk, and thereby change your family's diet instantly. But you will not be completely aware of the fat content of many of the foods you buy. Knowing how to read—and decode—nutrition labels guarantees that you can bring home food that is lower in all kinds of fat. If you eat packaged food—and I can't imagine a family that doesn't—you cannot lower the fat in your family's food *intelligently* without mastering the art of decoding packaged food labels.

But are you flustered and perhaps irritated when you look at the numbers and percentages of fat on the nutrition labels that appear on all packaged foods? You should be. They are ambiguous. However, Step One of The Lower-Fat Kids Plan continues your education to help you become label smart. If that is all you can consider attempting now, do just that much. By learning to decode labels, you can do the following things:

- You can determine at a glance which packaged foods are dangerously high in fat and which foods are truly low in fat.
- You will be able to decode all the literature regarding fat, including recipes in your local newspaper and in cookbooks.
- You will no longer be one of a large group of people who are successfully duped every day by misleading advertising and the camouflaging of fat.

DEMYSTIFYING THE LABELS ON PACKAGED FOOD

Since May 1994, nutritional information on packaged food (cans, jars, frozen food, processed cheese, processed meats, crackers, bread, dairy products, cereals—almost all foods wrapped by the manufacturer) must adhere to stipulations mandated by the Food and Drug Administration (FDA) of the United States Department of Agriculture. Nutritional values of food *must* now appear on most packaged food; this information is strictly monitored and standardized. There are some exceptions to this rule; if you see a packaged food without this information, ask. It is available.

Because of this mandate, certain information regarding fat is clearly represented. Sadly, as a result of the very same legislation, harmful trans fatty acids, the byproducts of partially hydrogenated oils, are not represented. This is a major deception.

Also missing from the label is the percentage of calories from fat contained in the food. You must figure it out for yourself. And knowing how will give you more information about the fat in the food you feed your child. This chapter will show you a simple method for determining the true content of packaged foods, but first, take a closer look at how misleading nutritional information can be.

WHAT IS "PERCENTAGE OF FAT"?

Take a packaged food from your pantry or freezer and look at the nutrition label. The ambiguity is in the column headed "% Daily Value" or "% DV." This is not the actual percentage of calories from fat for the portion of food you or your child will eat. Instead, it is the percentage of fat that the food contains in relation to the *total daily suggested allotment of fat for adults who are eating 2,000 to 2,500 calories per day!*

Most people understand this "Percent Daily Value" to mean the precise amount of fat in one serving of the food. Not true. This figure on the package is considerably *lower* than the *actual* percentage of calories from fat in the food.

The % DV, as represented on the package, is intended to be used by a pad-and-pencil-carrying adult who computes the fat grams and percentages and who is also counting all the calories he or she eats so as not to exceed 2,000 or 2,500, whichever the particular manufacturer has selected as its caloric base. If all the calories are not counted, if all the morsels consumed in the day are not written down, the % DV is totally useless.

A better system of nutritional labeling would have included a line that told the *true* percentage of total fat, saturated fat, and hydrogenated oils. Knowing whether a particular food is 10 percent fat, 20 percent fat, or 50 percent fat would make all the difference to the consumer; as would knowing the percentage of *saturated* fat and trans fatty acids. As it is now, the % DV never appears as high as the true percentage of fat the food contains.

HOW TO COMPUTE THE PERCENTAGE OF FAT IN ANY PACKAGED FOOD

Nutrition labels, while in some ways confusing, do give you two important and valuable pieces of information, if you know how to use them. I promised to show you the simple math equations that would help you successfully monitor your family's fat intake, and here they are. This simple math will add up to a lifetime of good health for your family. Here is the first equation.

Search the label on the packaged food you have selected and find:

- the number of total calories in each serving of the food
- the number of fat calories in each serving

These numbers are usually at the top of the label. Together, they will allow you to easily calculate the essential missing information: By dividing the number of fat calories by the total number of calories, you can determine the percentage of calories from fat in each food you select.

The following examples illuminate the fat content of some familiar foods.

When you read the % DV, you may come away with the impression that this popular baking mix is fairly low in fat—only 9 percent fat per serving (see Figure A). But is it true? Let's use the label to find out.

Nutrition Facts

Serving Size ⅓ cup (40g)
Servings Per Container 14

Amount Per Serving

Calories 170 Calories from Fat 50

% Daily Value*

Total Fat 6g   **9%**

Saturated Fat 1.5g   **8%**

INGREDIENTS: ENRICHED FLOUR BLEACHED [WHEAT FLOUR, NIACIN (A B VITAMIN), IRON, THIAMIN MONONITRATE (VITAMIN B₁), RIBOFLAVIN (VITAMIN B₂)], VEGETABLE SHORTENING (CONTAINS PARTIALLY HYDROGENATED SOYBEAN AND/OR COTTONSEED OIL0, LEAVENING (BAKING SODA, SODIUM ALUMINUM PHOSPHATE, MONOCALCIUM PHOSPHATE0, DEXTROSE, SALT, BUTTERMILK.

Figure A. Bisquick label.

The first line shows the total calories per serving as 170 and the calories from fat as 50. Compute the percentage of calories from fat per serving as follows:

50 (fat calories) ÷ 170 (total calories) =
29 percent of calories from fat

One serving of Bisquick mix is a 29-percent-fat food; that is, 29 percent of the calories are from fat, not 9 percent, as a consumer might believe. And, of course, this is before milk, eggs, and butter or margarine are added to make pancakes, biscuits, or waffles. Notice the hydrogenated oils in the ingredients listing; these are the oils that form trans fatty acids, the very worst kind of fat you can feed your family.

Now use the same formula to compute the calories from fat in your package.

☞ EXAMPLE 2: STOUFFER'S SPINACH SOUFFLÉ

Most of us feed our children frozen dinners at one time or another, some more often and some less. Some of those frozen foods seem as though they should be good for children because they include vegetables; actually many have high amounts of fat. Let's do the same math with a popular spinach dish, which would seem to be a 15-percent-fat food (see Figure B).

Divide the number of fat calories by the number of total calories:

90 (fat calories) ÷ 150 (total calories) =
60 percent of calories from fat

The real story: This food derives 60 percent of its calories from fat—that is, more than half the calories. It is a very, very high-fat food, and the suggestion that the package serves three makes for very tiny portions, less than

½ cup per person. If your child ate an ample serving, he or she would probably eat more than half the package—far too much fat to eat on a regular basis.

With 60 percent fat, unless this food is eaten as an occasional treat to satisfy an insistent urge or as an expedient meal for one evening, it is an extremely high-fat food. On the other hand, if your children were text-book material that day and only ate Grape-Nuts and bananas and nonfat milk for breakfast, a salad and a tomato and sprout sandwich for lunch with tomato juice, and if dinner was to be a baked potato, a salad, and the 60-percent-fat frozen spinach, with fresh fruit for dessert, the total saturated and nonsaturated fats for the day would not exceed what even the most rigid enforcer would advocate for a child.

But the kind of fat in this product raises another consideration. The ingredients show that the fat in the frozen spinach dish is mostly margarine, made from partially hydrogenated soybean oil. If the dish were homemade and the spinach were sautéed in water or broth, tossed lightly with olive oil and lightly sprinkled with Parmesan cheese, there would only be a minimal amount of saturated fat from the cheese, and the added oil would be monounsaturated fat; plus there would be a heartier helping of spinach.

Nutrition Facts

Serving Size ½ cup (118g)
Servings Per Container About 3

Amount Per Serving

Calories 150　Calories from Fat 90

	% Daily Value*
Total Fat 10g	**15%**
Saturated Fat 2g	**10%**

INGREDIENTS: SKIM MILK, SPINACH, EGGS, MARGARINE (PARTIALLY HYDROGENATED SOYBEAN OIL, SKIM MILK, SALT, SOY LECITHIN, VEGETABLE MONO- AND DIGLYCERIDES, ARTIFICIALLY FLAVORED, VITAMIN A PALMITATE ADDED, COLORED WITH BETA CAROTENE), MODIFIED FOOD STARCH, BLEACHED ENRICHED FLOUR (WHEAT FLOUR, NIACIN, REDUCED IRON, THIAMIN MONONITRATE, RIBOFLAVIN), SOYBEAN OIL, SUGAR, SALT, SPICE.

Figure B. Stouffer's Spinach Soufflé label.

It certainly won't be the same packaged spinach the children were used to seeing on their plate—too green, too many stem parts, not as much salty taste, and at least ten other negative responses they will invent with their uncanny ability to unsettle you. This is not the moment to regale them with the virtues of your recipe. Listen quietly if your composure is still intact; see if you can enjoy their brilliance as they observe and criticize. Don't try to make them eat it by telling them they must—they won't. They don't know (and you must never tell them) you shopped for the spinach, washed it, chopped it, sautéed it, measured the oil, grated the cheese, and prayed—all for them. At this moment they are not capable of empathizing with you. Maybe the next time the vegetable will seem less strange and they will feel less defiant. Perhaps next time they will even taste the spinach and like it. The downside of all this is they will take your suggestion to eat a carrot instead and with a peeler in hand will decorate the walls and sink with the scrapings. The upside—well, you get an extra portion of spinach.

These are the choices facing every parent every day. To cook from scratch or not; to shop for expediency or not; to learn to identify high-fat foods so you can modify your children's diet to allow for them.

To keep all harmful fats low—saturated fat and the hydrogenated oils that produce trans fatty acids—frozen foods and packaged foods are best avoided if the percentage of total fat in a serving, *after* you have calculated it, is higher than 15 percent. Also, read labels carefully and do your best to turn down foods with killer fats—partially hydrogenated oils and saturated fat. Keep looking. Manufacturers are feeling the pressure from an indignant community and are beginning to consider alternatives; seriously consider which foods you can do without and what can replace them.

☞ EXAMPLE 3: PEPPERIDGE FARM GOLDFISH

This favorite children's snack is frequently eaten by the handful and also used as pacifier food for toddlers. If you habitually stock this snack, you may be laboring under the delusion that you are feeding your child a food that is only 9 percent fat (see Figure C).

But let's do the math:

$$60 \text{ (fat calories)} \div 140 \text{ (total calories)} =$$
$$43 \text{ percent of calories from fat}$$

If your child is eating this snack, he or she is eating a 43-percent-fat food with almost half the calories from fat. Furthermore, the inclusion of polyunsaturated and monounsaturated fats on the label may suggest that some of the fat comes from healthy vegetable oils. The ingredients list shows, however, that the monounsaturated and polyunsaturated vegetable oils have been partially hydrogenated—resulting in unhealthy trans fatty acids. So most of the fat here is the worst kind.

Nutrition Facts
Serving Size 55 pieces (30g/1.1 oz)
Servings Per Container About 6

Amount Per Serving

Calories 140   Calories from Fat 60

% Daily Value*

Total Fat 6g	**9%**
Saturated Fat 2g	**10%**
Polyunsaturated Fat 0.5 g	
Monounsaturated Fat 2.5 g	

MADE FROM: UNBLEACHED ENRICHED WHEAT FLOUR [FLOUR, NIACIN, REDUCED IRON, THIAMIN MONONITRATE (VITAMIN B₁), RIBOFLAVIN (VITAMIN B₂)], NONFAT MILK, PARTIALLY HYDROGENATED VEGETABLE SHORTENING (CANOLA, COTTONSEED AND SOYBEAN OILS), SALT, YEAST, LEAVENING (AMMONIUM BICARBONATE, BAKING SODA, CREAM OF TARTAR, BUTTER, SUGAR, PAPRIKA, CELERY SEED, ONION POWDER AND SPICES.

Figure C. Pepperidge Farm Goldfish label.

☞ EXAMPLE 4: WHOLE MILK

How much fat is in regular whole milk (see Figure D)?
Again, let's do the math:

70 (fat calories) ÷ 160 (total calories) =
44 percent of calories from fat

So, whole milk, which seems to be 13 percent fat, is really a 44-percent-fat drink.

The milk is not only high in fat, but high in saturated fat. Choosing whole-fat milk as a daily or even frequent choice just doesn't make sense in this time of lower-fat alternatives. Healthy children do not need the extra calories from high-fat foods such as whole milk; extra calories can come from lower-fat or nonfat dairy products, fruit, and baked goods such as bagels, pretzels, or bread without added fats.

Nutrition Facts
Serving Size 1 cup (236mL)
Servings Per Container 4

Amount Per Serving
Calories 160   Calories from Fat 70

% Daily Value*
Total Fat 8g   **13%**

Figure D. Whole milk label.

☞ EXAMPLE 5: RITZ CRACKERS

Without knowing how to compute percentages of fat in packaged food, you could erroneously believe that a serving of a popular snack cracker has only 6 percent total fat per serving instead of the *actual* percentage of total calories from fat, which is 43 percent! (See Figure E.) If your child eats half a box (6 ounces) of this popular cracker while doing homework or watching television, he or she will consume approximately 840 calories (perhaps one-fourth of his or her daily calories), with almost all the 43-percent-fat calories coming from hydrogenated oils.

How did this label system happen? Ironically, the most important improvement on the "new" labels was supposed to be that the fat content of the foods would be immediately apparent to the consumer. With the % DV easily misread as the total percentage in a

Nutrition Facts
Serving Size 5 crackers (16g)
Servings Per Container About 21

Amount Per Serving
Calories 80   Calories from Fat 35

% Daily Value*
Total Fat 4g   **9%**
   Saturated Fat 0.5g   **4%**
   Polyunsaturated Fat 0 g
   Monounsaturated Fat 1.5 g

INGREDIENTS: ENRICHED WHEAT FLOUR (CONTAINS NIACIN, REDUCED IRON, THIAMIN MONONITRATE (VITAMIN B₁), RIBOFLAVIN (VITAMIN B₂)), VEGETABLE SHORTENING (PARTIALLY HYDROGENATED SOYBEAN OIL), SUGAR, HIGH FRUCTOSE CORN SYRUP, SALT, LEAVENING (CALCIUM PHOSPHATE, BAKING SODA), MALTED BARLEY FLOUR, SOY LECITHIN (EMULSIFIER).

Figure E. Ritz Crackers label.

serving, the labeling falls far short of what was promised and what was hoped for. The high saturated-fat and hydrogenated oil content of many packaged foods is alarming to nutritionists, physicians, and adults who can decipher the labels.

Recently, a journalist who writes a weekly column on food, with an emphasis on fat and health in general, described a major inconsistency of the Nutritional Labeling and Education Act, as it is formally called, as a "loophole." These "loopholes" are really large information gaps for parents. And the victims are parents and children.

Knowing how simple it is to compute the truth for yourself allows you to choose intelligently; this information is what you need to answer the question, "Just how fatty is the frozen pizza I brought home from the market yesterday? The ice cream I am contemplating today? The waffles? The mayonnaise? The chips? The chocolate milk? Or the foods that seem to be 'lower in fat'?"

Without adequate information, we tend to believe what seems like the best truth; if what we read is confusing, we explain it to ourselves so that it supports our supposition. When we know the facts, there is no argument and no confusion. Learning the truth about the fat percentages of the foods you feed your children allows your choices to be based on fact rather than ambiguous labels.

COMPUTING THE PERCENTAGE OF FAT IN RECIPES

With one additional skill, you can apply the same principle to recipes in newspapers listing the nutritional breakdown in grams. This is the second equation that I promised would help you keep better track of your family's health. This calculation will show you at a glance how much fat is in the recipe you select. For example, a *New York Times* recipe for Spicy Pork is listed as having 180 total calories per portion and *7 grams fat*. (Newspaper and magazine recipes usually indicate fat only in grams rather than in calories from fat.)

Every fat gram, no matter what kind of food it is in, has exactly 9.4 calories. Rounding it out to 10, as many people do, eases the computation. Multiply the 7 fat grams in the Spicy Pork recipe by 10 fat calories to get a very close approximation of the number of fat calories in each serving.

7 fat grams x 10 fat calories = 70 fat calories

Now, use the same computation method as you did for the packaged food: Divide the number of fat calories by the number of total calories.

70 fat calories ÷ 180 total calories = 39 percent of the calories
are from fat in the Spicy Pork recipe

You can do this simple math for every recipe in any book or magazine or newspaper that lists a nutritional breakdown using fat grams. You can know in just a minute approximately how many calories from fat a particular dish with a nutritional analysis contains. Fat grams do not have to be mysterious, mind-boggling mathematical obstacles. And as you become more expert at this endeavor, computation will become totally unnecessary. Clearly, recipes made with cream, eggs, butter, margarine, lots of oil, non-defatted stocks, bacon, beef, or chicken skin will be high in fat. In Step Four: Cooking for Your Lower-Fat Family, you'll learn how to modify recipes with these ingredients and see at a glance what substitutions you can make. *You* will determine the nutritional analysis of recipes.

DECODING THE INGREDIENT LISTING ON PACKAGED FOOD LABELS

All the ingredients on packaged foods are listed—almost always*—on the nutritional label, which may be found on the lid, on a tag attached to the box, on the box itself, or on the wrapper, as with bread. Some states have a law mandating that the ingredients also be listed for all bulk and take-out foods, including fast food. This list can be a quick way to judge the quality of the food and to learn which kind of fat it contains.

The major ingredient in the food, by weight, is listed first. As you begin investigating, you will notice that this ingredient is sometimes a virtual non-food, such as sugar or water. For salad dressings and mayonnaise (the full-fat versions), the major ingredient is oil, so naturally the oil is listed first. In the listing for most cookies, sugar is the primary ingredient. Breads always list the main type of flour used. If a product has three or four or five ingredients other than spices, and the added fat is last, you can assume there is a very low percentage of fat in that food.

---

* In my wanderings I have come across some foods, which, when compared to another in the same category, clearly do not have all the ingredients listed. Sometimes it is the size of the package that is the determining factor, i.e., a large box of cereal versus an individual size; a small soup can versus a large one. Generally, most manufacturers have complied with the labeling laws.

After you learn to decode labels, subtle changes in your marketing choices can demonstrate to your older children that lower-fat foods can be easily incorporated into the family diet, training your children to enjoy the taste of less fatty foods.

ADDED FATS AND INTRINSIC FATS

Intrinsic fats are those fats that occur *naturally* in a particular food. Animal foods are high in intrinsic fats, but plant foods have intrinsic fats as well, in varying amounts. For example, an avocado's fat level is very high, while the fat level of rice or a potato is very low, and in green beans, even lower. Getting to know which foods, especially which plant foods, are high in fat, is another assist for you in helping you choose a lower-fat diet for your children, and alerts you to foods you will want to offer less frequently. Don't eliminate these high-fat plant foods. Even if your children might not notice an avocado moratorium, resist this strategy; every food is unique. These foods, although very high in fat, all contain important healthy fats and other nutrients that are essential to your children's well-being and growth, and have a place in your children's diet. Begin to use olives, for instance, sliced and tossed with salad or rice instead of by the handful; think of avocado as a garnish rather than the entire substance of a sandwich, and guacamole as a less frequent snack; buy nuts for snacking in shells rather than in jars—they take longer to eat and determination is mandatory for consumption, not unconscious habit. And instead of constantly filling a sandwich with a thick schmear of peanut butter, consider using less and fill the sandwich with fruit slices or green pepper. Turning your own imagination to high can result in more inventions. Providing a broad assortment of foods throughout a week or month, rather than an everyday diet of Poptarts and egg sandwiches, is your goal.

PLANT FOODS THAT ARE HIGH IN INTRINSIC FAT

- olives
- avocados
- all nuts, including the legume, peanut
- all seeds such as sesame, pumpkin, sunflower
- all oils, such as olive, safflower, corn, peanut, canola, nut oils
- all nut butters including peanut butter

Added fats are the oils, butter, lard, shortening, partially hydrogenated oils, and/or margarine *added* to the food in processing and cooking. Sometimes the fat added is a healthy oil such as olive or peanut oil. Often, though, they are unhealthy fats resulting from the manufacturing process.

ANIMAL FOODS THAT ARE HIGH IN INTRINSIC FAT

- egg yolks
- beef
- lamb
- dark meat chicken and chicken skin
- dark meat turkey and turkey skin
- organ meats such as calf's liver, chicken liver, kidneys, sweet breads
- low- and whole-milk dairy products

FINDING NEW FOODS

Finding new foods for your children is always a challenge; besides needing to know just what is in the food, you want the food to taste good. As your children will clearly inform you, lower-fat food that tastes like unsalted rubber bands or overly sugared paper is not a win, only a loss. Return the food to the market if you or your kids don't like it; you can get a refund and continue your search. More information on maneuvering in the supermarket is in Chapter Six, "Making Friends with Your Supermarket."

Educating yourself about the percentage of calories from fat in the food you feed your children does not mean you must immediately stop buying familiar foods. The primary purpose of this information is to enable you to distinguish, with full awareness and perhaps some humor, highly saturated-fat foods from lower-fat foods. As you become more and more aware of the high levels of fat in some of your family favorites, you will begin to feel the urge to curtail the frequency with which you buy some of these foods. Making educated choices instead of purchasing in response to advertising and habit can be, if you let it, challenging to your imagination and exciting to master.

5

camouflaged fat:
don't be fooled by low-fat pretenders

The education process of Step One does not end with calculating percentage of fat. There is more information on the package waiting to be decoded. For example, in the rush to own a larger share of the burgeoning low-fat marketplace, many food manufacturers mislead you. As a result, you buy foods you *think* are healthy. Even with the new labeling mandate, manufacturers deliberately design clever package advertising to cloud your logic and lull you into purchases you probably would never make if you knew the truth. Here are some that I think will be of special interest to you in your effort to lower the fat in your family's diet.

LOW FAT? LOOK AGAIN:
MILK AND OTHER DAIRY PRODUCTS

Milk, in both its low-fat and whole form, is on the USDA list of the top ten highest-saturated-fat foods consumed by American children. Low-fat milk is a successful camouflage of a high-fat food.

Any intelligent person would believe that milk labeled "2 percent fat" contains just that: 2 percent fat, and 98 percent *not* fat (see Figure A).

When you make the computation, you see that low-fat milk is not 2 percent fat, as the name implies, nor 8 percent fat, as the label implies. It's 32 percent fat. The 2 percent refers only to the *weight* of the fat in the milk; *it has no correlation* to the percent of calories from fat or the degree of saturation of the fat. Here are the facts:

Nutrition Facts
Serving Size 1 cup (236mL)
Servings Per Container 4

Amount Per Serving

Calories 140   Calories from Fat 45

% Daily Value*

Total Fat 5g   **8%**

Figure A. Low-fat milk label.

- As you learned in the previous chapter, one glass of whole milk derives 44 percent of its calories from fat.
- One glass of 2 percent "low-fat" milk derives 32 percent of its calories from fat.
- One glass of 1 percent "low-fat" milk derives 17 percent of its calories from fat.
- One glass of nonfat, or skim, milk is a 0 percent fat drink, and it has the same amount of protein, calcium, and Vitamin D as the other milks.
- The same percentages are true for nonfat, low-fat, and whole-milk cottage cheese, yogurt, and buttermilk.

Knowing this, wouldn't it make sense to seriously consider a permanent shift to nonfat milk? Or at least a move to lower the fat in the milk and dairy products you purchase now? Even the tiniest reduction you make in your children's diet is a win in your goal to lower the saturated fat in the food you feed your children—and by lowering the fat in the milk you purchase, you lower the total amount of fat they consume.

If a child drank four glasses each day of 1 percent low-fat milk (or an equal mixture of nonfat milk and 2 percent milk) instead of four glasses of 2 percent milk, the child's consumption of total fat would be lowered by 90 fat calories each day, 2,700 fat calories each month, and 32,400 fat calories each year! Staggering, isn't it? If a child has a tendency to be chubby, this single dietary change can result in a slow, steady weight loss, while clearing his or her arteries of some of the fat burden they now carry. If the child drank an equal mixture of 1 percent milk with nonfat, or skim, to make .5 percent milk, the reduction would be even greater.

If the child also ate nonfat yogurt instead of whole or low-fat yogurt (or cottage cheese or ice cream), the reduction of saturated fat calories and total fat calories could be considerable. If you are willing to make *only one* change in the food you feed your children, the switch from whole to 2 percent or from 2 percent to 1 percent, or from 1 percent to .5 percent or nonfat milk would eliminate a major source of saturated fat calories and total fat.

If you currently give your children nonfat milk, you are already aware of the difference in the calories from fat in milk. If you haven't tried the other nonfat dairy products, why not bring a few home? You will be surprised at how similar in taste they are to the higher-fat versions.

If your children are used to drinking whole milk or 2 percent milk, the taste of nonfat milk will be different and the switch may be difficult. Because in my family our children were young when we began to feed them nonfat milk, taste was not an issue. Our eldest son found the change in the color of the milk container bewildering, but after several trips to the fridge he became content. After all, what came out was white, he drank it from the same cup, and he ate it with the same cereal. Two of our children did notice the difference and didn't like it, so we invented the combination method—mixing a bit of whole milk (there was no low-fat milk then) in with the nonfat. That worked for them, and for us. Gradually, we were able to eliminate whole milk entirely.

For your children, try reducing the amount of 2 percent or 1 percent milk that you mix with the nonfat over a two-month period. If a continuing reduction doesn't work in your family, then keep the half-and-half mixture in place. Even a small reduction contributes to your goal of lowering the amount of saturated fat you feed your children.

WHAT ABOUT "97 PERCENT OR 98 PERCENT FAT-FREE" PACKAGED FOODS?

When you see a label that says "97 percent fat free," don't believe that the food derives 3 percent of its calories from fat. You are most likely looking at the same old high-fat food in a new disguise. These seductive come-ons are warnings in themselves: All the foods with these advertisements have much higher percentages of fat than is suggested by the advertising. If the package is soup, the fat is often partially hydrogenated fat, and in some instances it may be as high as 35 percent.

Using your new skill at computing fat percentages, try it out on two or three packages and see what the results are. Deliberately select a food that claims to be

96, 97, or 98 percent fat free—perhaps one you have been purchasing because of this promise. Figure B shows an example.

Nutrition Facts

Serving Size 1 cup (240mL)
Servings about 2

Amount Per Serving

Calories 120   Fat Calories 30

                                    % Daily Value*

Total Fat 3g   **5%**
    Saturated Fat 1g   **5%**
    Polyunsaturated Fat 0.5g
    Monounsaturated Fat 1g

INGREDIENTS: CHICKEN STOCK, COOKED CHICKEN MEAT, WATER, CARROTS, CELERY, RICE, POTATOES, POTATO STARCH, ONIONS, CONTAINS LESS THAN 1% OF THE FOLLOWING INGREDIENTS: CHICKEN FLAVOR (CONTAINS SALT AND FLAVORING), TOMATOES, SALT, SUGAR, CHICKEN FLAVOR (CONTAINS SALT, FLAVOR, CULTURED WHEY, EGG ALBUMIN), POTASSIUM CHLORIDE, DEHYDRATED GARLIC, DISODIUM INOSINATE, DISODIUM GUANYLATE, LACTIC ACID, SPICE EXTRACT, DEHYDRATED PARSLEY, BETA CAROTENE FOR COLOR, SPICE.

Figure B. Campbell's Healthy Request Hearty Chicken Rice Soup.

You may think that when you open a can of soup you are feeding your children a healthy meal. The front label on this can of soup claims it is 98% fat free. But how much fat is in the soup? Let's do the division. The soup is listed as having 120 total calories and 30 fat calories per serving. To compute the percentage of fat, do what you have learned:

30 fat calories ÷ 120 total calories = 25 percent of calories from fat

Are you surprised by the results? This soup contains 25 percent fat, not the 2 percent the front of the label leads you to believe.

Finding out what's too much fat in the marketplace can be easy: Read the label, and divide the fat calories by the total calories. You will instantly see the truth.

The food-labeling law mandated that strict definitions be applied to certain terms used to advertise packaged food. Previously there were no restraints, and words such as low-fat did not mean anything specific. Following are the current definitions of four packaging terms:

- *Low-Fat* means no more than 3 grams of total fat per serving. A gram is a metric unit of weight. Three grams of fat equals about 30 fat calories. If the total calories per serving is, say, 60, the item could be a 50-percent-fat food—despite the "low-fat" label.

- *Light* means the food must have at least one-third fewer calories than a comparable product made by the same manufacturer, such as a maker of mayonnaise like Best Foods. Any percentage of these calories could come from fat.

- *Low-Calorie* means each serving must have less than 40 total calories. Any percentage of these could come from fat.

- *Fat-Free* means that the food is nonfat or contains less than .5 grams of fat per serving. If a package contains 8 servings, the food could contain 4 grams of fat if you ate the entire contents. The only way to tell if a food that is labeled "fat-free" is really nonfat is to read the ingredient listing.

chapter 5

CRACKERS AND THEIR CRUMBS

Except for the truly fat-free crackers for sale in the marketplace, some of which (without much sugar added) are very good, most crackers include hydrogenated vegetable oils. Mostly, these vegetable oils will have been partially hydrogenated—converted into trans fatty acids that act in your child's body, as you have learned, like the saturated fat in chicken, milk, butter, and cream. Or, the ingredient listing will say "margarine," which means the same thing, since (as you now know) most margarine is made from oils processed in this manner.

Look in your market for fat-free crackers. Use them in cooking as well as for snacks. Fat-free cracker crumbs made from crackers you purchase in the market are instant aids in thickening soups and tomato sauces, and in mixing with bread to make stuffings.

You can return the crackers to the store if your children don't like them. The market sends returns back to the manufacturer for credit. Get some friends to experiment with new crackers and other foods so you can expand your repertoire more immediately and at the same time develop a community of compatriots with a common goal.

6

making friends with your supermarket:
food shopping for healthier kids

Embarking on The Lower-Fat Kids Plan takes you into the supermarket for Step Two, Food Shopping for Healthier Kids, where you will put your new education to practical use. As you have noticed, the last five years have brought a proliferation of new package designs and labels for foods you have been purchasing for years. Wherever you look in your supermarket, you see the words and phrases "lower in fat," "low-fat," "less fat," "no cholesterol" "lighter," "lite," "nonfat," "98 percent fat-free," "healthy," "more fiber," "sugar-free," "only fruit juice used as sweetener," "less sodium," "salt-free." These foods are no longer in a special dietetic section as they once were, but are spread all over the market among all categories of food.

These foods are the result of the concerns you have indicated in your responses to questionnaires in the magazines and books you purchase, in the foods you buy, and in the spas, gyms, and restaurants you patronize. Your expanding concern about a healthful diet for you and your children has given rise to a mega-industry of low-fat, low-sugar, fat-free foods, as well as a mega-industry of foods that are not what you think they are. This is a far different market from the one I confronted when I first began a search for lower-fat foods.

ONCE UPON A TIME...

In 1962, when my husband and I began to lower the fat in our diet, hardly any supermarket foods were free of fat; we could count only on vinegar, skim (nonfat) milk, fruit, and vegetables! Nor was there anything in the supermarket that advertised itself as being lower in fat. In New York City, we could always purchase skim milk; it seemed to have always been there, even during my childhood. But when we ventured into the country, it disappeared from markets unless vacationing urbanites had demanded it.

In those days, we could find spaghetti sauces that listed oil or butter or margarine way down at the end of the ingredient listing, so we knew that there was less fat in that particular can than in one where the fat was the second ingredient after tomatoes. We could do the same with pretzels, bread, an occasional canned soup, and frozen food. It was a laborious task yielding very few victories, and even fewer tasty ones.

We made nonfat yogurt at home, carried nonfat milk powder into rural areas, invented margarine-free cookies, baked our own nonfat Irish soda bread, took salami and butter off our shopping list, made "ice cream" pops out of our own yogurt and strawberries and others out of pineapple juice. Our children begged us not to order pizza without cheese when their friends came over, and we didn't.

For a while, I was a fanatic—impossible to bear. Gradually, a wisdom of sorts came to me and life became livable for us once again. Every once in a while, I bought Kentucky Fried Chicken and everyone thought they had gone to heaven. We chose our baby-sitter for her way with kids, not her ability in the kitchen, and on those nights TV dinners were king. And every now and then, packaged bologna was in the lunch box of one or the other of our children.

Today, however, you can choose from a relatively extravagant selection of low-fat packaged meats, spaghetti sauces, tuna packed in water, low-fat desserts of every sort, and a huge variety of lower-fat and nonfat dairy products. You can find bread without added fats, cookies without added fats and without tons of sugar, pretzels and potato chips without added fats or sugar, soup without added fats, and every food you can think of in some lower-fat or nonfat permutation.

But still, the old high-fat reliables, along with new high-fat seductions, are on all the shelves. Soups, sauces, instant dinners, frozen foods, ice creams, tortillas with lard, breads and crackers with partially hydrogenated oils, high-fat mayonnaise, more cheese than ever, more kinds of packaged meats, more prepared foods with lots of oils and butter, more high-fat granolas, more high-fat cookies, and more salad bars with high-fat dressings, bacon, and sour cream.

But be heartened: With The Lower-Fat Kids Plan in hand, plus your new knowledge of where fat hides, and how to decode labels and recognize deceit, you can learn to navigate your supermarket with ease. Now you can find the camouflaged fat as well as the truly lower-fat foods. The supermarket can be your classroom. You now have new eyes for the market—you will see things you couldn't before because you didn't know where to look.

INVESTIGATING YOUR MARKET

If you are like most parents, time is in short supply. However, think of the time you spend on this part of The Plan as an investment in your family's health. You will use the information you discover on this expedition for years to come, and your children will benefit for the rest of their lives.

Try to set aside two hours to spend for your initial visit at the market. Find your warm clothes and comfortable shoes, and put a box of raisins in your pocket or eat a sandwich before you go. A growling stomach makes you less objective about food.

Before you go, look through your pantry for ten high-fat packaged foods you regularly purchase for your family or for your own snacks. Make a list of these foods on a pad and take the pad and a pen with you.

If two hours are impossible, plan to investigate just one high-fat food from your list on each of your next ten trips; the process will be slower but the results will be the same. Choose items you know your kids will love.

FINDING ALTERNATES FOR HIGH-FAT FOODS

Your task here is straightforward: Find the first item on your list of high-fat packaged foods, look at the nutrition label, and jot down the total calories and fat calories in your notebook. Now find one or more lower-fat alternatives—foods that you think your children might possibly like as substitutes—and jot down their names, total calories, and fat calories.

Using your notes about how to do the calculations, compute the fat percentages now. Do this for every item on your list if you're doing this in one trip. This simple act of *active* observation will make a significant impact on your future purchases. Remember: You don't have to buy now if you don't want to. Eventually, some of these newly investigated foods will become your new habits.

The following foods tend to appear on most people's shopping lists; on your exploratory trip to the market look for these food categories:

MAYONNAISE AND HIGH-FAT SALAD DRESSINGS: The mayonnaise and dressing shelves contain many high-fat products, as well as lower-fat substitutes you may not have considered. Look for a substitute you and your children might like, based on favorite ingredients or flavorings. Examine the nutrition label on the jar you usually buy and compare it to the label of your prospective purchase. Make sure your lower-fat choice lists fewer total calories and considerably fewer fat calories—at least half in the case of mayonnaise.

Remember, don't rely on the front-of-the-jar advertising. Check the ingredient listing, and do your math. Regular mayonnaise is practically all fat, as are regular salad dressings. The calories come mostly from the oils, eggs, and cheese used to flavor the dressings. Your substitute may contain liquids such as juice to replace fat, but avoid products with partially hydrogenated oils and margarine.

TUNA: Next seek out the canned fish section. Clearly canned tuna packed in water has less fat than canned tuna packed in oil. It is not necessary or of any benefit to buy tuna with added fat. Water-packed tuna tastes great and has the same nutritional value but less calories and fat. If for some reason you or your children feel you have to eat tuna with oil, add a teaspoon of olive oil when you prepare the water-packed version. You will still have considerably less oil than the oil-packed tuna, and of a quality you can count on.

CRACKERS AND COOKIES: You will put to good use all you have learned about hydrogenated oils in this section. Choose nonfat crackers over those baked with partially hydrogenated oils or high-saturated-fat butter or lard. Read the ingredient lists on the boxes and also check the calories from fat. Thinly spread with peanut or almond butter or a chickpea spread, children won't miss the additional saturated fat of the cracker. There are some really good fat-free crackers. Besides rice crackers, my family likes Nabisco brand fat-free saltines and matzos.

As you go from cookie to cookie notice the high-fat content of products. Select those with less or no fat such as Fig Newtons.

BREAD AND PACKAGED BAKERY GOODS: Your market will probably have bagels, breadsticks, and English muffins in the bread section. Traditionally these items are baked simply and without fat. Choose breads without hydrogenated oils, lard, or butter. Also select breads without oils as a major ingredient. This will be clear from reading the ingredient list. Remember that breads with added seeds, nuts, or whole grains are excellent choices for your growing children.

Most likely you will find the next several items clustered together in your market.

MILK PRODUCTS: Choose milk with a lower percentage of fat than your usual variety. (For more details, see the discussion on lower-fat milks in Chapter 5.) Do the same for yogurt, cottage cheese, sour cream, chocolate milk, and buttermilk. Select one or two products you usually take home—and compare the labels.

CHEESE: There are not many nonfat cheeses available at this writing, and most tend to be rubbery. The one we use at our house is Healthy Choice nonfat mozzarella. This cheese is similar to other packaged high-fat mozzarella, which is 75 percent fat, though it bears no resemblance at all to fresh mozzarella. Try it chopped or shredded with beans on a tortilla, melted on toast with herbs and served with soups, and melted and mixed with vegetables as an English muffin pizza. For an even better flavor, mix with a bit of Parmesan or Romano cheese. But look at all the brands, and perhaps you will discover your own favorites. More and more nonfat cheeses are being manufactured all the time. The difference in fat content between nonfat mozzarella (0 percent fat) and regular mozzarella (75 percent fat) is enormous, and so is the difference this will make to your children's health. The difference between a lower-in-fat mozzarella and a regular mozzarella is slight. You must check the labels; just because it says "lower in fat" on the front of the package doesn't guarantee a significant reduction; it may still be a 40- to 50-percent-fat food.

EGGS: You can't purchase lower-fat eggs, but you can make egg dishes lower in fat by using fewer yolks and more whites. To do this, you will have to purchase more eggs than you usually do. Double the recipe amount if discarding half the yolks, and one third more if you discard two yolks to every three whites. Cooking omelets this way is more than satisfactory. It is one case in which the reduction in fat (the yolks) can go totally unnoticed.

LOWER-FAT FROZEN DESSERTS: To select alternates for ice cream or low-fat frozen desserts (so-called "lower-fat" desserts are usually from 20 percent to 40 percent fat), begin to experiment with nonfat selections. Look at sorbets (which use no milk products), fruit sticks, nonfat "ice creams," and nonfat frozen yogurts. Compare what it says on the front of some containers to the actual truth on the label as you use your new skill to compute the percent of calories from fat. When you discover the enormous amounts of fat in regular ice creams as well as in the ones you used to think were low in fat, you will realize the importance of The Lower-Fat Kids Plan to help you streamline your kids' diet. Again, if you are the parent of a chubby child, the calories saved by combining low- and nonfat dairy foods, and eating nonfat frozen yogurt, nonfat milk, and other dairy products can produce a gradual weight loss over the course of a year.

HOT DOGS AND PACKAGED LUNCH MEATS: To select alternatives for hot dogs and packaged lunch meats, read the labels carefully. If you feel you need to continue to stock these foods as staples, look for products with half the fat of your usual brand and no hydrogenated oils, and look for vegetarian hot dogs and burgers that are low in fat. There are some really good frozen ones, but remember that not all vegetarian food is good for your children; manufacturers have found a way to put saturated fat and hydrogenated oils into vegetarian foods.

Do not be fooled by surreptitious advertising: Packaged chicken and turkey lunch meats and hot dogs are not always the "lower-fat" choices, even though the package says so. (Most traditional sausage-type foods in skin or a casing, such as franks, bologna, and salami, are usually very high both in fat— deriving about 70 percent of their calories from fat—and sodium, and can have unhealthy preservatives.) Again, in an attempt to seduce the consumer— you—packaged meat producers make claims that turn out to be deceptive. Sausages made from veal or turkey are advertised as lower in fat, and some, to a degree, are. Most, however, still have 40 percent to 50 percent total fat and derive up to 25 percent of their calories from saturated fat, because ground poultry usually includes dark meat and added fat.

OTHER CANNED AND PACKAGED FOODS: When purchasing packaged foods such as spaghetti sauces, soups, beans, chili, canned pasta, instant pasta and cheese dinners, stuffings, and instant potatoes, check the ingredient listing for fat. Again, eliminate products with partially hydrogenated oils if you can. If you must buy food with added fat, look for products with fat listed near the end of the ingredients list and where the fat is olive or nut oils such as almond or walnut. Keep searching for nonfat products. Several of them are very, very good.

CEREALS: To find alternative cereals, don't be swayed by the advertising, or unfounded claims on the front of the cereal box. You must read the ingredient lists to find out for sure whether fat is *added*. Many cereal manufactures include the fat intrinsic to the grains in the total fat percentage, and that can be misleading. There are granolas now with no added fats except perhaps for nuts. Choose those. Leave the granolas with added oils and coconut. Be vigilant. Just recently, I was food shopping with one of my sons in Durango, Colorado. Reading the labels on the bulk granolas, we discovered that they ranged from as little as 2 grams (10 percent calories from fat) of fat per serving to as much as 10 grams (50 percent of calories from fat) per serving! Many cereals are now made with minimal added fat or sugar and are sweetened with dried fruit. Check and compare some cereal labels. It's just not necessary, or wise, to choose high-fat cereal with a lot of added sugar.

Use the rest of your time to wander the aisles and look around with your new awareness. If you're expecting to go through the entire list, continue only as long as you feel up to it. This type of work, even though you are making discoveries, can be tiring. Notice what is being offered. At random, pick up a product that claims to be lower in fat and check to see if it advertises the truth. Use your new skills. Does the food you are considering have a high percentage of saturated fat? Does it contain hydrogenated oils? Notice your new proficiency at spotting camouflaged fats. Notice that you now know what you are buying or turning down. Now you are a consumer with your own educated judgments and label literacy.

LYING IN WAIT

In the freezer section of your market, along with some very healthy foods, are unhealthy, very high-fat foods, camouflaged with the words "spinach" or "chicken" or "lower-in-fat." After all, spinach is healthy, chicken has less fat than beef (sometimes), and anything lower in fat is automatically good, right?

But many of these foods have been fiddled with to produce tastes children love. The chicken is fried, the spinach is in cream sauce, and the cakes are dense with hydrogenated oils. On The Lower-Fat Kids Plan can you still use freezer foods to supplement your cooking? Of course. Look for the healthier choices. They are there: really good-tasting vegetarian soy burgers, truly reduced fat (less than 15 percent fat) main courses, herb flavored vegetables *without* butter, and nonfat frozen desserts. However, products do change regularly and some products disappear from the market entirely, usually the ones your children love. You cannot count on ingredients remaining the same. New food fads and market appeal determine what you will find in the marketplace, and in the freezer.

As the weeks go by, when you do your usual food shopping, select one category of food to investigate: packaged lunch meats, frozen desserts, chocolate cookies, granola bars or cereals, spaghetti sauce, veggie burgers or dogs, frozen vegetables, crackers, and so on. This should add only a few minutes to your visit to the market. Read the labels of as many of the foods in your category you have time for.

You don't have to make any decisions to buy if you don't have time. You are simply familiarizing yourself with high-fat products and lower-fat options. Remember, the market is your classroom. It is a tuition-free school for you. You can go to class anytime you want. You can take as long as you need to learn the facts; you can get your degree at your convenience. And if you want to, you can go on to even higher education whenever you have time.

A FEW WORDS ABOUT SUGAR

Since you're poised to look at fat in the food you feed your family, you may want to take a minute and consider sugar. Though not a concern in every family, sugar may become a larger part of your family's diet than you wish as you try to find substitutions for some of the high-fat foods you usually serve. For instance, if you eliminate French fries as a snack you may substitute a bag of nonfat candies or cookies with, obviously, much more sugar. High-sugar foods are filling, satisfying and a major American habit. Given a choice, and if they are offered or stocked as staples at home, too often children substitute high-sugar foods for healthier complex carbohydrates that have the nutrients they need. When our children eat more sugar calories than their bodies can use, the excess is stored as fat and can contribute to overweight. All sugar, whether it comes from a candy bar, fruit or honey, can also cause teeth to decay. Very young children, and many older ones, do not brush their teeth properly, or sometimes, at all. The longer the food sticks to the teeth, the more possibility for decay.

Sugar additives, along with fat, dominate processed foods. If eating too much sugar is a concern in your family, you can lower the sugar content of your family's diet by purchasing foods low in added sugar. Look for camouflaged sugar in the ingredient list: Whenever you see the words *malt syrup, maltose, dextrose, sucrose, fructose, honey, brown sugar, fruit juice or concentrate, or corn syrup,* the food has sugar in it.

Buy unsweetened orange, grapefruit, apple, and pineapple juice or any other unsweetened juice you can find instead of juices and fruit drinks with *added* sugars.

Begin to check labels for *added* sugars in soups, tomato and spaghetti sauces, beans, salsas, canned fruit, cereals, peanut butter, pretzels, bread, and crackers.

some instant ideas:
taking the fat out now

You don't have to complete all the steps of the Lower-Fat Kids Plan to start your family on the path to healthier eating. Even as you continue reading you may be surprised to discover how easily you can make some immediate shifts to lower-fat eating. One secret is the "deletion and substitution" method, which instantly converts you to a lower-fat cook. In Chapter 12, you will be introduced to lower-fat cooking. You'll see how you can revise your own recipes and newspaper and cookbook recipes by deleting some ingredients and substituting others. But first, here are some ideas that you can implement instantly.

If you choose just two of the following deletion suggestions, you will *markedly* lower the fat in your child's diet. If you choose four of the following deletions, you will *significantly* lower the fat in your child's diet. If you institute *all* of the suggestions for deletion and substitution that follow, you will accomplish a *major restructuring* of the entire family's diet. Note that some deletions will lower high-saturated-fat foods, high-fat foods, and some foods with hydrogenated oils.

CHANGING SOME OF YOUR HIGH-FAT COOKING HABITS—INSTANTLY

- If you're used to sautéing foods in butter and you are apprehensive about giving up the taste of butter, substitute olive oil or other healthy oil for half the butter. The percentage of the fat content will be the same, but the amount of saturated fat will be less.
- If you always sauté in olive oil, reduce the amount you use by half. (When you use olive oil for cooking, don't pour. Measure the oil by teaspoon—you can always add more. Also, try filling a spray bottle, the type you use to mist plants and dampen cotton before ironing, and spray a small amount of oil in your pan or simply brush some on with a pastry brush.)
- Delete all the oil you use for sautéing vegetables, and substitute non-fat chicken broth, vegetable broth, water, or a combination. As the vegetables are cooked with the broth or water, they will soften and brown as though you were using oil (you can always add 1 teaspoon of flavorful olive oil midway through the cooking or when the cooking is done if you feel you need the taste). As the cooking proceeds, you will need to add liquid by the tablespoon until the vegetables are cooked, then again at the end to make a sauce.
- Delete the whole or low-fat milk and dairy products you usually use, and substitute a lower-fat milk, yogurt, sour cream, or cottage cheese.
- Delete one-third to one-half the meat you usually use in stews and add twice the amount of vegetables.
- Prepare stews the day before and chill the gravy separately. The fat will solidify on top and you can easily discard it.
- Delete two of your family's traditional high-saturated-fat meals each week and substitute a simple-to-prepare lower-fat meal with minimal meat and more vegetables and grains.
- Delete half of your children's high-fat desserts and substitute nonfat frozen desserts or fruit. Do this by reducing the high-fat portion of the dessert and substituting a nonfat one, or by adding fresh or dried fruit to half a portion of regular ice cream.
- Delete bread with *added* fats and substitute bread with no added fats.

chapter 7

- Delete cereals with added fats if your family eats cereal regularly, and substitute cereals with no added fats.
- Delete half (or all) the cheese at restaurants where you can (for instance, on a pizza when you order it), and from take-out where you can (for instance, on hamburgers and sandwiches and on salads).
- In your own recipes, delete half (or all) the cheese—keep reminding yourself that cheese is a very high-saturated-fat food. When you do use cheese, add it as a condiment or combine nonfat cheese with regular cheese. (If your family eats cheese regularly, this will make a big difference.)
- Delete higher-fat (over 15 percent calories from fat) frozen foods, snacks, and main dishes from your shopping list and substitute frozen snacks and frozen main dishes that contain less than 15 percent of calories from fat. This will be more difficult if you are used to regular meals of frozen foods.
- Delete half the oil from your usual recipes, including the amount of oil you use to make salad dressings (replace oil in salad dressings with a fruit juice or stock or broth). (Although olive oil is the healthiest oil for your family, and delicious, most recipes and cooks use excessive amounts.)
- Delete half the cookies or crackers (high-fat or low-fat) your child eats and substitute fresh or dried fruit or nonfat cracker products such as saltines, rice crackers, pretzels, or melba rounds. With thinly spread peanut butter, plain crackers are transformed into filling snacks without as much saturated fat. With jam or fresh fruit slices, nonfat crackers are a no-fat snack.

Here are some more suggestions:

- Make an omelet with half the amount of yolks you usually use and twice the amount of whites. This will reduce the dietary cholesterol in your child's diet. (See the recipe on page 115.)
- Use cheese as a condiment rather than as a significant ingredient in a main dish.
- Use small portions of meat or poultry as a condiment. (For example, for six people, cook two portions of meat or poultry and toss with a rice, mushroom, and broccoli casserole.)

some instant ideas: taking the fat out now

- Always take the skin off chicken or turkey breast—the skin has more than 50 percent of the total amount of saturated fat.
- When you brown ground meat for a recipe, drain the grease from the pan before you begin cooking the rest of the recipe.
- To really remove the fat from browned ground meat, drain it on paper towels—they'll absorb a lot of the fat—then add the meat to your recipe.

WAYS TO CHANGE YOUR CHILD'S (AND YOUR OWN) LUNCH HABITS INSTANTLY

A diet lower in fat does not have to torture or embarrass your children. With some thought, you can lower the fat in their lunch boxes almost imperceptibly.

1. Delete some of the cheese and meat and substitute sliced raw vegetables on sandwiches. (Substituting vegetables for some of the meat and cheese adds fiber as well as an assortment of good-for-the-body nutrients to your child's diet.)

2. Use a nonfat sandwich spread: mustard, Our Nonfat "Mayonnaise" (page 161), or a packaged spread such as nonfat bean spread.

3. Alternate cakes or cookies with dried or fresh fruit, or a combination with a few walnuts.

4. Choose lower-fat milk, yogurt, and cottage cheese.

5. Substitute nonfat chips or pretzels for the high-fat versions.

6. Substitute homemade gorp (page 80) for candy bars.

7. Make sandwiches with bread that doesn't have added fats.

8. Make tuna sandwiches using tuna canned in water rather than oil, and half the usual amount of mayonnaise mixed with nonfat plain yogurt or Our Nonfat "Mayonnaise."

9. Make peanut butter and jelly sandwiches using half the usual amount of peanut butter and adding apple or vegetable slices. Ten to 15 percent of the fat of peanut butter is saturated. Because peanuts are quite nutritious and 85 percent of the fat in peanut butter is unsaturated, it is sometimes thought of as a "health" food, but no high-fat food is a "good" constant snack food unless you have a very young child going through a brief nothing-but-peanut-butter-eating stage. Vary your children's diet, and teach them how to do it themselves by reducing the amount of high-fat "healthy" foods they eat and filling those gaps with low-fat/no-fat healthy foods, such as fresh

fruits, grains, raw or cooked veggies, and other lower-fat snacks. Peanut butter and other nut butters can stay; used as light spreads along with other sandwich ingredients they become condiments rather than major ingredients. When you buy peanut butter read the label carefully. Avoid brands with added sugar, salt, and hydrogenated oils.

8

de-acquisitioning your kitchen:
what are the bad foods?

The next step in the Lower-Fat Kids Plan, shift to the kitchen. Stocking your kitchen with lower-fat and nonfat foods will definitely make the transition to a lower-fat diet easier. I will start by showing how to develop an overview of just what is in your kitchen, then to start to eliminate—or "de-acquisition"—high-fat foods. Remember, you will do this over a period of time. You can de-acquisition in an afternoon, or over the course of a week or month. The speed with which you do it is not as important as knowing that you will do it. Only you, in consultation with your family, can choose the actual time frame.

A ruthless de-acquisitioner will have a kitchen table full of high-saturated-fat ice cream, mayonnaise, butter, margarine, whipping cream, cheese, cream cheese, other high-fat (including "low-fat") dairy products, frankfurters, bologna, salami, ham, creamed or buttered homemade casseroles and lasagnas, cookies, crackers, chips, and lots of frozen foods ready to be evaluated and perhaps discarded.

But you probably won't be this enthusiastic, nor must you be. Remember, be gentle with your family. Tossing out loved favorites is not easy. These represent lifetime food connections, family traditions, and solidly entrenched habits. Make your decisions based on convenience, habit, necessity, health, and level of reluctance. If you are on a strict budget, you may decide to use the high-fat items on your shelves, but not replace them. On the other hand, you may choose to toss them out or give them away.

If you de-acquisition foods a few at a time, rather than making indiscriminate changes, your family can assimilate adjustments at their own pace, and make sensible—and personal—replacements. The point is for you and your family to become enthusiastic lovers of lower-fat foods, not dissatisfied victims.

YOUR REFRIGERATOR

Let's start with your fridge—not the freezer, just the fridge. First, separate the refrigerator food into three categories:

- NONFAT PACKAGED FOODS OR VERY LOW-FAT PACKAGED FOODS SUCH AS REDUCED-FAT COTTAGE CHEESE AND YOGURT, PLUS EGGS. Keep all of these items. Put them on one shelf during this exercise.
- HIGH-FAT AND "LOW-FAT" PACKAGED FOODS. If the "low-fat" foods are dairy products—whole milk, yogurt, milk, cottage cheese, sour cream—keep them until you have decided how you want to proceed. Make a note to yourself to reconsider the level or percentage of fat in the dairy products you want to stock. Sort out the other supposedly "low-fat" foods, such as salad dressings, "light" mayonnaise, or turkey bologna. Look at the labels to see if they contain partially hydrogenated oils, or if the packaged meat slogans compare favorably with the ingredients. You can keep these if it's inconvenient or too expensive to toss them, but they should eventually be on your list of foods to be replaced with more healthful substitutions. Now that you know how to read and calculate fat accurately, look to see what the percentages of calories from fat really are. Are your foods as "low-in-fat" as they claim to be?

Place all the high-fat foods you know you must consider tossing—mayonnaise, high-fat dips—in one section of the fridge. Make a list of each food to be replaced to make your shopping easier.

- VEGETABLES, FRUITS, NONPACKAGED MEATS AND CHICKEN, AND CHEESE. Unless it's nonfat, your cheese derives about 50 to 75 percent of its calories from fat. Don't throw it all out; again, look at it practically in terms of your family. What can the family give up now? Who in the family will not tolerate the absence (at least for now) of a favorite cheese? Keep the meat and chicken. You can skin the chicken and trim the visible fat from the meat and chicken later; the meat can also be divided in half or thirds and frozen for future use in lesser amounts. The fruits and veggies stay, of course. Ask yourself this question: Do you stock enough fruit and veggies to round out meals if you cut down on meat and cheese? Do you have the kind of fruits and vegetables that can be served simply for quick snacks straight from the fridge, such as apples, cut-up cantaloupe or watermelon, grapes, strawberries, carrots, cauliflower, green peas, green beans, radishes, bananas, cucumbers?

- HIGH-SATURATED-FAT FOODS YOUR CHILDREN LIKE AND FOR THE MOMENT YOU WOULD NOT CONSIDER TOSSING. Besides a favorite cheese and a lunch meat, you might have some butter or margarine you want to hold on to, chocolate or caramel sauces, or lots of partially eaten jars of artichokes in oil, olives packed in oil, high-fat dips, or a ham waiting to be cooked. What do you do? You know now that most of these foods have potential replacements, but it feels premature to de-acquisition them at the moment. Don't. But do add them to your list for possible discards and move them in the fridge, or freeze the ham and wait for a big party to cook it. Once you begin to look in the market and discover substitutes—such as artichoke hearts and peppers without the oil, nonfat bean dips (such as Santa Fe Olé Arriba brand), nonfat chocolate sauce (such as Chocoholics), and nonfat dairy products—discarding will be easier. Some high-fat foods will remain foods you know you won't live without—at least sometimes.

Reflect for a moment on who eats what in your family. Who will be most disappointed by which changes? Are certain foods as necessary as you think? Whose habit are you feeding? Are your children as stubborn as you believe? As you ponder these questions, you may notice that some of the foods are not significant omissions for your family, though some certainly will be. Even these foods do not have to be purchased as regularly—and there may be several lower-fat versions. You will begin to discover options you didn't know you had.

YOUR FREEZER

🖋 HIGH-FAT FROZEN LEFTOVERS. What is back there under the frozen vegetables and the pizza? Oh, lasagna from your favorite cook—your friend who cooks only with the best-quality butter, cheese, and meat. To toss or not to toss? No, not yet. Think about how to handle this dilemma. Perhaps this will be "sometimes" food made into a lower-than-usual-fat meal by the addition of a first course of sautéed or steamed vegetables as well as the salad you usually serve. Adding bulk in the form of a very low-fat first course before a high-fat main dish, and adding "healthy" fat—sunflower seeds, walnuts, pumpkin seeds, a little olive oil in salads or pasta—usually minimizes the amounts of high-saturated-fat food people crave.

🖋 HIGH-FAT PACKAGED FROZEN FOODS OF EVERY KIND. What can you rid the freezer of now? High-fat pizzas and tacos; chicken pot pies, ice cream and cake, cheese breads and cheese sticks, chicken a la king, and macaroni and cheese. Read and calculate the fat percentages of these foods. See how high in fat they really are? You don't have to toss them all at once, just don't restock them as you use them up. Cost *is* a consideration. Think about what you can dispense with, or how you can use this high-fat food to accompany grain casseroles and more vegetables. As you increase the carbohydrate portion of a meal— beans, croutons, pasta, rice, vegetables—you lower the percentage of total fat.

THE PANTRY

The pantry is another repository of high-fat foods. Go through it shelf by shelf, and ask yourself if you can de-acquisition the following high-fat items (select a space to keep the high-fat foods):

🖋 Tuna packed in oil (100 more fat calories than tuna packed in water!)

🖋 Potato chips you thought were "healthy" because the package says "cholesterol free," but which are as high in fat as your regular potato chips and are made with partially hydrogenated vegetable oils

🖋 Nuts roasted in additional oil (sometimes hydrogenated), doubling the amount of fat of nuts

- Pretzels with oil and sugar
- Spaghetti or tomato sauces with added oil as the second or third ingredient listed
- Cereals with enough added fats to make them derive 30 percent of their calories from fat (don't forget to check the granolas!)
- Any of the following products with hydrogenated or partially hydrogenated oils, butter, margarine, shortening, lard, or cream:

    Canned soups

    Cellophane-wrapped ramen type soups

    Packaged cookies, crackers, chips, pretzels and other snacks

    Instant dinners

    Pancake and biscuit mixes

    Instant pie crust mixes

    Chile, meat stews

    Dips

Here too, de-acquisition slowly. Toss now what you think you can, wait to find replacements for other foods, and when it seems a travesty to be without others, keep them for now.

restocking your kitchen: what are the healthy foods?

In this chapter and the next are lists of foods that are invaluable for lower-fat cooking and snacking. Most are available at markets across the country, though some may not be available everywhere. The energy you bring to this project will show results over time. As you learn of appealing foods ask the market in your town to stock them, or phone the companies yourself for information.

Large supermarket chains are stocked, to some extent, by their central office. In these instances you may be forced to wait patiently until your request is passed on; get some friends to ask too. Be persistent.

A friend who lives in Iowa City and has helped me research the availability of foods in less cosmopolitan places writes me that much is changing. My sister lives in St. Louis, and she tells me that more lower-fat products are available there now. And friends in places such as Yarmouth, Maine; Austin, Texas; and Gualala, California, are all reporting more and more lower-fat and nonfat supermarket foods. The lower-fat parade is marching into many communities where a sandwich without mayonnaise was once unheard of.

As you read about suggestions for restocking your kitchen, you may have a sense of déjà vu, and may say to yourself, wait a minute, I've read about cereals and baked goods and dairy products. Is she repeating herself? I want to assure you that in the previous chapters, the context for discussing these types of food was different. First you learned how to read labels on cereal boxes and packages of cookies. Additionally, I have taken you through the steps to follow on your investigative shopping trip where you compare labels on your customary items and then select some possible substitutes. In this chapter, you will begin to actually replace high-fat foods with healthier selections, if in fact you have not already begun to do so during the days you have been reading this book. I will start with the source of some much harmful fat in the typical American child's diet. Again, it is dairy products.

DAIRY PRODUCTS

Lowering the amount of total and saturated fat you feed your children is your major goal; choosing nonfat dairy products is one of the simplest ways to do this. With the high quality and good taste of most nonfat dairy products, switching may be easier than you thought possible. If your family has been eating high-fat dairy foods, as you have already learned, moving down from high-fat to low-fat dairy products will reduce the amount of fat you feed your family substantially. To refresh your memory regarding milk, you might want to reread the section on page 15.

Consider the following dairy products when you restock:

- Sufficient eggs (probably more than you are used to buying) so that you can use extra whites and discard some yolks
- Nonfat milk, yogurt, cottage cheese, sour cream
- Nonfat mozzarella cheese or other good-tasting nonfat cheeses you discover
- Baker's cheese (see below)
- Quark (see below)

BAKER'S CHEESE: Baker's cheese is an extraordinary find and worth the search to locate it where you live. It is less than .5 percent fat, which, based on the guidelines of the new label laws, means nonfat. And it is also tasteless. But therein lies its magic. You make its taste. You can add salt, pepper, fresh or dried herbs, sugar, cumin, turmeric, cinnamon, cloves, flaked leftover broiled or smoked fish, grated onion, olives, capers, mustard, salsa, finely chopped vegetables, lemon, and so on—even peanut butter.

Actually, you make its texture and bulk as well. When purchased, its consistency is a little stiffer than whipped cream cheese. You can change its

chapter 9

consistency by adding different amounts of items such as nonfat milk or yogurt, mustard, or lemon juice.

- 🍲 Mix it with lemon, mustard, horseradish, vinegar, spices, herbs, salt, and pepper to make a mayonnaise-type spread for bread. Bits of smoked salmon, a dash of lemon, fresh parsley, and freshly ground pepper makes a thicker spread for hors d'oeuvres or sandwiches.
- 🍲 Add some mild white vinegar like Japanese rice vinegar, fresh herbs, a bit of lemon juice, and some chicken broth to the cheese to make a creamy salad dressing.
- 🍲 Add sweetener, some milk, and perhaps cloves or fennel seeds to stuff figs, spread on green apples for dessert, or use as the filling for a crepe to be drizzled with melted jam or fruit syrup.

Although you may not have heard of baker's cheese, it is an old product, made from nonfat milk and lactic cultures. Traditionally, it was mixed with heavy cream, full-fat pot cheese, and perhaps an egg or two and used as the filling for cheese blintzes. Baker's cheese is available fresh or frozen. Finding it is worth the effort. The cheese is shipped in bulk containers to many parts of the United States; according to the distributors (see page 239), it is available nationally, but I have been able to find it only at smaller neighborhood cheese shops and in bakeries that use it for pastry fillings. If you don't see it, ask: your market cannot know you want it if you don't inquire.

QUARK: Quark, which is made from skim milk culture and rennet, is a fresh unripened curd cheese that is sold in whole-milk, low-fat, and nonfat forms. It is packaged in a container much like sour cream and looks like sour cream. Although it doesn't have the "sour" taste of sour cream or the tangy taste of yogurt, it can be substituted for both. It's another miracle product, and I think you will begin to find it in more markets very soon. The flavorings for baker's cheese, yogurt, and Yogurt Cheese (see page 160) can all be used to flavor quark. Again, if you can't find it, ask; also see page 238.

BREADS AND CRACKERS

All bread has small amounts of fat, because fat is intrinsic to grain. Breads with sesame seeds or poppy seeds have higher fat percentages because of the fat in the seeds, but do not eliminate these breads—seeds are good for you, especially in the small amounts contained in baked goods. Read bread labels to separate the breads with added fats and oils from those whose fat is intrinsic. Ingredient listings on packaged bread are very helpful here to notify you where partially hydrogenated fats lurk. When you check cracker boxes, remind yourself not to be fooled by the seductive advertising on the package. Rely on your own calculations and, of course, a package that says "nonfat." The words *lower-fat, no cholesterol,* and *98% fat-free* do not guarantee crackers without partially hydrogenated oil. Look for the following:

- Breads and crackers without added hydrogenated oils, butter, or margarine
- Nonfat rice crackers and other nonfat crackers (Note: Sugar has been added to some new nonfat crackers, but many do not have any sugar, or hardly any. These actually taste better to me and are another way to lower sugar.)
- Nonfat flour and corn tortillas

CANS, JARS, BULK FOODS, AND PACKAGES

Following is a list of basic foods I have in my pantry, refrigerator, and freezer. They can make or round out a meal, provide variety when you think variety is impossible, be dinner themselves (canned tomatoes and canned black beans), or be used as emergency snacks (canned corn, applesauce, garbanzos).

- Pasta
- Rice and other grains
- Instant nonfat dehydrated soups without monosodium glutamate
- Foods packed in jars without oil, such as red peppers, cauliflower, peperoncini, artichokes, pickles, cherry peppers
- Herring in wine sauce
- Chutneys
- Jams
- Chicken bones frozen in plastic bags for homemade stock
- Chicken-broth ice cubes frozen in plastic bags for just a small amount at a time
- Soups without added fat
- Nonfat chicken broth

- Nonfat vegetable broth
- Tomato juice, for adding to broth or heating with vegetables as an instant soup—and of course, drinking cold
- Nonfat spaghetti sauces and tomato sauce
- Dried beans (garbanzo, cannellini, kidney, and black)
- Canned beans (garbanzo, cannellini, kidney, and black)
- Nonfat "refried" beans
- Nonfat bean dips
- Nonfat dried milk
- Tuna packed in water
- Peeled and stewed tomatoes in cans or boxes
- Canned or frozen corn kernels
- Frozen green peas, spinach, and baby lima beans
- Unsweetened applesauce
- Sauerkraut
- Unsweetened pineapple juice, grapefruit juice, and other unsweetened juice
- Wheat bran (an instant fiber to sprinkle on cereals, mix with cookie dough, and add to pancake batter)
- Salsas
- Anchovies
- Dried bean soups in individual containers (try Nile Spice brand)
- Raisins, dried figs, and apricots
- Nuts in the shell
- Unsalted shelled walnuts and almonds
- Unsalted raw pumpkin, sunflower, and sesame seeds
- Nonfat snacking cheese
- Nonfat tortillas
- Vegetables
- Fruit
- A variety of nonfat dairy products: milk, yogurt, sour cream, quark, cottage cheese

NONFAT BROTHS

Canned nonfat chicken, beef, and vegetable broth are invaluable cooking staples. Use them in vegetable soups, sauces, stews; as a quick soup with cut-up or frozen vegetables; to liquid-sauté onions, leeks, shallots, celery; as an addition to salad dressings; as the cooking liquid for preparing mushrooms on toast; and, of course, right from the can as an afternoon snack with crackers. Read the label carefully. Choose fat-free low sodium broths.

DESSERTS

Once something sweet and fat has been tasted, like chocolate chip cookies and real ice cream, it is hard to replace. If you have a child who prefers to eat fruit for dessert, consider this a major advantage. If you don't, you will be, like most of us, looking for substitutes for the high-fat and high-sugar foods children love.

For sweet dessert staples without fat, try stocking:

- Fresh fruit for baking
- Nonfat frozen desserts, frozen yogurts, and sorbets
- Nonfat homemade yogurt pops
- Fruit juice pops without added sugar
- Nonfat "ice cream"
- Cookies without added oils or butter
- Dried fruit such as figs, dates, raisins, berries, apricots, pineapple
- Nonfat toppings (see "Nonfat Dessert Toppings Children Love," page 127)

STORE-BOUGHT NONFAT COOKIES AND CAKES

Nonfat cookies and cakes are rapidly becoming the bad snack habits of tomorrow. People mistakenly think that because they have no fat, they are healthy. This attitude encourages unlimited consumption. These cookies and cakes, however, can have more sugar than their high-fat counterparts and in some instances more calories as well. Unless these foods are eaten only as treats or desserts, they will add unneeded calories (empty ones at that) to the diet of anyone who gorges on them.

chapter 9

FRUITS AND VEGETABLES

Traditionally, children are not partial to vegetables, are somewhat accepting of fruit, and always embrace foods that contain sugar and fat. Abundant fruits and vegetables, however, are crucial to your children's diet as major sources of fiber and essential vitamins and nutrients. I would like to think that a history of overcooked green vegetables contributes to most children's dislike of them; I would also like to think that soggy fruit salads, dying bananas, and discolored apple slices (a little lemon juice will prevent browning) contribute to their lack of enthusiasm for fruit as dessert. Stock your kitchen with a variety of fresh fruits that are easy to keep, like oranges and grapefruits, grapes, melons, and apples; eat bananas before they turn brown and mushy. Buy frozen fruits and dried fruits without added sugars.

Be curious about vegetables. Try some new ones that you can sauté with chicken broth, vegetable broth, or water; or cook some old favorites with new-to-you spices. Most of all, be adventurous. It's just a vegetable or a fruit; you can eat it if your children won't. As you experiment and discover new vegetables and new ways to cook them, you will find a new excitement in the variety available. The monotonous supermarket vegetable tour you usually make—carrots, lettuce, potatoes, green beans—can become a background to fennel, bok choy, arugula, chard, and jícama. Here are some suggestions for interesting ways to add vegetables to your children's meals:

- Try carrots as soup (page 179).
- Liquid-sauté carrot sticks with fennel seeds and garlic and add a few drops of olive oil after cooking.
- Add spiced tomato sauce to green beans.
- Bake cauliflower with garlic, ginger, cumin, and turmeric.
- Buy sun-dried tomatoes in bulk and reconstitute them in water, or eat them dry as snacks.
- Thinly slice raw fennel into salads or toss with sliced mushrooms, olive oil, and mint, or leave out the mushrooms and add celery.
- Cut up regular bok choy or quarter baby bok choy, or even plain cabbage, and sauté it in chicken broth adding some olive oil and toasted cumin seeds when the cooking is complete.
- Buy broccoli, green peas, and green beans and make a steamed mix of green veggies.

GRAINS

For main-course dishes and side dishes, rice is the grain we turn to most often; it is time tested and guaranteed to please. When you look, you'll find that there are more grains than just white rice or brown rice (see list below) and these are an excellent source of fiber. And when you really look, you'll discover the truly wonderful world of grains. I choose grains like the ones listed below because I like to cook them, my family loves them, they are readily available in stores across the country, and they can substitute for rice in practically any instance. For more on cooking grains, see Chapter 13, "Cooking Grains, Legumes, and Vegetables." These are some grains that your children might enjoy.

- Short-grain rice (white or brown)
- Long-grain rice (white or brown)
- Arborio rice
- Wild rice
- Basmati rice (white or brown)
- Bulgur wheat—for tabbouli salad, or to cook like rice
- Pearl barley—alone or in soups
- Cracked wheat
- Millet
- Pasta

LOWER-FAT CONDIMENTS, SAUCES, AND FLAVORINGS

The following items can be purchased in most markets. Except for the olive oil, nuts, seeds, grating cheese, and olives, all are fat-free (read the labels; occasionally a manufacturer will add fat to a product that has been traditionally fat-free). A pantry of fat-free, good-tasting condiments is a treasure of tastes, textures, and flavors. A well-stocked pantry can save a last-minute trip to the market.

- Extra-virgin olive oil
- Assorted raw (unroasted) nuts and seeds
- Olives (try new varieties without added oil)

- Vinegars—plain and mild, such as Japanese rice vinegar or seasoned rice vinegar, or stronger, such as red and white wine, raspberry, tarragon, balsamic
- Soy sauce
- Worcestershire sauce
- Hot sauces and Thai curry pastes—to your children's tastes and tolerances
- Other sauces that appeal to your taste
- Ketchup
- Nonfat barbecue sauces or marinades
- Dried herbs and spices
- Candied ginger
- Parmesan cheese for grating (must be refrigerated)
- Store-bought bread crumbs without partially hydrogenated oils (or homemade bread crumbs, page 160)
- Dried mushrooms (separated into small packages for the freezer—frozen dried mushrooms stay fresher and defrost almost immediately)
- Unsweetened white grape juice for adding to fruit salads, and for making simple syrups
- Mild and hot salsa
- White horseradish in a jar for older children
- Pickled vegetables
- Marinated vegetables
- Capers
- Chutney—any kind you wish
- Mustard(s), wet
- Mustard, dry, such as Colman's
- Cans of nonfat vegetable, chicken, and beef broth
- Frozen or refrigerated homemade stocks

About Balsamic Vinegar

Balsamic vinegar can be costly if you look for it at specialty foods stores—sometimes as high as $100 for six ounces! That quality of balsamic vinegar should be savored in small doses—not used for everyday cooking. Balsamic from the supermarket, however, is much cheaper, only a few dollars per bottle. Balsamic vinegar imparts a distinctive taste to salad dressings, fruit sauces, baked fruits, soups, and grilled mushrooms. Just a few drops to ¼ cup of liquid will sufficiently flavor a sauce or dressing. Once you discover its pleasures, balsamic vinegar will become a staple even in recipes for your children.

NUTS AND SEEDS: Buy fresh raw nuts for cooking and garnishes, not nuts that have been "dry roasted"—which means they have been roasted in oils, thereby adding to their fat content—or cooked in other ways with additional oils. Make sure that the seeds you buy, such as pumpkin seeds and sunflower seeds, are raw also. Even though they are high in fat, nuts and seeds are healthy foods. Nuts can be healthy occasional snacks and substitutions for meat at some meals; try mixing them into casseroles or with bread crumbs to coat grilled mushrooms or eggplant.

CEREALS, HOT AND COLD: If your family eats cereal, check the boxes for *added* fats in the form of oils, butter, or coconut flakes. Cereals are mostly grains, but fats, as you have seen, are frequently added. These fats may be unhealthy saturated fats such as coconut oil or partially hydrogenated oils. Sometimes the fats are healthy fats, but are totally unnecessary to the cereal, resulting in a high-fat food rather than a low-fat one. Remind yourself once again that just because olive oil is considered the healthiest oil of all does not mean it is healthy to eat too much of it. In the bulk food section of your market, you will find granolas labeled with as little as an acceptable 2 grams of fat per serving all the way up to 10 grams of fat per serving. Take the lowest or the second lowest, but always check to make sure it does not contain partially hydrogenated vegetable oil. Granolas with 2 or 3 grams of fat get their fat from the oats and nuts, not from added oils. Granola with 5 to 10 grams of fat always has too much added fat, usually from coconut (which is highly saturated) and lots of nuts and too much oil. After all, cereals are supposed to be just that: grains. Boxed cereals, besides having added fats, can have large amounts of added sugars. Read the labels and choose the cereals with the lowest percentage of sugar, with the sugar listed lowest down on the ingredient list.

snack foods your children
will eat and love

Although delicious and healthy snack foods that you and your children will enjoy eating are commonly available in the market don't impulsively rid the house of your children's favorite foods as you wouldn't a favorite blanket or teddy bear. Replace them slowly, and include the children in the decision process. Even if your children are too young to consult, remember they will notice the absence of a favorite anything. Mix the familiar snack food with the new and gradually minimize the former. Ask them what they think will taste good, what actually does taste good, and what doesn't—their responses may surprise you. Children react well to challenge; given the task of invention, here again they will come up with ideas you might never have considered, such as freezing a berry in an ice cube and freezing banana slices.

Following are two lists of low-fat or nonfat snack foods you may want to keep on hand: those you can purchase ready to eat, and those that need some preparation. Note: Keep what you want the children to eat more of at *their* eye level—on the appropriate shelf in the fridge or in your cabinets, and on the kitchen counter or table. This works like magic if you select foods they will like. Remember, you have to use your best judgment when considering some of these foods for your children. Not all flavors, notably the spicier foods, will be appropriate for younger children.

READY-TO-EAT LOWER-FAT OR
NONFAT SNACKS FROM THE MARKET

- Dried fruits: dates, figs, raisins, berries, apricots
- Pretzels with no added fat or malted barley (a sugar additive)
- Corn tortillas
- Nonfat flour tortillas (be sure to check the label)
- Nonfat corn chips or potato chips
- Walnuts or almonds in the shell (shelling makes for lower consumption)
- Canned chickpeas (garbanzo beans)
- Nonfat crackers
- Raw seeds: pumpkin and sunflower
- Bagels made without sugar or eggs
- Jam
- Nonfat string cheese
- Peanut butter with no added salt, sugar, or oil
- Salsas
- Cereals without added fats (such as corn, rice, or wheat puffs, Grape-Nuts, and plain Cheerios)
- Jelly Belly jelly beans, in moderate quantities
- Bean spreads
- Any kind of food in a jar your children like or might like that is not packaged in oil—there are many
- Nonfat frozen fruit bars (look for all-fruit, sugar-free products)
- Frozen foods that derive no more than 15 percent of their calories from fat (you must calculate this yourself)
- Nonfat chocolate sauce
- Seedless grapes (these make great snacks when frozen fresh from the market and kept in small plastic bags)
- Canned fruit (look for fruit packaged without added sugar)
- Oranges, apples, bananas, and other fruits that can be eaten whole

SNACKS THAT NEED SOME PREPARATION

Cutting vegetables and fruits into small pieces and leaving the bowl on the child's-eye-level shelf of the fridge will encourage your children to eat these foods. Would my children ever cut fruit or vegetables for themselves at any age? Never! But when a pineapple or a melon or a carrot or a pepper was cut up for them, fruits and vegetables were gobbled as if they were candy. In fact, foods cut up for dinner had to be hidden.

The following list may cause slight tremors of hunger as you read it and discover the suggestions are not exclusive to the tastes of children. Why not begin to modify your own choices? Just because you are a grown-up doesn't mean you can't eat delicious lower-fat food, too, and substitute health for the Camembert, the pâté, and the cheese sticks.

- Cut-up vegetables and fruits.
- Nonfat milk shakes (page 180).
- Corn and nonfat flour tortillas cut into triangles and baked in the oven. Add cumin or chili powder and salt, if you wish, for older children. Flour tortillas, sprinkled with water and toasted in the toaster, puff up slightly; broken up they make hard-to-resist chips.
- Thinly cut bagel slices toasted and broken. Topped with salsa and a mixture of shredded nonfat cheese and a little Parmesan, these can be popped into the oven and come out "nachos."
- Air-popped popcorn tossed with some crumbled dried herbs. Be sure the popcorn has no added oil; some packaged popcorns have added hydrogenated oils, while the label reads "no cholesterol."
- Lower-fat cookie dough, ready to slice and bake.
- Nonfat pita bread to stuff with salsa, low-yolk scrambled eggs, skinless chicken breast and lettuce, or leftover vegetables with leftover spaghetti sauce.
- Cut-up vegetables on skewers ready to broil or to eat raw.
- Cut-up fruit on skewers—these too can be broiled lightly.
- Peanut or nut butter mixed with Grape-Nuts cereal—it will be crunchy without having nut pieces, and lower in fat because it's "stretched" with the cereal.
- Peanut or other nut butter mixed with baker's cheese.

snack foods your children will eat and love

⌖ Leftover or fat-free canned beans mashed with herbs and spices or hot sauce (great in pita bread with shredded lettuce and green peppers) (page 122).

⌖ Gorp, or trail mix (page 80). This mixture of cereal, seeds, and dried fruit can go to the movies, top nonfat frozen desserts, be packed in lunch boxes or mixed with nonfat yogurt or served as a group snack at field games.

A NONFAT MILK SHAKE

A delicious nonfat milk shake can be made with nonfat milk and fruits of all kinds (fruits color the milk shakes differently, and the variations delight children). Here's the basic recipe: In a blender, combine one cup nonfat milk, 4 strawberries or half a banana or ½ cup of cut-up pineapple or fruit of your choice, 1 teaspoon sugar, and 4 ice cubes. Blend until the ice is crushed and the milk is foamy. Taste for sweetness. Serve immediately. If you are out of fruit, use 2 teaspoons sugar and add 1 teaspoon vanilla extract.

GORP

2 cups oats
1 cup raw pumpkin seeds
1 cup raw sunflower seeds
½ cup M&M's
1 cup Grape-Nuts or other favorite cereal
1 to 2 cups raisins or cut-up dried fruit

Preheat the oven to 400°F. Spread the oats, pumpkin seeds, and raw sunflower seeds on a baking sheet and bake in the oven for 10 minutes, or until lightly toasted, stirring once.

When cool, combine with all the remaining ingredients and store in a sealed glass jar in the refrigerator. (The seeds can become rancid after a week or two if not refrigerated.) By the way, this is a popular way to give your children the pleasure of a popular high-fat, high-sugar treat—M&M's—by balancing them with a mix of very healthy ingredients.

chapter 10

11

kitchen equipment:
making lower-fat cooking easier

Take a moment to reflect on all you have accomplished so far in helping your family live healthier as they face the nutritional challenges of our high-fat world. You have made a commitment to good health for you and your children. You have become more than a wise shopper. You have stocked your kitchen with delicious foods and condiments that will not only please your children, but allow you to prepare lower-fat meals they will like and you will like to cook. Before I begin to discuss how to lower fat in your own recipes and in recipes from books and magazines, I'd like to share some discoveries I have made about equipment and tools that facilitate these new, leaner cooking methods.

Although you can cook lower-fat foods in most any kind of pan, the right kitchen utensils make a huge difference when it's time to transfer the cooked food to plates, and again when you have to wash the pots. When you cook with very little or no oil, and without butter, margarine, or lard, food sticks to ordinary pans.

Nonstick pans, pots, and baking sheets make cleaning a far less unpleasant chore. Absolutely nothing sticks to a good heavy aluminum pot or pan with a reliable nonstick lining. Coated aluminum is the pot and pan material used by many professional cooks; it conducts heat evenly and quickly. Reputable brands are guaranteed "nonstick" by the manufacturer. Don't purchase pots or pans without a manufacturer's guarantee. Even if the salesperson insists it is nonstick and long-lasting, insist on the guarantee. There is more than one expensive product on the market that pretends to be nonstick but isn't.

The lining on my pots is Silverstone Plus. (Since purchasing my pots, I have learned about an even more durable scratch-resistant lining called Ceramiguard.) Both are restaurant-grade heavy aluminum pans and pots with a blue rubber handle that I purchase at a restaurant supply store. Aluminum conducts heat very well, and since the pots are lined there is no problem with acidic foods. With good care, these pots last and last and last. When a soup or stew becomes dried or crusted in the pot, a one-minute soak magically loosens all the food and a soft sponge does the rest in a few seconds.

Good heavy aluminum pots and pans lined with this magical substance are expensive. Costly as this investment may seem, it will gradually pay for itself in time and energy saved and good humor preserved. If at all possible, try to purchase at least one such pan. Cooking without added fat requires many changes in your routine, and the utensils you use can contribute tremendously to easy cleanup. When cooking hamburgers or any meat in a pan, it is best to use a cast-iron skillet with "grill ridges" so that all the fat drops away from the meat. If you do use a lined pan when cooking meat, "blot" the meat with paper towels to absorb the fat released in cooking.

COOKING TOOLS AND CONTAINERS

These are utensils I use and recommend as more than helpful for your lower-fat kitchen. They are not all necessary, but they are extremely useful.

- A variety of nonstick pots.
- Large and small nonstick skillets.
- Nonstick baking sheets, such as Silpat or Exopat.
- A colander with a handle and hook.
- A Chinese bamboo steamer with two levels.
- Wooden spoons, forks, and chopsticks for mixing and stirring without scratching nonstick pans.
- A rubber spatula for use with nonstick pans.
- A food mill for pureeing and separating skins and seeds from pulp.

NOTE: Wearever heavy, restaurant-grade pots and pans with Silverstone Plus or Ceramiguard lining can be ordered from East Bay Restaurant Supply at 800-743-2526 extension 236.

- Wire whisks for making salad dressings, sauces, and whipped nonfat milk for cocoa and coffee.
- Mason jars to store beans, grains, rice, dried fruits, nuts, gorp, and other bulk foods.
- Plastic containers with lids for storage of refrigerated food.
- A very good pair of scissors for all sorts of kitchen tasks, from snipping fresh herbs to cutting the sharp tips off artichoke leaves to cutting up whole chickens—*not* poultry shears but good all-around scissors.
- Bamboo skewers for grilling vegetables, skewering fruit pieces for snacks, or making chicken or fish kabobs.
- A 1-inch-wide natural-bristle paintbrush or kitchen brush for applying olive oil to bread and vegetables.
- An ample supply of aluminum foil or parchment paper for steaming poultry, fish, and vegetables in the oven (see page 107).
- A gravy skimmer. These are plastic, look like a 1-cup measure, and have long spouts. They are easily found in hardware stores and kitchen supply stores.
- Cheesecloth for making yogurt cheese (page 160), or a plastic yogurt maker available at most complete hardware stores.
- A Japanese slicer made by Benriner. These come in two widths, are forever sharp, and quickly produce paper-thin slices of most any vegetable. This inexpensive slicer is easily found in Japanese hardware stores across the country and is a modern replacement for the heavy, very expensive, and cumbersome French mandoline. NOTE: Do not allow children to use these or any other sharp implements.

COLANDER WITH HANDLE AND HOOK

If you are using a fairly large soup or spaghetti pot, this type of colander will allow you to submerge pasta or vegetables in boiling or simmering water, cook the food, and lift it from the water instantly. This is especially convenient if you want to blanch vegetables for pasta in the same pot as the pasta is cooking. You can also blanch vegetables for garnish in the same pot if you are cooking a relatively clear soup.

Using a Chinese Bamboo Steamer

Our Chinese steamer joined our family when we moved to California from the East Coast and saw Japanese friends and restaurateurs using this marvelous utensil. I find it indispensable for easy fat-free cooking. When you're not using it for cooking, it holds fruit and vegetables, bills, and homework. Most steamers come with two levels and a lid; two levels let you steam extra vegetables, or steam fish or chicken at the same time as the vegetables.

If you own a wok, fill it with about 2 cups of water, bring it to a boil, and set the steamer inside the wok; the slanted sides of the wok make it a perfect holder for the steamer. If you don't have a wok, a pot or a skillet holds the steamer just as well.

Lay the vegetables directly on the bamboo grid, putting the ones needing more cooking time in the bottom layer. Lightly salt and pepper the vegetables or add any spice or herb you wish; vegetables can be left whole (small carrots, beans, peas, ears of corn, whole broccoli florets, tiny potatoes) or sliced, julienned, or cut into chunks. If you wish to combine some vegetables with a sauce (such as slivered scallions with soy, curry powder, and a few drops of water, stock, or broth), mix the vegetables with the sauce, put the mixture on a plate small enough to leave one inch between it and the sides of the steamer and proceed to cook. Also use a plate when cooking fish or a mixture of raw chicken slices and slivered vegetables. Place the plates on the bottom level of the steamer and use the top level to cook another part of your dinner—or something to refrigerate for the next day.

To clean the steamer, simply rinse it with warm water. If you live in a dry winter climate this kind of cooking creates an added bonus—humidity—that is very kind to your face and hands.

Quick-cooking vegetables or sliced or julienned vegetables can cook in three minutes. Potatoes, squash, and beets, of course, take longer but that also depends on how they are cut before cooking. Always use the steamer cover during cooking; it keeps most of the steam circulating around the food. If you are cooking food that takes more than ten minutes, check the water level occasionally to make sure it hasn't evaporated.

Kitchen Scissors

A good pair of scissors reserved especially for kitchen use can produce miracles. Buy a pair of Fiskars brand scissors, *not* the come-apart "kitchen" type. Fiskars-brand scissors can be purchased in most hardware stores, sewing departments, and notion sections of department stores. They cost between eight and fifteen dollars, depending on which of the many kinds you select. I use mine to cut herbs and flowers from the garden, fat and skin from chicken, and fat from meat—not to mention string, tape, and, on occasion, the children's hair.

chapter 11

lower-fat cooking anytime:
revising your recipes

T his chapter introduces cooking methods that will use the wholesome, leaner ingredients you now stock in your kitchen to prepare delicious, no fuss meals for your family. First, though, I'd like to tell you about a book that helped me learn to cook healthful—but scrumptious—foods for my own children.

The English-language edition of Michel Guerard's cookbook *Cuisine Minceur* was published in this country in 1976 (New York: William Morrow). Before then, I had never realized that it was possible to reduce the fat in so many dishes while creating delicious and even elegant food for special occasions. *Cuisine Minceur*—the phrase means "slimming" or "spa" food—offers many basic recipes and ideas for cooking healthy foods, with an emphasis on lowering fat content. As you know, since the seventies, hundreds of cookbooks with an emphasis on lowering fat have appeared with new techniques for preparation. More and more they reflect the sophistication of contemporary tastes. Leafing through *Cuisine Minceur,* I find it continues to reflect a serious and excellent understanding of lower fat cooking. It would be a good addition to your library if cooking is a major interest of yours.

Opening my copy of the book back in 1976, I knew I had a lower-fat miracle on my counter—an answer to broadening what I had up to that time been able to accomplish. I wasn't, after all, a particularly accomplished cook, just a mom who happened to like cooking, did it fairly well, and was on the lookout for any help I could get to enlarge my repertoire of lower-fat recipes. Guerard uses egg yolks, cream, and butter, but he uses them sparingly and you can use even less than he does. Some of the many special tips I learned from Guerard were cooking on the grill or in the coals in aluminum foil; using non-fat milk as a substitute for cream; and preparing sauces using only vegetables and broth.

TAKING THE FAT OUT OF NEWSPAPER AND MAGAZINE RECIPES

As you know, almost all newspapers and many magazines have a cooking section or cooking column. I scan those pages looking for an appealing recipe that is not too complicated and not too high in fat, and I imagine you spend time with this section as well. Until recently, finding lower-fat recipes was a difficult search, but today, many recipes and food columns are devoted solely to lower-fat cooking. Still, so many recipes in newspapers contain high amounts of oil, no suggestion for defatting stocks, and unnecessary butter and cheese. Adding saturated fat to ingredients like fish, tomatoes, pasta, grains, vegetables, and beans, or using extravagant amounts of olive oil is especially outrageous when the recipe is billed as a healthy one.

Are the columnists who print high-fat recipes advocates for the dairy industry or the oil consortiums? I don't think so. They, and many illustrious cooks and cookbook writers, operate in the world of butterfat and eggs. The world of low-saturated-fat food, as popular as it is becoming, is not the domain of many food writers and chefs. At the same time, extraordinary cooks have been the source of many of my most sublime food experiences—both low-fat and high-fat recipes from their cookbooks, at their homes, and at their restaurants—and for that I am forever grateful.

As you become more familiar with deleting and substituting ingredients and using lower-fat cooking techniques, you can adapt not only your family recipes, but the recipes created by extraordinary cooks. You will be able to revisit the cookbooks of famous chefs and prepare exquisite food while deleting much of the fat. As you become more proficient in this manner of cooking, you will be able to tell, with a brief look, which recipes are best suited for adaptation.

In the years when Pierre Franey wrote a weekly syndicated column, we used his high-fat but quick and simple recipes as a model for deletion and substitution. Not every recipe lent itself to this modification, but when they did we could take his dishes and convert them into satisfactory new versions. Now, Marion Burros does it for us, turning out truly delicious lower-fat recipes week after week. Look in your newspaper and begin to adapt recipes appearing in your food columns. Notice when fat is unnecessarily high and when saturated fat can be eliminated, and clip out recipes you think are possibilities.

Lower-fat cooking magazines, magazines interested in good health, and even magazines not devoted to health but to fashion can be a source of recipes to be modified. Not all food writers are created equal. Not all have the knowledge or interest to develop good-tasting lower-fat food, but you will after reading this book.

A major part of this book discusses using wholesome fresh or packaged foods to substitute for high-saturated fat foods. Using these substitutions you can prepare delicious, mostly no-fuss meals for your family using as little saturated fat as possible—and as little extra time.

Keep in mind that there are differences between saturated fat and unsaturated fat and that saturated fat is the fat you want to drastically reduce if your family eats large portions of meat, egg, cheese, and high-fat dairy products. If your family has already curtailed saturated fat, look at just how much they do eat; you may only need to make reductions in some areas. Some families already have made the shift to a very low saturated-fat diet without actually being aware of it.

Most, but definitely not all, recipes will take well to simply deleting fat and substituting other ingredients and still retain their character. I love casseroles such as chicken pot pie and authentic lasagna, which use large amounts of cheese or butter or milk, and choose not to adapt them for this exercise. Instead I save them for rare treats. Pastries and cakes are also more difficult to adapt to lower-fat cooking, and are not addressed in this book. The following important changes to your cooking methods will simplify deleting unnecessary fat from all your recipes.

LIQUID-SAUTÉING

Why add extra fat to a recipe right at the beginning? Any recipe that calls for browning, softening, or sautéing vegetables in a pan can be modified to substitute water, nonfat chicken broth, or nonfat vegetable broth in place of oil.

To start, add liquid to the pan to a depth of ¼ inch. Then add chopped or sliced vegetables (onions, shallots, garlic, celery, carrots, green beans, carrots, peppers, fennel) and begin cooking over medium heat. Watch the pan, as you would when you cook with butter or oil. As the liquid evaporates, add more by tablespoons, adjusting the heat as necessary, until the vegetables reach the desired state of doneness: a golden brown, or just softened. Add a little more liquid to make a sauce, if you like. Adding 1 or 2 teaspoons of olive oil to a finished pan of vegetables is also an option.

DRY-BROWNING MEAT

Any recipe that calls for browning meat in oil can be altered to use much less oil or none at all. Usually, at least 2 tablespoons of fat are used to brown meat in a 10-inch pan. Two tablespoons of fat contain about 220 fat calories, or 22 grams of fat; if you use butter, vegetable shortening, or lard, most of the added fat will be saturated. Using one of the following methods will eliminate these unnecessary fat calories.

BROILER METHOD: You do not have to use any oil at all, but if you wish to, lightly toss the meat with just a bit of olive oil. Preheat the broiler with the hot broiler pan in place. Quickly brown the meat or chicken pieces very close to the heat on both sides. If your recipe calls for a light coating of flour, herbs, salt, and pepper, add it after browning.

PAN METHOD: Heat a nonstick pan over medium-high heat. Lightly wipe olive oil in the pan with a wadded-up paper towel. Lightly salt and pepper the meat or chicken. Add the meat or chicken to the pan, taking care not to leave too much space between the pieces (bare spots tend to burn over high heat). Quickly brown the food evenly on both sides. Lightly flour after browning if your recipe calls for it.

GRILL METHOD: If you are cooking other food on your outdoor grill, at the same time brown meat or chicken for the next day. Whenever I am sufficiently organized, I try to put extra food on the grill: vegetables, skewered chicken for salads or for adding to grain casseroles, skewered meat to brown for the next day's stew. Put the meat or chicken over hot coals and sear on both sides. Let cool on paper towels before refrigerating—some of the fat will be absorbed by the toweling.

HOW TO REVISE A FAVORITE RECIPE

You can lower the fat in many main-course dishes, and still maintain the integrity of the dish. In some instances, a simple change such as replacing half the grated cheese with a nonfat substitute when serving pasta, or making a marinade with chili paste, lemon juice, and nonfat broth instead of coconut milk and oil, can be guaranteed winners. Depending on how many children and adults you are cooking for, use less oil than the recipe calls for—maybe half the amount. Most people (and most recipes) use much more oil than is necessary for sautéing. Even though olive oil is monounsaturated, heavy doses of fat are just not necessary when other ingredients such as water or nonfat broth are available. Your children will choose plenty of fat in treat foods such as olives and nuts and ice cream, extra cheese, hamburgers, fast food, muffin snacks, and food they eat when visiting friends. If you think they are particularly hungry on a particular day, simply add more olive oil to your cooking.

To begin, select one main-course recipe that is a family favorite. In your mind or on paper, make the deletions necessary to eliminate or lower the saturated fat: milk, cream, egg yolks, cheese, butter. Don't eliminate all the fat; remember, we are not working toward eradicating fat, only lowering saturated fat.

Here are a few ideas for using the fat-lowering suggestions described throughout the book. If the recipe calls for vegetables sautéed in butter:

- You can lower the saturated fat by using half butter and half heart-healthy oil. Or, if you prefer, use only oil. The taste will be different but very good. You will be deleting the harmful saturated fat from this step, while still using the same amount of total fat.
- Use less oil than the recipe calls for: 2 tablespoons of oil instead of 3, and if possible reduce the amount to 1 tablespoon. Most people use too much oil for sautéing.
- Use water, vegetable broth, nonfat chicken stock or broth, or a combination in place of oil. Liquid-sautéing vegetables works well and yields a pure vegetable flavor. You can always add 1 teaspoon or tablespoon of oil for additional flavor at the end.
- Use only defatted homemade stock or nonfat canned broths.

If the recipe calls for cream, whole milk, or any whole-milk dairy products:

- Use 2 percent, 1 percent, or nonfat milk.
- Use nonfat yogurt or quark, or a combination of the two.

If the recipe calls for meat and chicken:

- Use the white meat of poultry more frequently—it has half the fat of dark meat.
- Introduce your family to leaner cuts of meat—pork tenderloin instead of ribs or back; round of beef or flank steak instead of marbled steak, and lamb leg instead of high-fat chops and shoulder.
- Cut all the visible fat off meat. Many butchers trim to leave ¼ inch of fat. You don't need it for your recipes.
- Remove the skin and the fat from chicken—use your scissors and literally cut the yellow fat away from the flesh—you will be reducing the saturated fat, in some instances, by more than half.
- Reduce the amount of meat in a stew or casserole.
- Increase the amount of vegetables in the recipe to make up for the deleted meat.
- Serve extra vegetables when you prepare a roast to reduce the size of the meat portions.

If the recipe calls for eggs:

- Delete some of the yolks, substituting 1 white for each deleted yolk.
- For omelets, delete half the yolks, substituting 2 whites for each deleted yolk.

If the recipe calls for butter, lard, or rendered chicken fat:

- Delete any of these and replace entirely with olive oil. This doesn't lower the fat content of a dish, but it does change the fat from mostly saturated to mostly unsaturated.
- Many recipes call for more oil or butter than actually is necessary. Even if your recipe calls for healthy oil rather than butter, consider reducing the amount you use.

If the recipe calls for heavy cream, sour cream, or a high-fat sauce to use as a thickener or sauce, try one of the following ingredients:

🌿 Yogurt is a useful substitute for lower-fat cooking (replacing cream, sour cream*, and whole milk), but it does add an acidic taste to foods, and overuse can make this a wearisome substitution because its taste is so distinctive (adding a tablespoon of nonfat milk to a cup of yogurt will sweeten the taste). Used judiciously, yogurt can be a good base for some dishes; it works really well as the base for a spicy marinade, for example (see below). Use it to marinate 1-inch-thick vegetable slices, fillets of white fish such as halibut or rockfish, or skinless chicken breasts. Marinate for at least 1 hour, then grill or broil, slicing the chicken breasts and vegetables to serve.

SPICY YOGURT MARINADE

1 cup nonfat plain yogurt
2 shallots, minced
1 tablespoon fresh lime juice
1 tablespoon unsweetened white grape juice
4 garlic cloves, minced
1 teaspoon cumin seeds, crushed
1 teaspoon ground turmeric
1 teaspoon Colman's mustard
Kosher salt and freshly ground pepper to taste

In a medium bowl, beat the yogurt with a fork. Blend in all the remaining ingredients. Cover and store in the refrigerator for up to 2 days.
Makes about 1 cup.

Yogurt cannot be boiled. Unless flour is added to it, it will curdle and ruin your sauce. Keep the heat at no higher than a simmer when adding yogurt to a dish.

* Nonfat sour cream frequently has, as a major ingredient, sugar in the form of corn syrup. For this reason it is not suggested as a substitute for the regular product.

🌣 Yogurt cheese (page 160) is less acidic than yogurt because the whey, and consequently most of the sharp taste, is eliminated in the draining process. Yogurt cheese is especially good to add to a puree of sweet red peppers or to a green sauce such as Green Herb Sauce (page 165). Yogurt cheese will also curdle if boiled.

🌣 Baker's cheese is a good thickener and also a good filling for omelets, baked pasta dishes (mixed with shredded nonfat mozzarella) and dessert crepes (mixed with ground cloves, sugar, and ground cinnamon). It will separate if boiled.

🌣 Bread crumbs are one of my most favorite ingredients not only as a substitute for thick cream in sauces but because they work so well without changing the taste of food. Try fresh (untoasted) bread crumbs to thicken shrimp bisque or crab chowder or roasted tomato soup (page 188). Lightly toasted crumbs can be tossed with a grain casserole, be used as a topping (page 160) for many dishes, be used as an ingredient in a dry marinade for meat or vegetables, or form the crust of baked chicken breasts (page 214). Bread crumbs don't dissolve, fall apart, or curdle; they thicken, add crunch when they are toasted, and stretch spreads, casseroles, soups, and stuffings. (Fine grains such as leftover couscous or millet, pressed through a sieve, are also useful as thickeners for some sauces and soups, and unpressed can stretch another grain such as rice or barley.)

With these suggestions in mind, revise your selected recipe, serve the food, and check the results. The best result, of course, is when your family doesn't even notice the difference, and the next best is when they approve. If your revision is not successful, perhaps you deleted too much of the familiar ingredients. Rethink the preparation or try another recipe.

SOME POTENTIAL PROBLEMS

🌣 If you deleted all the meat from a spaghetti sauce, perhaps you need to add some back or substitute "meaty" vegetables such as mushrooms.

🌣 If you deleted all the cheese from a pizza, perhaps you need to use a little of a leaner cheese (try nonfat mozzarella) and use extra sauce.

🌣 Did you overwhelm a recipe by adding too many vegetables?

- Did you prepare a potato salad without mayonnaise and serve it to an unsuspecting audience? Try mixing half genuine mayonnaise and half Our Nonfat "Mayonnaise" (page 160), or try a potato salad with Vinaigrette (page 163) or Green Herb Sauce (page 165). As you gradually introduce the family to more nonfat and lower-fat choices, chicken salad and potato salad made without mayonnaise will begin to taste good.
- Did you serve a vegetarian meal unannounced to a family that eats meat at all meals?
- Did you make too many changes at one meal and besiege the family with health talk?

If you have reconsidered and retried the recipe and it still doesn't work, perhaps this is a recipe that needs all of its fat to taste authentic. If so, you don't have to toss it from your recipe collection, just relegate it to less frequent appearances on the family menu. It will definitely be appreciated when you serve it.

Stews and grain casseroles work very well. Paella, for instance, can be prepared without sausage and chicken and just with shrimp, or even with just vegetables (page 222). Because of the saffron and the distinctive flavor of fresh vegetables, the result will still be delicious. And a braised vegetable stew can replace a beef stew.

Consider what vegetables, grains, beans, or pastas you can serve with dinners. Will an assortment of vegetables or black beans be the main portion of the meal? Or will they be equal portions along with meat, poultry, or fish? A meal that is predominantly grains and vegetables or beans and vegetables one night usually has leftovers that can be the accompaniments to a grilled chicken breast the next. Or if your children are eating a primarily vegetarian diet, or the family has opted for less meat and poultry, topping a bean casserole with a salsa of chopped red onions, cucumber, and radish (my daughter Sarah's favorite), mixed with any flavored vinaigrette you choose, can be Wednesday's dinner. Thursday the leftover beans mixed with canned, chopped tomatoes, baked and topped with bread crumbs and a combination of three-quarters nonfat mozzarella and one-quarter grated Romano cheese presents as a truly different meal. Chili made with very little meat or an assortment of beans (page 220) can be a filling dinner with a salad of carrots, peppers, and onions. With less saturated fat in your children's meals, and with less fat in general, there is room for bread, potato, grains, pasta, and beans—all significant sources of fiber and B vitamins for your child.

What spices and flavors or toppings (page 127) will make grains and beans more appealing to your children? Consider spices and flavors such as toasted seeds (fennel, cumin, coriander, sunflower), and for older children red pepper flakes and cayenne, Thai curry paste mixed with fresh lime, or simply use some ground cinnamon to convert a bowl of rice into a new food. Until I began to keep a very well-stocked pantry, most of my grain cookery was grains and water and not only did my children dread the monotony of the food, I dreaded cooking it. Starting with a stocked pantry, the scatterings I could add to the cooking or as toppings became endless as I became more adventurous. You can also flavor foods with sliced olives, almonds, walnuts, sesame seeds, pumpkin seeds, chopped fresh garlic, chopped dried fruit, fresh and dried herbs, grated citrus zest, slivered anchovies, hot sauces, cool sauces. Also simple, but with just a bit of preparation, are quick sauces made from broth, citrus juices, chopped shallot or onion, dried herbs, dried spices, curry pastes, Asian sesame oil, garlic, or fresh parsley.

HEALTHIER BEEF, LAMB, OR CHICKEN STEW

Most families have a favorite recipe for beef, lamb, or chicken stew. Unfortunately, the level of fat in homemade stew is often high. Here are some ideas for reducing the fat in your stew without sacrificing flavor. Revising a stew in this way has a number of advantages: The stew is a familiar dinner to the children. You can cook a larger amount and make enough for two dinners— one for the day of cooking or the day after, and one for the end of the week or for the freezer.

- Prepare the stew the day before serving so you can remove and discard the congealed fat from the surface of the stew before reheating. To further reduce the fat, chill the stew liquid separately from the meat and the vegetables—this makes skimming easier and much more thorough.
- Reduce the amount of meat or poultry by one third or by half. By this single alteration, you will reduce the fat content markedly.
- Remove all the skin and fat from poultry, and cut off all visible outer fat from lamb or beef.

🖋 Substituting vegetables for the deleted meat, your stew will remain an ample dinner, perhaps along with a salad and warmed bread. Per person, the vegetables you can conveniently substitute for meat, in addition to what the original recipe calls for, are 1 small potato, 2 carrots, 1 small turnip, ½ onion, and 4 mushrooms. The variety, of course, is almost endless. You can add chard, spinach, shallots, green beans, or leftover black beans, garlic cloves, leeks, assorted peppers, or cabbage.

🖋 Use homemade defatted stock or canned nonfat broth in place of regular stock or broth. Use a mixture of homemade defatted stock or canned nonfat broth, and water.

🖋 Dry-brown the meat (see page 88). This procedure is simple, *and* it works without a sacrifice of flavor or time.

🖋 To substitute calories for the deleted meat or poultry, serve whole grain bread and unbuttered rice or noodles with the stew.

ROASTED ONION AND GARLIC CLOVES

As a garnish for stews, roast extra onions (quartered) and garlic cloves (separate the cloves but do not peel them) in some nonfat chicken, beef, or vegetable stock or broth, covered, in a preheated 350°F oven for 1 hour. There should be about ¼ inch of liquid in the baking dish. The liquid will evaporate and leave a lovely carmelized glaze. The onions and garlic can cook while the stew does and be served as a garnish.

TWO RECIPES USING DELETION AND SUBSTITUTION

I prepared each of the following original recipes before creating new lower-fat versions. Each high-fat original and each new very-low-fat version was delicious.

Puffed Biscuits
(New York Times Magazine, 11/12/95)

Yield: about 30 biscuits

4 packages active dry yeast

About 5½ cups sifted all purpose flour

2 cups whole milk

3 tablespoons sugar

3 tablespoons unsalted butter, plus butter for greasing the bowl

2½ teaspoons kosher salt

In a large bowl, combine the yeast and 2 cups of flour. In a medium saucepan, combine the milk, sugar, butter, and salt and cook over medium heat, stirring constantly, just until the butter melts.

Pour the milk mixture in the bowl with the flour mixture and beat well. Continue to beat vigorously for about 3 minutes, scraping the sides and bottom of the bowl often. Stir in enough of the remaining flour to make a moderately stiff dough.

Place the dough onto a floured surface and knead until smooth and elastic. Place in a greased bowl, turning once. Cover; let rise in a warm, draft-free place until doubled in size, about 45 minutes. Punch down, cover and let rest 10 minutes.

Preheat the oven to 350°F. Form the dough into balls about 1½ inches in diameter. Press each one into a circle about 3 inches in diameter. Place on ungreased baking sheets (you may need to bake in batches) and bake until puffed and lightly brown, about 10 minutes. Cool on a cloth-covered surface until the biscuits can be handled. Serve while warm.

LOWER-FAT VERSION

Substitute 2 cups nonfat milk, plus ½ cup dried nonfat milk for the whole milk.

Substitute 2 tablespoons olive oil for the 3 tablespoons butter, and use 1 teaspoon oil to grease the bowl.

Add the dried milk to ½ cup of the nonfat milk to dissolved. Add the remainder of the nonfat milk and mix well. Stir constantly when heating, as skim milk powder has a tendency to stick to pots when the milk is warmed. Continue with the recipe as directed.

ORIGINAL RECIPE

Spiced Potato Chips
(New York Times Magazine, 1/7/96)

Yield: 8 servings

½ cup unsalted butter, melted

8 medium baking potatoes, thinly sliced

½ teaspoon dry mustard

½ teaspoon hot paprika

¼ teaspoon chili powder

I small onion, peeled and minced

2 teaspoons kosher salt

Preheat oven to 425°F. Generously butter 2 baking sheets. Overlap the potato slices in single rows. Stir the spices and onion into the remaining butter and drizzle it over the potatoes. Sprinkle with salt and bake until the potatoes are golden, about 45 minutes. Serve.

LOWER-FAT VERSION

Delete the butter and substitute 2 tablespoons extra-virgin olive oil.

If you have one, use a nonstick baking sheet for this recipe and wipe it very lightly with olive oil. Add more oil if using a regular baking sheet.

Toss the potatoes, the spices, and the onion with the remaining olive oil. Overlap the potato slices in single rows. Sprinkle with salt and bake until the potatoes are golden, about 45 minutes. Serve warm.

cooking grains, legumes, and vegetables

Plant foods, as well as containing almost all the nutrients human beings need to grow and thrive, are extremely low-fat foods. Grains, legumes (soybeans, lentils, peanuts, peas, beans), and vegetables are the basic diet of most of the people in the world. Americans, who eat so much meat, have tended to overlook the wonderful variety of plant foods available. To them, *grains* usually means rice, *beans* means green beans, and *potatoes* means fried or baked. But as you'll see, there are so many more varieties to choose from—and all with only the small amount of fat nature gave it. In addition, as you add grains and vegetables as substitutes for high-saturated fat food (meat, dark meat poultry, cheese dishes, and frozen meals) you will automatically add fiber to your children's diet as you lower the fat.

GRAINS AND HOW TO COOK THEM

The grain most parents cook for family dinners is rice. The grain most parents cook for family breakfasts is oats. Today, with the proliferation of bulk food items for sale in the most ordinary of supermarkets and in smaller stores across America, you can be confronted with unfamiliar grains with strange-sounding names—and not the least idea of how to turn them into dinner. But it's worth learning how: Grains are one of the basic foods that can be substituted for high-saturated fat foods while still guaranteeing your children the protein, vitamins, minerals, and fiber their growing bodies need.

All grains are the dried seeds of grass plants. Without even being conscious of it, we eat grains daily, ground into flour for bread, rolled into oats or pressed flat into flakes for cereal, and ground into flour for pasta. We purchase ground grains (bleached or unbleached white flours and whole-wheat flour) to prepare home-baked cookies, other pastries, and bread, and for homemade pancakes, dumplings, waffles, and stuffings.

Wheat, corn, rice, oats, and rye have become staples in our lives. Rice is the most familiar grain; it is convenient, filling, and a time-tested, guaranteed winner. But if you embark on a new eating regimen of a higher proportion of plant foods and cook just rice, your diet may become monotonous. Other terrific grains such as fragrant Basmati rice, sweet millet, and nutty wild rice, will add interest and liveliness to your meals.

The main difference between cooking rice and other grains is the amount of liquid and the cooking time. You can use the same pot you use to cook rice (or use your new miracle nonstick pan or pot), and you can cook on top of the stove or in the oven—whatever you are used to.

Following is a chart of approximate cooking times for grains you can purchase in practically any market, either in bulk or packaged. Cooked, grains will keep in the fridge (tightly covered) for several days. Cooked al dente, grains can all be used cold as additions to salads; cooked until tender, they can be mashed into spreads for sandwiches (see page 16), added to soups or bean dishes such as chili, or made into soups themselves with the addition of some stock or broth and vegetables. Cold rice, leftover oatmeal, and other grains can even be made into delicious hot pancakes (see page 117).

Taped inside one of my kitchen cabinets is a list of the various grains I cook, the cooking times, and the amount of liquid needed. This list is no longer the pristine compendium it once was. Today it is a wonderful mass of annotations of my discoveries over the years.

My list attests to almost unending possibilities of cooking with grains: longer or shorter cooking times depending on how the food is being used (drier if it is accompanying a stew and will absorb some of the sauce; more porridgelike if it is the main ingredient of a meal-in-a-bowl with chicken or vegetables added to it); new and different flavorings; and many possibilities for newly invented additions, some from friends, some from cookbooks, and some out of desperation. Your own annotations will gradually turn your list into a valuable quick reference resource, scribbled over but fortunately decipherable to you.

COOKING TIMES FOR GRAINS

1 CUP GRAIN	AMOUNT OF LIQUID	COOKING TIME	YIELD
Pearled barley	3¼ cups	45 minutes-1 hour	3½ cups
Hulled barley	4 cups	2 hours	3½ cups
Cracked wheat	2¼ cups	2 hours	2¾ cups
Wheat berries	2½ cups	2½ hours	2¾ cups

(Soaking hulled barley, cracked wheat, or wheat berries for 5 hours or overnight will reduce cooking time.)

Couscous	1½ cups	10 minutes	3 cups
Bulgur wheat	2 cups	15-25 minutes	2½ cups

(To cook bulgur wheat or couscous, pour boiling liquid over the grain, cover, and steep. Fluff with a fork.)

Millet	3 cups	30-40 minutes	3½ cups
Rye flakes	3 cups	1 hour	3 cups
Cornmeal	4 cups	10-15 minutes	3-4 cups
Buckwheat groats	2 cups	15-20 minutes	2½ cups
Buckwheat kasha	2 cups	10-12 minutes	2½ cups
Wild rice	2½-3 cups	1¼ hours	2¾ cups
Quinoa	2 cups	15-20 minutes	4 cups

BUCKWHEAT, QUINOA, AND WILD RICE

Buckwheat and quinoa (pronounced keen-wah) look and taste like grains but are not; they do, however, cook like grains. Both are the seeds of green plants. Wild rice, while thought of as rice, is the grain of a marsh grass native to the Great Lakes Area and now cultivated in Northern California.

Grains do not have to be bland and uninteresting. Consider the following suggestions to vary the taste of the grains you cook.

chapter 13

- Use vegetable or chicken stock or broth as the cooking liquid, or add a teaspoon or two of soy sauce or Asian sesame oil and chopped onion to the cooking liquid.
- Sauté finely chopped onion, shallots, or garlic and add it before cooking grains.
- Experiment with spices: For instance, add ground cinnamon to rice and chili flakes to millet.
- Crumble in some dried herbs before cooking begins.
- Add minced fresh herbs after cooking.
- Add liquid-sautéed finely chopped celery and chopped dried fruit such as apricots to rice.
- For a meatless meal, toss some freshly toasted walnuts and sautéed mushrooms into cooked barley, rice, or wheat berries; they can be a nice substitute for the chewiness of meat.
- Add some leftover slivered chicken and fresh or frozen green peas and some olive oil flavored with herbs.
- Add foods such as minced fresh parsley or cilantro, baby lima beans, chopped green peppers, liquid-sautéed chopped spinach or chard, chopped scallions, and chopped red onion; these colorful additions can be prepared at the same time the grain is cooking.
- See "Topping for Casseroles," page 127, for additional suggestions.

The above preparations are not only simple; they can all be prepared while the grain is cooking. With the addition of a large salad and whole-grain bread, any one them can be a healthy and delicious dinner. Invent simple sauces you can add to cooked grains; one I frequently make follows:

A Sauce for Grains

1 tablespoon fresh lime juice

3 tablespoons extra-virgin olive oil

¼ teaspoon red pepper flakes

2 minced garlic cloves

Kosher salt and freshly ground pepper to taste

Whisk together lime juice, olive oil, red pepper flakes, garlic, salt, and pepper. Makes ¼ cup, enough to toss with 3 to 4 servings of any grain.

COOKING LEGUMES

A legume is a flowering plant; the part we eat is the seed. Legumes (beans, lentils, peas) have, on the average, double the protein of grains and an adequate concentration of other healthful nutrients. This ordinary and inexpensive food is good for you and your children. Just as many cooks limit their grains to rice, most people's repertoire of legumes is limited by habit. There are also fresh shell beans to consider, quick-cooking lentils, and dried beans that can cook while the rest of life goes on.

HOW TO BUY AND COOK FRESH SHELL BEANS

It's not unusual to have never seen a fresh shell bean. The "in season" time ends quickly, and over-mature or old shell beans are not particularly attractive. If you are inclined to try them and are willing to devote some of your time and your children's time to shelling, you will discover a real treat.

Fresh baby limas, cranberry beans, fava beans, flageolets (the tiny French beans traditionally served with roasted lamb), and soybeans* can be found, seasonally, in many markets around the country. Ethnic markets can be counted on to stock one or more of these beans when they are in season. But freshness counts. Like corn, these beans begin to lose sugar—and sweetness—as soon as they are harvested. Buying them from a reliable source and cooking them the same day, if you can, guarantees a return that makes shelling, for me, a worthwhile trade-off. Shelling can be a family activity before dinner, or during the day while other activities are in progress.

Once you've found the source for the beans, buy the smallest—they're usually the youngest. To cook shelled beans, boil and salt the water, put in the beans, and after a couple of minutes taste a bean for doneness. Young beans can cook very quickly, sometimes in 2 minutes; older beans are tougher and

---

*Soybeans can be steamed in the pod until tender (30 to 40 minutes) and eaten as a snack from the pods. Frozen soybeans (in the pod) can be found in Korean and Japanese markets; they are worth looking for, as they are simple to prepare, healthy, and so delicious. Follow the directions on the package.

will take longer to cook (5 to 10 minutes). Use as little water as possible when you cook fresh shell beans—just enough so that the beans have space to move around. If you should overcook the beans and they come out too mushy, drain half of the cooking water, add some chicken or vegetable stock or broth, puree in a blender or food processor, and pour over thickly sliced toasted bread to eat as soup.

As a casserole, mixed with rice or another grain, or served alone as a first course with chopped fresh tomatoes, some lemon, sweet onions, and a small amount of olive oil, fresh shell beans are outstanding. My favorite preparation is to steam the beans briefly, add just the barest amount of olive oil and salt and pepper, toss with minced fresh herbs—perhaps mint or oregano—and just gobble them up.

If the thought of shelling beans is just too much to consider, try a box of frozen baby lima beans. They are frozen at the moment of freshness. Cook barely any time at all, and proceed as suggested above.

HOW TO BUY AND COOK DRIED LEGUMES

Dried legumes available in our markets commonly include black beans, cannellini beans, kidney beans, garbanzo beans, different varieties of white beans, pinto beans, mung beans, soybeans, split peas (green and yellow), and lentils (green, brown, and pink).

Depending on the legume, the cooking time can be as little as 5 minutes for tiny pink lentils or as much as 3 hours; black beans, cannellini beans, and navy beans are the least predictable, taking from 1½ to 3 hours *after* soaking! The disparities, as with grains, have to do with the freshness and storage of the dried beans before purchase, where they were grown, and how long they are kept at home before cooking. If they cook quickly remove them from the hot cooking pot and mix just a bit of fresh lemon juice with them; they will wait patiently and take well to reheating, as lemon juice slows the cooking. So does salt. For this reason do not add salt until the beans are halfway cooked. Dry lentils, split peas, and mung beans cook more quickly, usually within 30 to 40 minutes.

To soak beans, rinse and soak them overnight in 4 times as much water as beans. Discard the soaking water and proceed using the chart below, keeping in mind that the times are approximate.

APPROXIMATE COOKING TIMES FOR DRIED LEGUMES

I CUP SOAKED DRIED BEANS	LIQUID	COOKING TIME	YIELD
Baby lima beans	2 cups	1-1½ hours	1¾ cups
Chickpeas (Garbanzos)	4 cups	3 hours	2½ cups
Black beans	4 cups	1½-2½ hours	2 cups
Fava beans	3 cups	2-3 hours	2¼ cups
Kidney beans	3 cups	1-1½ hours	2 cups
Navy beans	3 cups	1½-2½ hours	2 cups
Pinto beans	3 cups	1½-2½ hours	2 cups
Soybeans	4 cups	2½ hours	3 cups
Cannellini beans	3 cups	1-2 hours	2½ cups
I CUP UNSOAKED LEGUMES			
Lentils (brown and green)	3 cups	30-45 minutes	2½ cups
Lentils (pink)	3 cups	5-10 minutes	1½-2 cups
Mung beans	2½ cups	1-1½ hours	2 cups
Split peas (green and yellow)	4 cups	40 minutes	2½ cups

Basic Recipe for Soaked Dried Beans

Makes 4 to 6 servings

6 cups water

2 cups soaked dried beans

1 bay leaf

5 unpeeled garlic cloves

Kosher salt and freshly ground pepper

Minced fresh parsley or chives for garnish

In a large pot, bring the water to a boil. Add the soaked beans, bay leaf, and garlic. Cover, reduce heat to a strong simmer, and cook for 1 hour. Add the salt and pepper to taste and continue cooking, covered, until tender, about 30 minutes to 1½ hours.

Remove the bay leaf. Peel the garlic cloves and puree them in a blender with ½ cup of the cooked beans and some of the liquid. Return this mixture to the beans. Taste and adjust the seasoning.

chapter 13

- Liquid-sauté 3 tablespoons finely chopped carrot, 6 tablespoons finely chopped onion, and 6 tablespoons finely chopped celery. Add to the beans along with the bay leaf and garlic.
- After cooking, add one or more of the following: any leftover grain or shredded meat, chopped cucumbers, bell peppers, onions, garlic, tomatoes, fennel, radishes; barely cooked cabbage, broccoli, carrots, potatoes, grilled tomatoes. For toppings, try grated Parmesan, salsa, minced fresh parsley or cilantro, a bread crumb topping (see page 160), or an herb sauce (see page 165).
- While cooking, add any one or more of the following for different flavors: 1 whole onion, peeled and stuck with 4 cloves; 2 minced shallots; thick peeled apple slices; minced fresh tarragon; 1 minced seeded jalapeño chili; chicken stock or broth, vegetable stock or broth. When cooking is completed, always remove and discard the bay leaf. The other solid ingredients, including the clove, can be pureed with ½ cup of the beans and some of the cooking broth and mixed back into the beans.

A Basic Recipe for Green or Brown Lentils

Handful chopped onions or shallots

2½ cups water, stock, or broth, plus more for sautéing

1 cup lentils

1 bay leaf

Salt and pepper to taste

½ teaspoon crumbled dried sage

Liquid-sauté a large handful of finely chopped onions or shallots in ¼ inch water, stock or broth over medium heat until tender. Add 2½ cups boiling stock, broth, or water; lentils; leaf; salt and pepper; and sage. Bring the liquid to a boil, skim once or twice, lower heat to a simmer, cover, and cook for about 40 minutes, or until the lentils are tender.

VARIATIONS

- To make a soup, briefly blend the cooked lentils with 2 cups stock or broth, 2 tablespoons grated fresh ginger, and 1 teaspoon minced lemon zest; heat on high simmer. Top with slivered fresh basil leaves.
- Toss warm lentils with a light vinaigrette, then add finely chopped red onions and minced fresh parsley.
- Add finely diced red or yellow bell peppers.

cooking grains, legumes, and vegetables

COOKING POTATOES YOUR FAMILY WILL LOVE

Potatoes are my favorite comfort food. Steamy baked potatoes; casseroles of chunky, browned potato pieces; potatoes mashed with garlic, stewed with pepper, mixed with turnips, or browned like French fries; and most of all potatoes as the basic ingredient of winter soups. My family eats potatoes practically every day, and so do most Americans. But many families eat potatoes a very high-fat way—and they don't have to.

Did you know that hash browned potatoes, as prepared in most restaurants, derive 60 percent of their calories from fat? That French fried potatoes derive 35 percent of their calories from fat and in fast food restaurants are usually prepared with partially hydrogenated oil? Did you know that a ½-cup serving of traditional potato salad gets all of its fat from mayonnaise?

Can baked potatoes be enjoyed without butter or sour cream? Is there a way to cook potatoes—beside French-fried—that your children will want to eat? Yes! Following are five ways to cook potatoes that my family really enjoys, and that you may want to try:

BAKED "FRIES": Cut unpeeled baking potatoes, sweet potatoes, or yams into a thick French-fry shape. Salt and pepper the pieces and bake them uncovered, skin-side down, on a wiped-with-oil baking sheet in a preheated 400°F oven for about 1 hour, or until the potatoes are puffed and golden brown. Everyone loves these. We even serve them as hors d'oeuvres.

MASHED/BAKED POTATOES: Cut baked potatoes in half and let cool for 5 minutes. Scoop out the insides, mash with salt and pepper and a little chicken or vegetable stock or broth, and return the mashed potato to the skins. Bake in a preheated 400°F oven until the tops brown, about 15 minutes.

CRUNCHY BAKED POTATO SKINS: Remove baked potato insides from the skins and refrigerate for another use. Season the inside of the skins by making a paste of mixed herbs, chicken or vegetable stock or broth, salt and pepper, and the barest amount of olive oil. Place a small piece of parchment paper or aluminum foil over the skins and bake in a preheated 450°F oven for 10 minutes, or until crisp and brown.

Unlike the potato skins in most restaurants, these are not fried in fat. Fried skins, which are touted as "baked" skins in many restaurants, are loaded with fat before you consider the cheese or other additions!

BROKEN POTATOES WITHOUT BUTTER: Boil some quartered unpeeled red or white potatoes in salted water until tender. Break the potatoes up with a wooden fork or wooden spoon; these are not to be mashed, but broken. Season with salt and pepper. Just before serving add minced fresh parsley and some extra-virgin olive oil. To prepare in advance, oil a casserole dish, coat it with bread crumbs, add the potatoes, cover, and keep warm in a 200°F oven for up to 30 minutes. Add the herbs just before serving.

BAKED POTATOES WITH TOPPINGS: Choose toppings for your baked potatoes from the list on page 107. Some children's favorites include salsa, nonfat yogurt mixed with chopped onions or scallions, leftover spaghetti sauce, crumbled baked potato chips, chopped nuts or seeds, or a combination of toasted bread crumbs and grated Parmesan.

MORE VEGETABLES

Some children naturally love green and yellow and orange vegetables, but many children find vegetables "yucky" or worse. One problem may be the way they're cooked. Some children (and most adults!) don't like mushy, over-cooked, pale green vegetables, but find they love lightly steamed vegetables that are still a bit crisp and have color. Some children who won't eat a sliced tomato will eat that same tomato when it's chopped up in salsa. And children who won't eat lettuce will eat a chopped salad of cucumbers, carrots, celery, and zucchini.

The following cooking suggestions may begin to change the way you and your family think about vegetables. And they will provide substitutions for the meat or chicken you deleted from your recipes. For ideas for fresh-vegetable salsas, see page 162.

VEGETABLES FOR STEAMING: Asparagus, broccoli, cauliflower, corn on the cob, artichokes, celery, baby turnips, potatoes, carrots.

VEGETABLES FOR SAUTÉING: Onions, garlic, chard, spinach (or any bunch of green-leafed vegetable in the market), asparagus, mushrooms, fennel, sum-mer squashes.

VEGETABLES FOR STIR-FRYING WITH A MIXTURE OF OIL AND STOCK OR BROTH: Cabbage, sliced broccoli and cauliflower, asparagus, snap peas, leeks, onions, garlic, green and red bell peppers, milder chilies such as Anaheim, baby bok choy.

VEGETABLES FOR GRILLING: Scallions, asparagus, onions, mushrooms, fennel, all kinds of peppers, tomatoes, mushrooms, corn on the cob, steamed potatoes, chunks of turnips, and winter squash. All these vegetables (except corn) can be threaded on wooden skewers. This makes turning easier, and prevents losing vegetables to the coals. Grilled vegetables are great as a side dish, and wonderful served on baguette toasts as sandwiches, or with rice or grain main courses.

When grilling, I usually grill extra vegetables for the next day. Adults, especially, like cold grilled vegetables on sandwiches. For your own lunch, try grilled scallions and green pepper slices with fresh tomato (or marinated red peppers from a jar) on toast with Our Nonfat "Mayonnaise" (page 161); or try grilled potato slices, onions, and asparagus with our mayonnaise. Grilled vegetables can be the main dish for summer lunch anytime, whether cooked fresh or left over from dinner. Grilled vegetables need a little oil to keep them from drying out. Pour oil into a glass and, using a brush, coat them lightly.

chapter 13

children and fish:
a combination that doesn't
always work

When I was small, fish was something white and soft with very little taste under quite a bit of melted butter. It was always served with carrots and was not my favorite meal; actually, I hated it. During World War II, patriotic Americans ate fish once a week. All our sacrificed meat was consigned to the armies of men fighting the war. I was a chubby child who loved food and who "starved to death" on fish Tuesdays, our family's fish night. Today, children don't have to groan as deeply as I did on Tuesdays because so much delicious fish is available. However, don't force children to eat fish if they don't like it. The Lower Fat Kids Plan offers many alternatives.

If you can, buy your fish in a good fish market. Fresh fish glistens. It has no smell even after being kept in your fridge for 2 days. The eyes of fresh fish are bright, not cloudy. Defrosted fish can also be delicious and should look and taste as though it were fresh. The flesh, when pressed, should be springy, not mushy.

If you are stuck with a meager supermarket supply of limp, dull-looking fish, make friends with the fishmonger and share your concerns. Perhaps your interest will spark the store to stock fresher fish, or to tell you when fresh fish arrives. If not, go elsewhere if at all possible.

Frequently, small pieces (chunks) of cold-water fish such as swordfish, halibut, bluefish, shark, and tuna are available at the fish counter; marinate them in dry spicy marinades or soy-based or lime marinades; you can grill or broil these fish pieces with lots of vegetables on wooden skewers. Serve the fish with a grain or bean casserole or with a filling vegetable soup.

If you do not consider yourself a pro at fish cookery, think of your beginning forays as necessary adventures in becoming expert. Cooking fish scares many people. When I first cooked fish, I experienced uncertainty and alarm. However, I found that ultimately, fish can be one of the simplest foods to prepare. If cooking fish seems like an adventure you want to postpone, wait until you have the time and inclination. If the children haven't been eating fish, or if learning to cook it is distasteful to you, waiting longer won't even be noticed. If you are determined to include fish in your family meals and have up to now not succeeded, the following suggestions may be useful:

- Most kids love burgers, so the next time you grill, buy some fish too. Bread the fish, grill it (see below), and serve it with a hamburger bun and salsa.
- Thread fish and vegetables on wooden skewers, then marinate the kabobs in a marinade the children like, or brush the kabobs with a favorite bottled sauce.

GRILLING FISH

BROILER GRILLING: There aren't many kids who don't enjoy barbecued food. This might be the best way to introduce them to fish. Remove the fish from the refrigerator 30 minutes before cooking; it will cook more evenly at room temperature. Preheat the broiler with the broiler pan under it until the pan is very hot, then wipe the hot pan with olive oil using a wadded-up paper towel. If the fish has not been marinated, salt and pepper it just before preheating the broiler. Broil the fish until it flakes when tested with a fork, unless you are deliberately cooking the fish rare. A 5- to 6-ounce fillet will cook in 5 to 8 minutes, depending on the heat of your broiler and the thickness of the fish. Do not turn the fish—the hot broiler pan will cook the fish on the underside while the broiler cooks the top.

OUTDOOR GRILLING: Using a charcoal chimney can give you hot coals in 30 minutes, so, except for rain or snow, there is almost no excuse for not being able to start a fire in a grill. If you have easy access to an outdoor grill, consider using it as an all-year-round method for grilling fish (or anything else). I grill large (3- to 5-pound) whole fish so that they partly steam and the underside is brown with a crunchy skin.

Wrap the fish in a double thickness of aluminum foil, leaving a narrow opening along the entire top length of the package. Check after 20 minutes. The juices should be simmering, not boiling. If the juices are bubbling too fast, move the package further away from the coals. A 3-pound fresh salmon will take about 45 minutes to cook until it flakes. The fish can be cooked simply with nothing added, or it can be salted, peppered, and stuffed with fresh herbs and lemon slices.

If you are grilling fillets, lightly oil each fillet, top and bottom, and place it directly on the grill. Turn once to cook evenly.

QUICK FISH STEWS AND SOUPS

Most chicken stew or tomato-based vegetable soup recipes can be transformed into quick low-fat fish stews or soups. Delete any butter and cream from the recipe. Buy inexpensive white fish such as cod or rockfish, and perhaps some shrimp or other shellfish if your family likes them. Remove the fish from the refrigerator 30 minutes before cooking. Add the fish to a barely simmering soup. The fish pieces will cook in 4 or 5 minutes, when the fish becomes opaque and the shrimp turn pink.

For extra liquid, add bottled clam juice or some white wine. Serve the soup with garlic bread or croutons, extra vegetables with lemon, and a salad with low-fat dressing.

breakfast can be healthy

Wtanglehen you make the shift—in some cases gradually, in others quickly—to lower-saturated-fat cooking, your children may worry that meals will be very different, and they are right, some will be. Breakfasts, however, will look *almost* the same. Your children can still eat eggs, cereal, fruit, toast, milk—no barley casseroles with shredded fish! No beans and rice at breakfast (unless that is what they are used to eating).

The differences in appearance and taste at breakfast will be minimal, but the milk will have less fat; the cereal will have no saturated fat if you are diligent; the scrambled eggs and omelets will use fewer yolks; and the toast will be spread with jam or a nut butter, not the harmful highly saturated fat of butter or the hydrogenated oils of margarine.

You can make good-tasting pancakes and crepes and waffles with olive oil instead of butter or margarine. Talk to your children about eliminating butter and adding quark flavored with choices of your own (see page 69), whipped "cream" for pancakes (see page 129), or even cut-up dried fruit. Dribbling maple syrup over these foods is hard to avoid, but look and see how much your children actually pour—½ cup of syrup is not unusual. This syrup is 100 percent sugar; cutting the amount by half makes a huge difference. You'll be surprised at how interested children can become in solving these problems *with* you. The facts will be startling, even to them.

chapter 15

WHAT ABOUT EGGS

Egg yolks are a very high-cholesterol food. With about 220 to 250 mg in each yolk, they contain almost the maximum 300 mg recommended as the daily allowance for an adult. For decades dietary cholesterol was believed to be a major source of elevated blood cholesterol levels, and consequently, heart disease. The American Heart Association (AHA), in response to early, highly documented research, strongly recommended that egg yolk consumption be limited to no more than three egg yolks per week for both adults and children over the age of two, thinking correctly that whole eggs were a major food source for Americans. They urged that egg whites be substituted for egg yolks whenever possible.

Recent studies, as a result of more sophisticated clinical techniques and the discovery of cholesterol receptors by the Nobel prize winners Michael Brown and Joseph Goldstein, have shown that it is *not* dietary cholesterol in isolation that raises blood cholesterol, but rather high intakes of saturated fat and trans fatty acids that accompany the dietary cholesterol.

But does this new information make egg yolks a good, regular food for your child?

- A whole large egg, surprisingly, is a 65 percent (total) fat food (80 calories and 6 grams of fat).
- A whole large egg is 15 percent *saturated* fat, the fat that raises cholesterol levels.
- The egg white alone has half the protein of a whole egg without *any of the fat at all.*
- The protein in two large egg whites is equal to three-quarters of a cup of nonfat milk or half a cup of nonfat yogurt.

From this information you can see that the whites of the egg are a more preferable choice if you want to cut down on fat of any kind. Serving a whole egg to your children once or twice a week or even three or four times is not a vice. It's a familiar food that is low in total calories, high in protein, and low in cost. But your children eat more fat each week than they need for healthy growth. Egg yolks do not have to be a staple food, or, as some parents think, a necessary food. Serving whole eggs as frequent light meals, daily lunch box snacks, and typical afternoon snacks is conditioning your child to select a

breakfast can be healthy

food that is a source of saturated fat. True, eggs are a relatively lower-fat food compared to other choices such as roast chicken, hamburgers, and lasagna. If those are the only options, then whole eggs are the best choice. Another problem with serving whole eggs frequently is that the foods that usually accompany eggs, both at home and in restaurants, are hashed brown potatoes, buttered toast, and cheese, all high in harmful saturated fat. Some suggestions follow for minimizing egg yolks and lowering fat in general in the accompanying foods.

- Toast and jam instead of butter.
- Nonfat cheese as the predominant cheese in omelets with sprinklings of a more flavorful Romano or Parmesan.
- New and inventive side dishes for eggs to replace fried and hashed brown potatoes—beans, grilled tomatoes, oven baked "fries," grilled toast with olive oil, fresh fruit or grilled pineapple.
- 1, 2, or 3 yolks and 6 to 8 whites to make an omelet for three people.
- 1 yolk and 3 whites to make fried eggs.
- 3 egg whites and 1 yolk to make egg salad for 2 sandwiches.
- Substituting whites for yolks when you can in frittata-type dishes.

One frittata I still prepare for my children as a light Sunday supper or lunch goes like this:

Scramble 8 egg whites with 2 yolks and ¼ cup nonfat mozzarella and 1 tablespoon or two of grated Parmesan cheese. Add salt and pepper (or chili flakes) to taste.

Chop a cup or two of any greens (chard, spinach, arugula, watercress), or onions if you are out of greens, and water-sauté briefly, until they just begin to wilt. Season to taste.

Add 1 teaspoon of olive oil to the greens and mix. Cover the greens with the egg mixture and turn the heat to medium, cover, and cook for about 7 to 9 minutes, or to the doneness you prefer.

What do you do with the yolks? Compost them. Throw them away. They cannot save the lives or fill the stomachs of starving children in India or here. If you are bothered by the idea of waste, egg substitutes without fat are available in the market. Some people find them a preferable solution, though the taste is not the same.

For a truly delicious weekend breakfast or light supper, try Bob's Egg-White and Tomato Omelet, below. You can grate some Parmesan on top

chapter 15

of the omelet either during or after cooking. This small amount of cheese adds a familiar taste and will not invalidate the huge fat reduction in this type of cooking.

Bob's Egg-White and Tomato Omelet

This omelet is made just like an omelet that uses yolks; we use all whites, but 2 to 3 yolks and 6 to 8 whites will work well and lower the fat by more than half.

Makes 2 omelets; serves 4

TOMATO FILLING

¼ cup finely chopped onions

¼ teaspoon dried thyme, marjoram, or oregano, crumbled

¾ cup well-drained chopped fresh, canned, or grilled tomatoes

1 teaspoon extra-virgin olive oil

Minced fresh parsley for garnish

8 egg whites

2 egg yolks

Salt and freshly ground pepper to taste

Grated Parmesan (optional)

In a small skillet or omelet pan water-sauté the onions over low to medium heat until softened. Add the herbs and the tomatoes and cook over medium heat until the tomatoes give up most of their water. Add olive oil. Remove to a separate bowl and set aside. Wipe pan clean with a paper towel. In a small bowl, beat the eggs. Heat an oiled pan briefly. Pour the eggs into the pan and stir gently until they begin to set, about 1 minute. Add the tomato mixture, lift the edges of the omelet to allow the eggs to run under it, fold the omelet, and cover the pan. Cook for 4 to 8 minutes over medium heat, depending on the doneness you prefer. Turn the omelet out onto a warm plate with the browned side on top.

OTHER SUGGESTED OMELETTE FILLINGS AND FLAVORINGS
- Sautéed spinach and mushrooms
- Shredded nonfat mozzarella cheese mixed with 2 tablespoons grated Parmesan and crumbled herbs

breakfast can be healthy

- Onions and leftover potatoes sautéed until browned
- Any leftover vegetables
- I teaspoon drained and rinsed capers and ½ teaspoon Dijon mustard beaten into the eggs

LOWERING THE FAT IN PANCAKE AND WAFFLE MIXES

When you buy pancake and waffle mixes for your family, make sure to read the labels. One famous brand offers four kinds of pancake mixes, one of which contains partially hydrogenated oil. Boxes that look alike don't necessarily adhere to the same standards. The recipes on some mixes call for saturated fat and hydrogenated oils to be added in the form of whole eggs, margarine, or butter.

Transforming pancakes into lower-saturated-fat food is possible. Here's how you can lower the fat without lowering the taste:
- Substitute nonfat milk for whole milk.
- Substitute ½ tablespoon of oil, such as olive or almond, for each tablespoon of butter or margarine.
- Substitute 2 egg whites for each whole egg. (Beating the whites briefly with a whisk adds air to the whites and results in a fluffier pancake.)

SOME LOWER-FAT BREAKFAST IDEAS

High-fat breakfast habits include foods such as granola bars (which can derive 40 percent of their calories from fat), leftover cheese pizza, bacon and eggs, high-fat cereals, or (as one mom shared with me) potato chips and peanut butter. I know breakfast is a hard meal to keep healthy—and sane—when you are rushing in the morning, which makes high-fat convenience foods hard to resist.

Following are some quick suggestions that may work in your house:

- Fresh fruit, toast, and lower-fat milk
- A fresh fruit drink (blended fruit, nonfat milk, nonfat yogurt)
- Cereals without added fats
- Bagels with a nonfat spread, or a mixture of peanut butter, Grape-Nuts, low-fat yogurt, or quark
- Microwaved baked potatoes

And for less hurried times:

- Pancakes or waffles made with less fat and fewer egg yolks, with Grape-Nuts or a similar cereal or wheat bran added to the batter
- French toast made with egg whites and nonfat milk, cooked with minimal olive oil and spread with fresh fruit slices or jam
- Oatmeal pancakes with fresh fruit or jam or cinnamon topping (recipe follows)

OATMEAL PANCAKES

Using 1 cup of leftover cooked oatmeal, make about 5 small patties with your hands. Cook them over medium heat in a nonstick pan coated with a little oil until browned on both sides. The pancakes can be seasoned before cooking with salt and pepper or after cooking with a sprinkling of cinnamon and sugar.

what's for lunch?
the secrets of sandwiches

For most children—and most adults—lunch means sandwiches. Sandwiches seem indispensable to our busy lives, and we have passed this habit on to our children. According to the USDA, hamburgers are ordered more frequently in restaurants than any other food. Ham sandwiches, hot dogs, peanut butter and jelly sandwiches, and turkey and cheese sandwiches are also among the top ten food choices ordered in restaurants by Americans.

But sandwiches without mayonnaise, hamburgers, cheese, avocado, bacon, salami, corned beef, or cream cheese can also be great food choices. Like breakfast, lunch can still look like lunch although what's inside the sandwiches will change.

SANDWICH PROBLEMS AND
SANDWICH SOLUTIONS

Most kids' sandwiches are composed of lunch meat, cheese, and mayonnaise, foods that are quickly combined and need no preparation. Next in popularity is tuna salad, which typically means canned-in-oil tuna mixed with and accompanied with mayonnaise. And then there's peanut butter and jelly, which children quickly learn to make for themselves.

Usually the meat that goes on made-at-home sandwiches is a packaged, store-bought, high saturated-fat, high-sodium product. The cheese, if you are one of the millions of families counted by the USDA, is American or Cheddar, both very high in saturated fat. The mayonnaise derives 77 percent of its calories from fat. And the bread is a primarily white-flour bread, which is low in fiber.

These sandwiches are good-tasting, familiar, easy to prepare, and filling. The problem is that these ubiquitous foods are causing havoc with our children's health. Let's look at some high-fat problems and some lower-fat solutions.

HIGH-FAT PROBLEM: One tuna salad sandwich prepared at home with a 3-ounce can of tuna in oil, 1 tablespoon of mayonnaise for the salad, and 1 tablespoon of mayonnaise for the bread contains 350 fat calories, calculated conservatively. That sandwich derives 75 percent of its calories from fat! Depending on the ingredients of the bread you use, you may or may not add more fat. With a candy bar and whole milk, that sandwich lunch becomes an out-of-sight mostly saturated-fat meal.

LOWER-FAT SOLUTION: By using tuna canned in water and Our Non-fat "Mayonnaise" (page 161) or plain mustard, you can reduce the amount of calories derived from fat to about 10 percent, or what is in the tuna itself. Or, toss the tuna with a mix of half mayonnaise and half nonfat plain yogurt. For the extra nutrition and fiber your child needs, add lettuce, tomato, and carrots (or any vegetable that is convenient and your child likes) either to the sandwich or in a baggie, and perhaps a nonfat pretzel or two and dried and/or fresh fruit. Or make two sandwiches. Calories do not have to be provided by added fat; tuna has sufficient fat all by itself. Commercially made reduced-fat mayonnaise *sometimes* has as little as half the fat of regular or as *much* as half the fat as regular mayonnaise. It's all in the way you regard it.

HIGH-FAT PROBLEM: A bacon, lettuce, tomato, and avocado sandwich made with mayonnaise is a high-fat sandwich. The bacon and mayonnaise are the saturated-fat culprits. But no one who loves this sandwich wants to give it up entirely.

LOWER-FAT SOLUTION: Make a sandwich that is mostly vegetables—lettuce, tomato, cucumber, sprouts—with only 2 slices of crisp bacon on toasted bread spread with Our Nonfat "Mayonnaise" (page 161) or with mustard. Omit the avocado when adding bacon. Made this way this sandwich will contain less than the amount of saturated fat in a glass of 2 percent milk.

HIGH-FAT PROBLEM: Some packaged meats, including many of the lower-fat turkey varieties, are typically quite high in saturated fat and extraordinarily high in sodium. Read the labels on the back, not just the advertising on the front.

LOWER-FAT SOLUTION: Prepare sandwiches with leftover home-cooked chicken or beef, or sliced fresh-roasted chicken or turkey breast, or beef from a delicatessen (no nitrates or excessive sodium). Use less meat, and load up the sandwich with sliced, raw vegetables. Use Our Nonfat "Mayonnaise" (page 161), or just use mustard. Nonfat mozzarella cheese can be added, if you like.

HIGH-FAT PROBLEM: Many brands of peanut butter are made with added oils and frequently partially hydrogenated oil, added salt, and added sugar. And, as you are well aware, peanut butter frequently is offered "crunchy" style, with added nuts. No one needs these additions, especially your children.

LOWER-FAT SOLUTION: Buy peanut or other nut butter without added oil, added sugar or added salt. This type of peanut butter will taste different to children who have been used to grossly adulterated peanut butter, but they usually adapt quickly because it really does taste very good. To resolve the crunch problem, try adding a nonfat cereal such as Grape-Nuts or roasted soy nuts to the peanut butter. This restores the crunch some children miss while "stretching" the peanut butter and lowering the fat in the sandwich. Peanut butter mixed with one quarter quark or baker's cheese further reduces the fat in this sandwich without hiding the taste. Peanut butter is a high-fat food. Thinking of it in that way will help you take it off your everyday sandwich menu, and perhaps off your everyday snack-time menu.

As a "spread" rather than as the primary filler for a sandwich, peanut butter goes with lots of foods: apples, bananas, pineapple, papaya, dried fruits, and cereals—even peppers, onions, and/or chilies—and even lettuce (it is better shredded). Apple slices (sprinkled with lemon juice to retard browning) are a great addition to most sandwiches. Also try cucumber slices, banana slices, jícama, sliced plums or dates.

USE HIGH FIBER BREAD FOR SANDWICHES

Some breads are better for your children than others. Many are made of enriched white flour or a combination of white and whole-wheat flour. The more *whole* grain—wheat, rye, corn, oats, millet, buckwheat and others—a bread has, the more fiber it has, which is crucial to your children's well-being.

Some whole-wheat breads taste much better than others; experiment to find the ones your family will enjoy eating.

High fiber diets promote healthy arteries and decrease the risk of certain cancers. In addition, fiber cleanses the digestive system efficiently and naturally by keeping food moving through the body. Digested food that remains in the intestinal system too long produces gases and other products that irritate the colon. White bread is a very low source of fiber, but white-flour bread in its many forms, including baguettes, is too good to give up. Eating a variety of breads, including whole-grain breads for sandwiches, will add to your children's general health.

MORE HIGH-FIBER FOODS

Bread isn't the only high-fiber food. All of us, not just our children, need a rich supply of various types of plant foods for the daily requirement of soluble and non-soluble fiber. High amounts of fiber are found in the following foods:
- Dried fruits such as dates, figs, and apricots
- Seeds and nuts
- Cabbage, broccoli, cauliflower, dark green leafy vegetables, corn
- Apples, cantaloupe, strawberries, persimmons, raspberries, oranges
- Grains, dry cereals (read the labels), wheat bran
- Dried or fresh beans, lentils

GREAT-TASTING BEAN OR GRAIN SPREADS

Used as a dip for sliced vegetables, grain or bean spreads can become a family favorite (see the following recipe). They are also good stuffed in pita bread or spread on whole-grain bread and topped with sliced raw or cooked vegetables and/or lettuce.

The bean spread, hummus, is traditionally made with large amounts of sesame paste and/or large amounts of oil—sometimes as much as 1 cup oil to 1 cup of beans! Make your own lower-fat version by adding 1 tablespoon olive oil for each cup of pureed cooked chickpeas (garbanzo beans). Add cumin seeds, red pepper flakes, and garlic to taste and a bit of stock or broth to make a spread or dip that is delicious and much better for you than the fat-rich hummus you are used to.

what's for lunch? the secrets of sandwiches

This delicious spread is easily made from leftover cooked beans.

Makes 2 cups

2 cups cooked beans

½ cup nonfat vegetable or chicken stock (page 159 or 158) or
    canned nonfat broth

⅓ cup Our Nonfat "Mayonnaise" (page 161)

Salt and freshly ground pepper

Tabasco sauce, red pepper flakes, or ground turmeric to taste

1 to 2 teaspoons extra-virgin olive oil (optional)

In a blender or food processor, blend the beans with as much broth or stock as necessary to make a smooth puree the consistency of peanut butter.

Add the "mayonnaise" and blend well. Stir in the salt, pepper, and other seasonings to taste. If using, stir in the optional olive oil, and serve.

LOWER-FAT VERSIONS OF FAVORITE SANDWICH FILLINGS

- Sliced fresh-cooked turkey breast from your kitchen or deli, with lettuce, bell pepper, vinegar-marinated red peppers, and Our Nonfat "Mayonnaise" (page 161).
- Tuna canned in water, with chopped celery or green pepper and Our Nonfat "Mayonnaise."
- Leftover home-cooked or deli-cooked chicken or turkey breast or lean meat, with lettuce, onion, green pepper, and tomato making up most of the sandwich.
- Lettuce, tomato, cucumber, grated Parmesan, shredded nonfat cheese, and Our Nonfat "Mayonnaise."
- Two parts shredded nonfat mozzarella mixed with one part full-fat shredded cheese. Sprinkle on bread, top with sliced tomato, green pepper, onion, or sautéed mushrooms and another slice of bread, and cook in your toaster oven instead of frying in butter or oil.

MORE IDEAS FOR SANDWICH FILLINGS

- Thinly sliced green bell pepper and red onion with Our Nonfat "Mayonnaise" (page 161)
- Leftover grilled fish, chopped and mixed with Our Nonfat "Mayonnaise," with sliced Anaheim pepper
- An open-faced sandwich of finely chopped tomatoes mixed with lemon juice, salt, and pepper
- Pureed cooked bean spread topped with lettuce, avocado, and onion
- Pureed cooked bean spread with red onion, green bell pepper, and nonfat cheese
- Peanut butter topped with cucumber slices, celery sticks, fennel slices, jícama sticks, apple slices, or banana slices
- Leftover baked potatoes broken up and browned in just a bit of oil, piled in a pita bread half with shredded lettuce tossed with a tangy vinaigrette

READY-TO-EAT FOODS FOR QUICK PICNIC LUNCHES

- Low-fat meats such as skinless turkey breast or roast beef without visible fat
- Three-ounce cans of packed-in-water tuna
- Jars of marinated red peppers and artichokes without oil for layering on sandwiches
- Leftover baked chicken breasts (see page 214)
- Leftover grilled vegetables
- Fresh fruit
- Fresh vegetables
- Pita bread for stuffing with all of the above
- Nonfat pretzels or chips

PICNIC DISHES NEEDING SOME PREPARATION

- Vegetable kabobs prepared the day before, wrapped well, and broiled in the morning; let cool to room temperature before packing
- Fresh bread picked up on your way (Fresh bread with lemon, salt, pepper, and tomato makes a wonderful sandwich)
- A low-fat bean spread (see page 122)
- Freshly sliced vegetables tossed with extra-virgin olive oil and lemon juice
- Fruit salads such as Flat Salads (page 196)

SUBSTITUTES FOR MAYONNAISE AND BUTTER

- Our Nonfat "Mayonnaise" (page 161)
- Quark or yogurt cheese (page 160)
- Fresh lemon juice (on vegetable sandwiches)
- A "sauce" of grated cucumbers, lemon, and, if your children like it, horseradish
- Baker's cheese with salt and pepper
- Bean spread mixed with Our Nonfat "Mayonnaise"
- Nut butter mixed with yogurt cheese, baker's cheese, or quark
- Mustard
- Low-fat or nonfat salad dressing
- Salsa
- Fresh mint leaves
- Fresh herbs
- Liquid-sautéed cabbage lightly tossed with extra-virgin olive oil
- Sesame, sunflower, or pumpkin seeds, mixed with Our Nonfat "Mayonnaise"

chapter 16

what's for dinner?
keeping hamburgers on the menu,
and a few other ideas

It's hard for most children to even contemplate giving up the foods they have grown to love—it's like giving up a favorite blanket or teddy bear before it's time. They don't have to; even hamburgers and hot dogs can be part of a lower-fat diet when they are prepared and served as part of meals with ample servings of vegetables. Preparing familiar meals differently requires just a moment's thought because the changes are so simple: vegetables without butter, potatoes without fat, hamburgers without French fries and mayonnaise.

Your children are healthy. Maintaining that status is your goal, without robbing them of everything they crave. Knowing how to balance high-fat "treat" foods with lower-fat foods means that you never have to banish hotdogs from your table.

The following comparison shows how it is possible to serve a hamburger dinner that is very similar to the one you are probably used to eating, but which has far less fat and does not leave you feeling deprived.

A TYPICAL HIGH-FAT HAMBURGER DINNER: Notice how much fat other than the hamburger is in the following menu: butter, high-fat salad dressing, butter *again*, and ice cream.

what's for dinner? keeping hamburgers on the menu, and a few other ideas   125

- Tomato juice with scallions or instant gazpacho soup made with tomato juice, salsa, chopped bell peppers, onions, and cucumbers
- Four ounces ground chuck
- Regular hamburger bun
- Baked potatoes with 2 tablespoons butter
- Chopped vegetable salad with carrots, cucumber, and celery
- Two tablespoons regular salad dressing
- Onions and tomatoes for the hamburger
- Ketchup and mustard for the hamburger
- Frozen Italian beans or green peas with 1 teaspoon butter
- Ice cream

This dinner has 49 percent of its calories from fat.

A HAMBURGER DINNER WITH NO-ADDED-FAT ACCOMPANIMENTS: The hamburger itself is the only saturated fat food in this version.

- Tomato juice with scallions or an instant gazpacho made with tomato juice, salsa, and chopped bell peppers, onions, and cucumbers.
- Four ounces ground chuck
- No-fat-added hamburger roll or baguette
- Baked "French fries" (page 106), or baked potato with yogurt cheese (page 160), herbed quark, or salsa
- Chopped vegetable salad with carrots, cucumbers, and celery
- 2 tablespoons low or nonfat salad dressing
- Onion and tomato for the hamburger
- Ketchup and mustard for the hamburger
- Frozen Italian beans or green peas with lemon
- Grapes or nonfat frozen yogurt

This dinner has 23 percent of its calories from fat, a little more if you add oil to the salad dressing.

Vegetarians in the family can eat everything in this meal except of course the hamburger. Substituting low-fat veggie burgers or perhaps sautéed vegetables and melted nonfat cheese on toasted hamburger rolls makes a relatively quick alternative to the meat. Stuff potatoes with a variety of broiled, sautéed or frozen vegetables.

HOT DOGS AND BAKED BEANS

Hot dogs, like veggie burgers, are now available in lower-fat versions (including some very low-fat and vegetarian ones) and with lower sodium. According to my nephews—and their dad—they can be really, really good. You must check the labels, as the variations in fat content are wide.

Instead of canned baked beans made with lard (that white square you see when you open the can is pure fat), try vegetarian baked beans—your children will not even notice the difference. When making baked beans at home, substitute olive oil for bacon if you insist on adding fat; at least then the fat will be the one *you* add, and it will be monounsaturated, the healthier choice. Adding a salad, vegetable, and fruit or nonfat frozen dessert makes a relatively simple meal out of a can of beans.

TOPPINGS CHILDREN LOVE

Toppings can make any food more interesting and fun for children. If the ingredients are readily available in your kitchen, children will often create new combinations on their own. These are some of the toppings we use at home.

TOPPINGS FOR GRAIN AND BEAN CASSEROLES AND PASTA:
- A mixture of chopped onions and green bell peppers
- Two parts toasted bread crumbs mixed with one part grated Parmesan
- Equal amounts of minced garlic, minced fresh parsley, and toasted bread crumbs (add some grated lemon zest to top black beans)
- Chopped seeded cucumber, tomato, onion, and bell pepper
- Frozen green peas and frozen corn, rinsed quickly under hot water (this is an especially good topping for bean casseroles)
- Canned black beans, rinsed and mixed with minced fresh herbs and a little olive oil; mixed with a few sunflower or pumpkin seeds for crunch; or mixed with chopped tomatoes or chunky salsa as a filling for tortillas, a topping for baked potatoes, or a topping for all kinds of grains
- Salsa

- Hot sauce
- Leftover lentil soup or any bean soup (perfect for topping grain casseroles)
- Chopped lettuce or cabbage sautéed for 1 or 2 minutes in a few tablespoons of chicken stock or broth and tossed with 1 teaspoon olive oil
- Canned or leftover chili

DESSERT TOPPINGS FOR FRUIT:
- Chopped dried fruits
- Candied ginger cut into very fine strips with a knife or scissors (the fiery taste of ginger may not be for every child, however)
- Raisins
- Sliced almonds
- Quark or nonfat yogurt mixed with just a bit of jam, or ground cloves, or cinnamon, or just simply by themselves

DESSERT TOPPINGS FOR FROZEN DESSERTS AND NONFAT PUDDINGS:
- Crumbled nonfat, low-sugar cookies
- Chopped dried fruits
- Chopped dried fruits mixed with chopped chocolate
- Nonfat, low-sugar chocolate fudge sauce
- Chopped nuts or sliced almonds
- Praline Topping (recipe follows)
- Fresh fruit slices or berries
- Crushed or whole grain cereal
- One nonfat, no-sugar pretzel, crushed (the salt and ice cream are delicious together, and children love it)
- A few finely chopped M&M's
- Puffed rice, wheat, and corn cereal
- Nonfat Whipped "Cream" (recipe follows)

chapter 17

NONFAT WHIPPED "CREAM"

In a food processor fitted with the knife blade, process 1 cup nonfat milk, 4 teaspoons sugar, vanilla extract, and 6 ice cubes for 1 to 2 minutes, or until the mixture is stiff. Serve immediately, as it separates quickly.

PRALINE TOPPING

In a medium saucepan, combine 4 cups sugar and 2 cups water. Stir over medium-high heat until the sugar dissolves, then cook to the hard ball stage (265°F, or until a small amount dropped into a glass of water solidifies to a hard ball). Quickly add 1 cup nuts, mix, and pour out onto a pastry marble, a baking sheet, or a plastic cutting board. The praline will harden quickly. Pry the praline off the surface, break it up, and crush it finely in a food processor. Store in an airtight jar in the refrigerator indefinitely. This is a high-sugar topping, and so sweet that 1 teaspoon is a big treat.

AN IDEA FOR LIGHT DINNERS OR WEEKEND LUNCHES

Offer grilled or steamed vegetables and spreads such as Our Nonfat "Mayonnaise" (page 161), yogurt cheese mixed with pureed beans or an herb sauce (see page 160), and salsa (page 162). Crunchy, warmed whole-grain breads or baguettes filled with these combinations can be supplemented with a fresh salad tossed with thin celery slices and crisp red onion rings. Adding "fried" baked potatoes (see page 106) to this meal pleases children.

If this seems too drastic a departure from the meals that are traditional in your family, introduce the idea gradually by offering sliced turkey breast, or tuna salad made with vinaigrette. For heartier meals include a quick lentil salad or a filling soup.

feeding your vegetarian child: eating well without meat

Have you noticed what your vegetarian child is eating? Are all meals enhanced with large servings of cheese or other high-saturated-fat dairy foods in an effort to provide sufficient protein? And are you saying "yes" to pints of the richest, creamiest, "in" ice cream, hoping to provide more calcium and alleviate your fears about insufficient nutrients?

You know that your child needs protein and calcium, and you're glad that he or she drinks milk and eats cheese. Even your pediatrician suggests cheese as a substitute food for meat! Unfortunately, cheese and many other dairy products are awfully high in saturated fat—but what are the alternatives?

Your vegetarian child is on an accepted track in looking for a way to eat lower down on the food chain, but it can possibly create another problem for you. Unless your child eats a vegan diet, which excludes fish, chicken, meat, *and* dairy, the risk is that his or her vegetarian diet will be too high in saturated fat. The typical diet of a child who has eliminated meat, fish, and chicken, but who *includes* all dairy products in his or her regimen is frequently higher in saturated fat than that of children who eat chicken breasts, steak, fish, and turkey sandwiches!

Perhaps you haven't taken the time or don't have the time (you think) to investigate a meatless diet that will work for you and your child in all ways. Or perhaps you have investigated and come away with the sense that what is needed is impossible without the investment of lots of time and attention—which you may not have the energy for just now.

At age eight, one of our sons announced that he was never eating meat again. I certainly wasn't enthralled, given our family's orientation toward meat and what seemed like the difficult task ahead. In the beginning, feeding him did require extra thought and extra time for me—vegetarian cooking seemed formidable. I bought cookbooks to teach myself the art of tofu loaves and soybean pancakes, most of which did not touch the hearts—or the stomachs—of my children. I was impatient, rushed in my own life, and generally uninterested in vegetarian diets.

But I was proud of the determination of our youngest child to insist on support. I straightened my shoulders, took a few breaths, and began to develop a way of cooking that fit our family, a way of cooking that could nurture a vegetarian and not alienate the rest of us. Today, with the blessed help of so many more vegetable choices, so many foods available in bulk, so many canned and packaged, good-tasting nonfat foods, the ubiquitous burrito, and many other takeout foods, lower-fat vegetarian cooking can become smoothly integrated into your never-ending list of parental responsibilities.

PROVIDING PROTEIN AND CALCIUM

Parents of vegetarian children often worry that their children are not eating enough protein or calcium, but in most cases, this is a needless concern.* Average American children and adults, both meat-eating and vegetarian, eat far more protein than is necessary for their continued good health. There are always exceptions to any rule or generalization, however; diet does not exist separately from our way of life, but is a part of it. Diet, along with mood and exercise, has profound effects on our feeling well, successful, and fulfilled. Children should be encouraged to notice when their energy levels are high and when they are low, and which foods seem to deplete them and which sustain them. Children eat more when they use more energy playing or engaging in strenuous work; *their* body is telling *them* that it needs more calories. Because

*The diets of children who follow strictly macrobiotic or vegan diets are sometimes found to be lacking protein and calcium. Families undertaking this kind of regimen must pay extremely careful attention to the diets of their growing children, and are best advised to consult with a physician regarding adequate nutrients.

protein and calcium needs vary with each person and age group, the USDA recommendations are set *above* what is actually needed.

In the sixties and seventies the theory of combining grains, legumes, nuts, and seeds at each meal to form a "complete protein" was the generally accepted vegetarian rule. Having vegetarian children in those days required a lot of investigation to satisfy oneself that one could feed and nurture a vegetarian child without subscribing to this often difficult manner of cooking and eating. Quickly, I found doctors and nutritionists to side with me and assure me my children could get all the protein (and calcium) they needed without what looked then like being bound to the kitchen. Now, the American Dietetic Association in its position papers of 1987 and 1993 absolutely states that any "conscious feeding of grain and legumes in the same meal is not necessary" and that the essential amino acids children need to grow can be obtained from various foods, and at various meals.

HOW MUCH PROTEIN DOES YOUR CHILD NEED?

The protein requirement for children is based on their age and weight. An average small young child might need 20 grams of protein each day, which three cups of nonfat milk would provide, while an average pre-adolescent might need 45 grams. This is the amount of protein found in 5 cups of milk, or 4 cups of yogurt, or 2 cups of cottage cheese, or 4 egg whites. *Nonfat milk products have just as much protein as whole or low-fat products.* If your child drinks a quart of milk each day or likes yogurt and eats that regularly, most of his or her protein requirements will be satisfied. Vegan children usually live in vegan households when they are young and learn to eat soy products (tofu, soy milk, tempeh, miso, soy burgers) as replacement for dairy products and meat. Vegan households also pay a lot of attention to maintaining an intake of essential fats by including moderate amounts of walnuts, almonds, sesame seeds, pumpkin seeds, sunflower seeds, and oils made from those plants in their diet.

Rice and other grains also have protein. Buckwheat, millet, and bulgur all have about twice as much protein as rice. On the other hand, wild rice has more protein than any other grain. One cup of cooked beans will provide the same amount of protein as an average glass of milk. And ordinary vegetables have protein: About ¾ cup of cooked lima beans, green peas, corn, kale, broccoli, or mushrooms has the same amount of protein as a glass of milk.

HOW MUCH CALCIUM DOES YOUR CHILD NEED?

A healthy daily diet for the average growing child should include approximately 800 milligrams of calcium at age two, increasing to 1,200 milligrams of calcium at age twelve. Twelve hundred milligrams of calcium is the amount present in 4 cups of milk *or* 2½ cups of yogurt. Calcium is also available in small amounts from plant foods such as watercress, broccoli, and spinach. However, the body does not absorb the calcium in plant foods as easily as the calcium in dairy products, which is why milk products are the ideal source of calcium for your children. Calcium-fortified orange juice is a convenient way of getting calcium, but since this drink doesn't contain protein it should not be a substitute for milk.

Vegetarian and non-vegetarian children who eat and like fish and shellfish can also get calcium from salmon and sardines canned with the bones (the bones supply the calcium), and from clams and oysters. These choices may not be suitable for younger children, of course.

WHAT ABOUT THE NUTRITIONAL VALUE OF LOWER-FAT DAIRY PRODUCTS?

All milk products, whether nonfat or whole, provide the same amounts of protein and calcium. Some states have regulations allowing or insisting on the fortification of low-fat and nonfat milk; in those states, low-fat and nonfat milk is fortified with dry nonfat milk, resulting in those milks having additional protein and calcium.

WHAT ABOUT CHEESE?

Cheese—whether domestic or imported, Cheddar, Swiss, feta, blue, Fontina, mozzarella, Brie, goat, or American—is a very high-fat food: between 50 percent and 80 percent of the calories are from fat. Even when you purchase bulk cheese marked "lower fat," or packaged cheese labeled "⅓ the fat," you are bringing home, on an average, a food deriving 30 to 50 percent of its calories from fat, most of it saturated.

Instead of cheese, try topping foods like casseroles, vegetable stews, and pastas with some of the toppings on page 127. The task now is to lower the amount of cheese your child substitutes for meat and to gradually introduce main-dish foods that are delicious and filling without cheese. Use high-fat cheeses sparingly—as condiments for grains and beans, as sprinklings on pasta and soups, and mixed with bread crumbs (page 160). And, once in a while, enjoy a big, fat, cheese sandwich! Remember, we are *lowering* the fat in your child's diet, not eliminating it. When cheese is the only answer, serve it. When there are other choices, eliminate it.

FILLING YOUR VEGETARIAN TEENAGER'S STOMACH

Throughout this book my emphasis has been on lowering the saturated fat and hydrogenated oils you feed your children without drastically changing the look and the "feel" of their food. In my family this has led (over time) to considerably more meatless meals. And if one or two of your children have proclaimed themselves vegetarians, you probably will find it mandatory to prepare less meat and poultry just to keep your kitchen from turning into a restaurant!

Many recipes for main courses need only minor adjustments to become vegetarian dishes; conversely, vegetarian dishes need only a side dish of a chicken breast or a chop to satisfy those who want meat. Cooking for your vegetarian child can be a matter of adding more vegetables, a broader variety of grains, more filling soups, more meatless chilies, and more meatless sandwiches. Scouting your market for cans of no-added-fat foods—spaghetti sauces, beans, chilies, spreads and dips, soups—can make meals simpler for you to prepare and in some cases, more appealing to your children.

The most significant aspect of feeding a vegetarian child is providing foods that contribute bulk and calories as well as nutrients. Following are a few suggestions for dishes and foods that will provide calories for snacks or for meals without relying on high-saturated-fat dairy products. Depending on the particular likes and dislikes of your children, your list may look very different. Keep reminding yourself that cooking is constant invention, and shopping for a broader range of foods encourages more creative results.

- Grain and bean casseroles with new toppings (page 127)
- An assortment of no-added-fat pitas, corn tortillas, flour tortillas, and pizza crusts for instant snacking and simple suppers

- Foods that will make low-fat nachos such as sauces, nonfat cheese, vegetables, and bagel slices ready to go in the freezer
- Favorite breads always on hand in the freezer in portion-sized pieces or slices; the bread can be toasted quickly or used as the base for an instant pizza
- Nonfat sauces—salsa, marinara sauce, spaghetti sauce, dips
- Baked potato skins to fill quickly with a selection of canned foods or favorite leftovers
- Fresh fruit
- Fresh vegetables
- Nonfat frozen treats

Young children will eat what you stock; they are captives. Some younger children won't or don't eat everything and my guess is that you think they were born that way. Once in a great while that is true for a very young child, especially a child who has allergies to certain foods that make him or her feel ill. My own idea is that most healthy children with fussy food habits developed their attitudes because of parental (or caretaker) dislikes toward certain foods: making a face when feeding a toddler squash; tasting a food and expressing disdain to your child, verbally or facially; or simply not feeding certain food to your child at all. Another way to encourage food dislikes is to feed your child practically the same foods every day, which many parents do for various reasons. These subtle expressions of parental likes and dislikes create the attitudes and habits of our children. Noticing what your predilections are toward food will assist you to remember that your children, even very young ones, learn most of what they know from you.

Older children have many eating choices: They can bring food home, eat out, or eat at a friend's house. They are also more verbally equipped to turn you down and invalidate your ideas; older children need more time to make the decision to choose lower-fat food for themselves but will probably not complain if you feed it to them—that way they are not *adopting* the idea, only complying. In a more benevolent state, and if their peers are also somewhat accepting, your adolescent and teenage children will support the plan to lower fat and join with you to generate lists of suggestions. Capitalize on their interest: check your pantry with your teenager for food combinations that will result in snacks and meals they will like. Develop shopping lists together. If you have the time, put your heads together to turn out some lower-fat alternatives to their favorite meals. If your vegetarian teenager is talking "health" and lower-fat with you the probability is "health" is "in" in her or his group. If that is true, they don't want to be the only kid on the block with ice cream and Cheddar cheese to come home to. Why shouldn't your child have a wide range of foods available at home? If he or she doesn't, it may only be because you aren't aware of the possibilities. Taking the stand to eat a vegetarian diet is a courageous adventure for a child in a non-vegetarian household; your partnership will echo the admiration and respect you show your child's other endeavors.

chapter 18

eating in and eating out: restaurants, birthday parties, and celebrations with friends

Entertaining and dining out present new and different considerations when you want to feed your family *right*. This chapter is designed to assist you on those special occasions, as well as suggest healthy alternatives on just about every restaurant menu. Keep in mind that the Lower-Fat Kids Plan stresses flexibility and wisdom, not rigidity. You *can* make your children's eating adventures at any festive occasion food for fond recollections, rather than an unintentional punishment because of an overly restrictive nutritional regimen.

While most restaurant, delicatessen, and take-out food is not deliberately camouflaged, it does not pretend or even attempt to be low in fat. The menu food offered frequently contains more fat, the fats we have all become accustomed to, and the amounts cooks are accustomed to adding. What kinds of fat? All kinds, especially the fats that are *bad* for your child: the saturated fat of butter, whole milk, cheese, cream, and lard, and the trans fatty acids of hydrogenated oils. But, instead of butter in more upscale or health conscious shops and restaurants, many of these foods are cooked and dressed with the "healthy" fats, the largely monounsaturated oils—olive, canola, walnut, almond. Consuming these fats in unnecessarily large amounts is gradually becoming the new fat habit. There is no evil intent in these preparations, no motive other than a basically good-natured one to produce the best culinary wins along with the luscious, and familiar, taste of fat, and to ensure returning customers: you.

And you don't actually see the fat. That is a big win for you when your objective is peace and the comfort of not cooking. You are in a restaurant or in a take-out shop for convenience and for a respite from the chores of shopping and cooking, not to think about fat. You want to loll in the luxury of a meal prepared for you, one selected by you based on its appeal, not its health benefits.

In that context—the expectation of comfort or a special indulgence— you ignore fat easily as you make your selection. As a matter of fact, fat isn't even a consideration. At this moment, you are determined to celebrate your emancipation from the kitchen and to revel in your momentary freedom, and you are determined not to look for problems or obstacles. So mayonnaise in tuna salad becomes invisible; cooking oils disappear in soups, stews, sautéed onions, and eggplant; butter disappears in mushroom sauces and in mashed potatoes; fats don't exist in the crusts and cakes of desserts; partially hydrogenated oils are eradicated from your short-term memory, even though they glisten on French fries and donuts; smoked fish is gobbled up with cream cheese as "healthy." And because we have been propagandized to think of *all* chicken as "low-fat," we purchase brown, crunchy-skinned barbecued chickens without a thought other than pleasure.

INDULGENCE: ITS RIGHTFUL PLACE

Do you even want to change these luxurious moments? Probably not. Who has the inclination to create revolutions at moments like these, to undo the pleasure of restaurant occasions, to ruin the indulgence of being freed from a day of shopping, cooking, and thinking about food? It is time to relax, to snuggle into the opulence of being cooked for. High-fat, good-tasting, filling convenience food, whether eaten in a neighborhood restaurant or on vacation or carried from a take-out shop, helps us to survive as parents. Hardly anything—certainly not the "right" food—is worth sacrificing warm, easy, generous, sane, family time—sometimes.*

*American families are eating more meals in restaurants (all kinds) and eating more take-out or delivered food than ever before. For two-worker families, time is scarce, scarcer than money sometimes. Eating out has become a necessary habit. If your family eats food in restaurants or from take-out places more than twice a week, however, perhaps you need to consider limiting your "treat" nights.

chapter 19

What *has* changed significantly is your awareness of high-fat foods. You can't pretend any more. You will know what you are carrying when you bring home barbecued chickens, Big Macs, and potato salad; corned beef, salami, French fries, chili, and chicken chow mein; lasagna, pizza, and frittatas; barbecued ribs and enchiladas. And you will know all about the fat in the foods your children are eating in hamburger places, delis, pizza palaces, Italian restaurants, Mexican cantinas, and the perfectly elegant restaurants you introduce them to. Now you have the ability, the skills, *and* the knowledge to balance eating-out overindulgences with an intelligently thought-out household regimen. You have learned to make substitutions at home for the high-fat foods you used to stock and cook. You know how to read labels, guaranteeing you won't be duped by package advertising and ambiguous amounts of fat. You are an informed parent, an informed shopper, and an informed cook.

If you are, however, determined to not abandon your lower-fat crusade; if you feel confident that you can lower the fat in your take-out choices or at restaurants so that it will not be viewed as a deprivation for the family; and if you feel up to handling the opposition you may get from your children or your partner, consider some of the survival hints on the next few pages. But first ask yourself: Are the substitutions significant payback for the sacrifices? If the answer is yes, keep on your warrior hat. Restaurants are used to special requests; they want you and your children to be satisfied; they want you to come back again. You are, after all, what keeps them in business. Let's look at what's served at some popular types of restaurants families enjoy.

"HEALTH" FOOD RESTAURANTS

Many people don't realize that some of the so-called "health" food served at "health food" restaurants or take-out counters is very high in calories and in saturated fat (cheese, whole-milk yogurt drinks, mayonnaise, high-butterfat cookies). Vegetable salads may be overdosed with mayonnaise; vegetable or tofu-loaf offerings are often prepared with considerable fat; yogurt drinks are typically prepared with high-fat or low-fat yogurt and milk; and cookies, though made with whole-wheat flour, may have so much oil or butter that they are as much as 70 percent fat. Some snacks and side orders, of course, are lower in fat, such as dried fruits, skim milk and fruit drinks, nonfat yogurt, lightly dressed vegetable salads, and fruit salads.

Again, there is no deliberate camouflage here—just an honest desire to provide good-tasting vegetarian food. Unfortunately, the amount of fat in the food has not always been taken into consideration by these purveyors of "health." When analyzed, an avocado, cheese, mayonnaise, tomato, and lettuce sandwich on sesame oil bread from a San Francisco "health" bar turned out to derive almost 80 percent of its calories from fat—almost 30 percent more than a Big Mac! Without the cheese and the mayonnaise it would be a different sandwich, of course, but by themselves avocado, lettuce, and tomato, with fresh lemon juice on the bread, would result in a good-tasting sandwich without any added saturated fat. You could modify the sandwich in yet another way. Order it without mayonnaise, with one third of the cheese, with half of the avocado, and with the tomato, lettuce, and a very low-fat salad dressing. When making substitutions, consider keeping some of the high-fat ingredients or replacing them with additional vegetables. Keep reminding yourself that just a little of a high-fat ingredient can provide a lot of flavor to your children's sandwiches.

FAST-FOOD GIANTS: DELIBERATE CAMOUFLAGE

Fast-food chains are industrial giants that make billions of dollars of profit out of your need to be fed inexpensively with relatively good-tasting quick food. The fat content of these foods goes down whenever the giant is running scared, but mostly these foods are high in fat, satisfying consumers' urge for taste and familiarity.

During the past ten years, consumer groups have pressured fast-food franchises to lower the fat in hamburger meat; to take the lard and hydrogenated oils out of French fries and salad dressings; and to declare themselves on the lower-fat march. They have made that declaration, but if you look closely you will see the deceptions.

The present intent of these consortiums is not to serve lower-fat food because it is healthy, but because—for now at least—the perception of the public is that lower-fat food is essential. Today "healthy" food means more profit. The public is clamoring for "health." And the public needs to know that the fat content of food has been reduced—or at least they need to *think* it has. It does not matter to the general public exactly how much fat is eliminated, just that it seems as though some has.

But the public also wants tastes that are familiar. If a deluxe lower-fat hamburger doesn't taste as good, and doesn't fill your children's tummies as well as the original, it won't sell and the financial loss can be catastrophic to the company. With public attention focused on lowering the fat in hamburger meat and eating the new health fad, chicken, as an alternative to beef, some *deliberate* addition of fat by the food manufacturers is necessary for customer satisfaction. The fast-food people know how to add fat when you are not looking.

- One fast-food giant added whole milk to what used to be a perfectly healthy nonfat shake and instantly transformed it into a high-saturated-fat one. Perhaps the new shake adds just the right amount of fat calories to make up for the ones taken out of the hamburger!
- One major chicken franchise added enough mayonnaise to its advertised "healthy" chicken salad sandwich so that, in terms of fat calories, the mayonnaise raised the fat content of the benign chicken sandwich to rival that of two large portions of French fries.
- Another franchise offers chicken to appease the health-conscious, but it's roasted with the skin and fat and served with high-fat gravy and buttered vegetables. The same franchise offers a chicken sandwich with bacon, cheese, and mayonnaise!

Given the foods generally available, eating regularly at fast-food stops can be treacherous forays for your children's health (though maybe essential as occasional treats or outings). These restaurants, as you know, remain convenient and inexpensive (relatively). Like Kleenex, they are often house-hold habits. If they are your family's habits, you probably will want to educate your children about the fat added to a seemingly healthy sandwich. The quickest and simplest way to minimize high-fat fast food meals is to eat them less frequently. Look around you; there are probably other restaurants to try—places with more meatless, less fried, and healthier choices. When your family does eat traditional fast food, here are some ways to make it lower in fat:

- Skip the fried chicken nuggets, fried chicken-breast sandwiches, and fried-fish sandwiches. You are better off with a plain hamburger. If grilled chicken or fish is offered order it instead, but remind your children and yourself to look at what else is on your sandwich, such as mayonnaise or bacon, and perhaps delete these additions.

- Skip the cheese and bacon on hamburgers or share the bacon and avocado from one hamburger with another person. Consider ordering your hamburger with only one high-fat addition instead of three.
- Ask for unbuttered or oiled buns without mayonnaise, or "secret" sauces. Substitute fresh lemon or a low-fat salad dressing.
- Share orders of French fries.
- Order an extra salad and stuff your sandwiches with the vegetables to replace deleted or reduced high-fat ingredients.
- More and more fast-food restaurants are offering salad bars with lower-fat dressings and true lower-fat sandwiches and platters. Find them and eat there!

SANDWICH SHOPS

It's so natural to order a sandwich when you go out for lunch. They are easy, quick, and familiar take-out meals. Sandwiches of some sort are available in practically every restaurant, even upscale ones, as "bruschetta," "croutons," or "open-faced," and sandwiches or half sandwiches accompanied with salads or soups are found on almost every lunch menu. Are familiar sandwiches—a BLT, turkey with Russian dressing and coleslaw, pastrami on rye, egg salad and bacon, or smoked salmon or lox and cream cheese—your family's high-fat habits? Below are some guidelines for reformulating sandwiches, reinventing the choices that have become family habits.

MAYONNAISE: Mayonnaise, the most common high-fat spread, is automatically put on the bread of most restaurant sandwiches, and is a major ingredient in tuna salad, chicken salad, vegetable salad, and turkey salad. Mayonnaise is also a staple ingredient in pasta salad, potato salad, coleslaw, and various other side dishes served with sandwiches, side dishes your children have come to expect and love. It is also occasionally a sauce for green salad.* Ask for sandwiches without mayonnaise on the bread. If it seems too radical to eliminate completely, ask for it on the side and teach your child to use it sparingly. Aioli, or garlic mayonnaise, is served frequently now as the sauce of

---

*Green salads can be the best and the worst. Dressed lightly with only a little house dressing or dressed with a mix of the house dressing and extra lemon or vinegar, they can be perfect. Covered with large amounts of high-fat dressings and fried croutons, salads are no better than hamburgers.

chapter 19

choice, especially on grilled fish, chicken, and vegetable sandwiches. Reserve it as an occasional treat, not a habit, or ask for it on the side and choose the amount *you* want. To avoid conspicuous torture of your child and that gloomy "you ruined my lunch" look, keep some of the high-fat side dishes for now. Teaching one modification at a time is a substantial shift for most children. Congratulate them. They are warriors. This may be hard for them.

BACON: Bacon is frequently added to cheeseburgers, egg salad sandwiches, and grilled cheese sandwiches, one of the sandwiches my children coveted. Even crisply cooked bacon adds unnecessary saturated fat to the above sandwiches, which are already high-saturated-fat foods. Remember that each high-saturated-fat ingredient you eliminate means a healthier sandwich for your child.

That said, you may be surprised and delighted to find out that bacon by itself is a better choice than some other high-fat foods. A three-strip bacon sandwich with lettuce, tomato, and maybe cucumber, without mayonnaise or butter (try some lemon juice squeezed directly on the bread), can be a much lower-fat choice than a hamburger, an egg salad sandwich, a small pizza with cheese, or, in most instances, a pasta salad. This is not a bacon endorsement, but rather information to assist you with your children's choices.

AVOCADO: Categorized as a fruit, eaten as a vegetable, loved as a sandwich food, avocado has been elevated into a "health" food most children adore. But avocados, depending on the variety, can derive 75 percent of their calories from fat. True, the fat is a largely unsaturated vegetable fat, but eaten as a daily ingredient on sandwiches, sliced on the side (with mayonnaise), or as guacamole with high-fat tortilla chips, avocado becomes a not-good-for-your child addition. Eaten in moderation, and especially with lots of other vegetables, avocado can be a highly acceptable treat. If you order avocado on sandwiches, for example, specify that you want less or no cheese, butter, or mayonnaise and request lots of other vegetables, such as tomato, lettuce, cucumber, sprouts, or carrot. Your child will still get to eat avocado but without the saturated fat in the cheese and mayonnaise.

CHEESE: Too bad cheeseburgers are so delicious. Resist them if you can. To ease into cheeseless hamburgers or vegetarian burgers, start with ordering half the amount of cheese. If your child must order a grilled cheese sandwich, a little extra ingenuity is necessary. Grilled cheese sandwiches are usually cooked in some kind of unknown grease on a kitchen grill, usually with a very high-fat cheese such as Cheddar. Ask for a baked grilled cheese sandwich, with half the regular amount of cheese and with tomatoes and other vegetables added for a far healthier version of the old familiar sandwich.

HAM: The combination of ham and cheese, like that of hamburger and bacon or cheese, makes a sandwich high in saturated fat, exactly what you don't want to teach your children to eat. Teach your older children to order a thin slice or two of ham on a vegetable sandwich instead. They can much more easily regulate the amount of ham than the cheese, which may be cut in thick slabs rather than slices. As your older children begin to learn that some deletions are very easy to accomplish, they will begin to feel empowered to make more inventive adjustments on their own.

MEATBALLS: Order a *sauce* sandwich rather than a meatball sandwich, with shredded lettuce and other vegetables. One meatball, on the side, if absolutely necessary, can be divided between two children. What I noticed when my children and I were up against some hard decisions in fat-friendly eating places, was that leaving choices and invention up to them frequently resulted in selections I would never have thought of, for instance the sauce sandwich. The flavor remains, the bread is dripping with sauce, the missing meat is hardly noticeable, and the sandwich becomes a delicious and tasty substitution.

OTHER LOWER-FAT SANDWICH SUGGESTIONS

- Ask for sandwiches with less meat or poultry and more vegetables (lettuce, tomatoes, sprouts, cucumber).
- Order lower-fat meats such as skinless turkey or chicken breast, or plain roast beef. Lean roast beef has one-half the fat of chicken salad, pastrami, or corned beef, and considerably less fat than salami, chopped liver, or egg salad.
- Most sandwiches are overstuffed; if the restaurant is sufficiently informal you can order one sandwich, extra bread, and make your own second sandwich to share.

chapter 19

A REFLECTION ON TEACHING YOUR CHILDREN ABOUT CHOICE AND INVENTION

Remember that a restaurant or coffee shop or take-out counter will custom-make your sandwich or other food; your request is one of the many special orders they want to fill. One of the ways children learn is from example. As your children begin to order for themselves, both when they are with you and when they are out with other families or friends, they will recall your manner—the ease with which you asked for special food and got it. They will recollect the willingness of the waitpeople to help out. With these reminders, they may be able to withstand peer mockery or they may succumb for the moment rather than deal with their friends' teasing. This is not an unusual stance. Prepare yourself for it and be sympathetic to your children at these times. You are not, at this time, who your child wants or needs to please. Belonging is their only goal. What you can do is continue your behavior in restaurants when you are with your children. Kids want to know the ins and outs of survival. They will respect your guidance and gradually change their behavior as they observe and experience your wisdom in other ways, even children who are somewhat recalcitrant at first. What I noticed as my children were growing up was that one of the ways their self-esteem thrived was through their *own* initiative of specific and concrete solutions to problems. Personal invention became fun and challenging for them. Like us, children love to win.

WHEN YOU TAKE YOUR CHILDREN TO RESTAURANTS

I am amazed at how many children I see eating in restaurants now— pizza and pasta restaurants; Asian restaurants; sit-down, table service franchises; Mexican cantinas; and upscale restaurants offering delectables such as boeuf bourguignon and crab soufflé. What's happened? Could it be that baby-sitters are more expensive than restaurants; that dinner time for many families is more compatible, less interrupted out than in? Or maybe it's the issue of time once again—less time to cook or why use time *to* cook. Whichever or how many reasons there are, children of all ages are eating in restaurants more than ever before.

What can you do about lowering fat in these circumstances? My restaurant choice is usually based on how much readily available lower-fat food is on the menu. At other moments I have been known to opt for the divine. But this is your call: the future health of your children and your family hinges not on what they eat tonight for dinner (in a restaurant or at home) but rather on what you put in place as a model for their diet—and their life.

PIZZA AND PASTA RESTAURANTS

Sometimes there is so much cheese on (and now *in*) our American version of pizza that dinner can jump to 85 percent of calories from fat. But with all the variations possible, pizza can be a lower-fat choice to me. This is one dining-out situation where substitutions seem too simple not to ask for. To most pizza chefs such requests are a creative challenge rather than the old solution: saturate the pizza with another can of sauce. Consider these simple requests: asking for one third the cheese; asking for no cheese with extra vegetables *instead* of cheese; or ordering a half-and-half pizza so everyone gets a piece or two of the familiar.

Eating pasta in restaurants is one of the times it is probably best to leave the dishes as they are, unless you know that whoever is in the kitchen produces winner spaghetti with lower fat. Of course eating in a restaurant with an accomplished pasta chef managing your order opens more opportunity for delicious modifications, but that is not where you frequently eat with your children. Choosing baked pasta dishes such as lasagna and baked ziti is treacherous because so much cheese and fat is baked in with the sauce. However, some pasta restaurants will feature a "low-fat" or "heart-healthy" choice based on a variation of tomato sauce. And with your newly acquired skills at determining where fat is and what questions to ask you can make more knowledgeable choices.

ASIAN RESTAURANTS

Steamed whole fish, fish salads in vinegary sauces, raw and marinated fish, clear soups with lotus blossoms! These were Bob's and my occasional choices. But our children's? Never! It was the curries, the stir-fries, the tiny barbecued ribs, the chicken with almonds, the mu-shu pork, and the vegetable tempura that tempted them. Now that they are older their repertoire includes more of the exotic but not when they were younger. Our children tended to eat plainer, simpler foods when they were small, as most children typically

chapter 19

do. But by the time they were teenagers their interests began to expand to include spicier and unusual food.

Many Asian foods, along with delicious tastes, have lots of added fat. It is found in the sauces, the soups, the curries, and of course the sautéed and fried foods. It is unfortunate, given that these offerings taste so good and families can eat them relatively inexpensively. The best you can do without spoiling the dining adventure of eating Asian food may be to order a steamed vegetable dish or two to accompany the delectable higher-fat choices. Avoiding deep fried foods and soups and sauces using large amounts of coconut milk are ways to keep saturated fat and trans fatty acids lower. Traditional Japanese food, with the exception of tempura, uses the least fat: delicious beef or fish soups with see-through noodles; grilled fish or beef or chicken with a never-ending supply of rice; steamy bowls of soup with vegetables and thick "udon" and "soba," the Japanese versions of pasta; and of course sushi and sashimi. This is not food all children like, but based on the numbers and the wide variety of ages I see at my favorite Japanese restaurant, many do.

MEXICAN RESTAURANTS

Lately my husband and I find ourselves choosing a local cantina for a casual and quick dinner. Now that our children are grown and living away from home, we belong to one group of patrons, the other being families with children of all ages, lots of children making happy noises. Mexican restaurants have something for every child; from a simple plate of rice to burritos, tostados, grilled meat or chicken, taco plates, and tortas (sandwiches). What's particularly appealing to me is that I can delete or add ingredients to burritos, tostada salads, taco plates, and tortas. With beans made without fat, grilled meat, sautéed vegetables, and piles of fresh lettuce and cabbage, so many menu choices are actually healthy choices. If you are going to limit your own fat on this outing and suggest limiting the fat in your children's orders, it is easy to ask for burritos without cheese (or meat), not as easy to modify the nachos, and only if you are a magician will you be able to limit the chips that come with the salsa. Perhaps your family can share an order of nachos? Or a smaller order of guacamole with steamed corn tortillas—not fried? Or one burrito *with* cheese but cut into thirds or fourths and shared along with a cheeseless burrito?

As time passes you will see how differently your children begin to emulate your ordering in restaurants or ask you to order it the "right" way. Not perhaps in all instances, but in many—enough to begin to make a difference in their future health. Children who understand the wisdom of lowering fat will adopt a lower-fat orientation for the rest of their lives. Their choices will be determined by will, by mood, by hunger, by education, by temptation, by peer advocacy, and by availability—at home and in restaurants. They will not always choose lower-fat but they will always know they have a choice.

HOLIDAYS AND COMPANY DINNERS

Inviting friends to dinner, lunch, celebrations, or holiday meals always implies, at least to me, not only sociability but an abundance of delicious food. Most of our friends and our children's friends would much rather we serve them scrumptious meals than ruin a feast with our lower-fat concerns. At the same time, these same friends are now beginning to eat fewer high-fat meals themselves. They now welcome, and ask for, steamed, baked, and grilled foods instead of teasing us about the absence of roast goose and braised lamb shanks, just so the food, they say, doesn't taste as though *they* were on a diet.

So, today, for company of all ages, including little children and big ones, we mainly serve simple grilled and baked and roasted foods, primarily fish or chicken and vegetables, usually accompanied with a grain cooked or embellished with fruits or nuts and spices and an abundance of fresh herbs. Most of our entertaining now also includes contributions from our guests. In all our busy lives we find that gracious and abundant entertaining is easier when we all participate. Friends bring gorgeous salads, vegetables with unusual vinaigrettes, soups, and casseroles of warmed fruit. Usually we can count on one fine baker to bring an outrageous dessert full of chocolate and butter for those who would miss this kind of treat. We have learned not to be afraid of experimenting with vegetables and it seems as though we are always inventing potato dishes (see recipes, page 106) and coming up with new ways of combining them with other foods. For large dinners or holiday meals, I always add an extra potato dish—potatoes fill in gaps for vegetarians. They also provide filling food for particularly hungry people, and satisfy children who are finicky vegetable eaters. These kinds of company meals are easy to prepare, without much last-minute preparation, and are especially simple when there are extra hands and hearts helping in the kitchen.

chapter 19

At our house, Thanksgiving dinner and other rich holiday meals were our major concerns when we began to reconsider how much fat was in the food we served. Pleasing the children and the adults at dinner, lowering the fat, and keeping the celebratory aspect of the food was a challenge. Like every family we have food traditions associated with Thanksgiving and I would never meddle with a beloved definition of Thanksgiving, or any holiday dinner. But our traditional turkey, I realized, did not have to be *stuffed* in order to roast. The stuffing could be prepared and baked in two baking dishes using defatted stock instead of butter and without the fat from the turkey dripping into it during cooking. Without major alterations we still were able to enjoy our familiar and longed-for stuffing of bread, millet, walnuts, dried apricots, mushrooms, and onions.

When the turkey is out of the oven and resting for the last forty-five minutes, the two baking dishes will fit comfortably in your oven along with a casserole or two. For simpler meals with many guests another recipe I like is Herb Baked Chicken (page 214) because it too must rest for awhile and will keep its heat for 30 minutes while another dish or two finishes in the oven.

For Thanksgiving dessert we always serve fruit tarts or pies, and traditionalists that we are, we usually mimic those desserts at other celebrations such as Christmas and July Fourth. For Passover we serve flour-free desserts in keeping with the tradition of the holiday, so along with baked fruit we add a sinful cake made with a pound of nuts but revised to use three yolks instead of ten! A delicious fat-free alternative at all our pie-for-dessert festivals is Thanksgiving Oranges (page 225).

Around holiday times all newspapers and magazines are full of dessert recipes, gift foods, casseroles, and salads; some are newly invented, some take-offs of familiar favorites; some are delicious, and some tragic failures. Some of these recipes are specifically geared to children's fantasies of holiday foods; some can be adjusted to conform to those desires. Look for what appeals to you, scan the recipe for excess fat, decide what you can eliminate and still keep the integrity of the idea, and perhaps try it out earlier than the day of the party. This year one day during the week before Christmas, in one newspaper alone I found the following four recipes adaptable to revision:

> 🍲 Cornbread and Apple Stuffed Onions: eliminating the ground pork and the butter from this recipe worked perfectly.

- Parsley Root and Pureed Potatoes: We eliminated the whole milk, cream and butter, and substituted nonfat milk and olive oil.
- Grated Carrot and Medjool Date Salad: Eliminating the Gorgonzola cheese and the ½ cup olive oil and substituting 1 teaspoon of oil per person and 1 teaspoon for the bowl, resulted in a lovely salad.
- Dried Fig and Apricot Stuffing: All this stuffing needed was the deletion of 2 tablespoons of butter and the high-fat chicken stock.

BIRTHDAY PARTIES

Birthday parties are sacred. When our children were small, our cardinal rule was never to change a *noticeable* thing—unless the children suggested it. As our children became more aware and involved in our diet goals, they did make some suggestions that both surprised us and delighted us. Our daughter Sarah suggested that we use chocolate syrup in the skim milk so the other children wouldn't notice the absence of creamy milk, and that we use cookie cutters for sandwiches so guests would be more interested in the shapes of the sandwiches than in the omission of salami and cheese. These two ideas became birthday party traditions, along with a few other simple changes I made over those years. These practically invisible alterations were initiated when my children began to celebrate their birthdays with friends. Our children were various ages when these celebrations began—the boys began late and ended earlier. The girls began celebrating sooner and still are! They never balked at this list of substitutions.

- I deleted yolks from the birthday cake.
- I deleted some sugar and yolks from the frosting if I made it from scratch, or deleted the frosting altogether and decorated the cake all over with real flowers. Served with ice cream the missing frosting was hardly noticed! (Now, with the nonfat frozen dessert choices available this is an even lower-fat treat.)
- Our children loved peanut butter sandwiches, jam sandwiches, or any sandwich with fresh vegetables such as sliced carrots, cucumber, and celery and my guess is your children do too. I spread the bread with mustard or with Our Nonfat "Mayonnaise" (page 161) to anchor the vegetables. A little Parmesan adds the taste of cheese with minimal fat. And of course the cookie cutters.

chapter 19

🍃 I served lots of air-popped popcorn.

🍃 I ordered pizza with considerably less cheese, the absence of which was never commented on except for conspiratorial nods from my son.

Today, there are many lower fat and nonfat sweet and savory foods to include at parties, many of which I'm sure you've discovered at your market. Some that I like are nonfat chocolate sauce for frozen desserts and to use as cake icing, Jelly Belly's jelly beans, nonfat pretzels, nonfat potato chips, nonfat cookies, nonfat sorbets, and nonfat frozen yogurts and "ice creams." But then again, birthdays are holy days and if Häagen-Dazs and Ben & Jerry's make them more special, why not?

Once I took my children to a birthday party where steamed rice squares decorated with candles were brought out as the birthday cake. The idea and good will of the mother who thought she would do the "right" thing for the "health" of it resulted in a calamity for our children, who, united in their indignation and disappointment, sulked. Sitting here now many years past this disaster I am reminded of those rice squares—rice, some milk, some flour, sugar, cinnamon—something like that. But more, as I sit here at my desk, I am reminded of the sweetness of that time of pink party dresses and ribbons and batmobiles crashing; those are my very tender memories; the rice squares, well, they have their place in my memory too, and especially the mom who baked them just for us.

lower-fat recipes from my kitchen

As you have learned as you read along with me, preparing lower-fat dishes for your family is simple using the deletion and substitution method. You have learned to scan the food section of your favorite newspapers and magazines and instantly recognize which fats can be deleted from seductive recipes. You know how to revisit the books of famous chefs and wisely delete from, and substitute, foods in their recipes. Elizabeth David, Julia Child, Alice Waters, Richard Olney, Marion Cunningham, Jacques Pepin, and James Beard can all be your friends. And you have the best skill of all: you can transform what have been traditionally high-fat dishes in your family—the ones you have been preparing for years—into delicious and substantial food that is considerably lower in fat.

Why, then, this recipe section? I thought to offer some recipes from my kitchen that have the fat already reduced and in several instances totally absent— as a convenient resource for you on a day when you don't want to think, just cook, or to suggest a combination of ingredients you hadn't considered. Some of the recipes are perfect for simple family meals; some are more appropriate for the times you have more leisure.

Several of the recipes in this section come from the collections of dear family and friends, and some are from the chefs with whom I have had the opportunity to apprentice at Chez Panisse restaurant, but most are recipes invented in my kitchen, often because necessity prompted creativity. All of these recipes have brought the pleasure of simple cooking to my friends and family.

Nutritional analyses have been deliberately omitted. The guiding principle of this book—reducing oil, butter, and other high-fat foods—enables you to cook without having to count fat grams or fat calories. You now have the ability to manage your family's fat consumption by your judicious selection from the vast marketplace, along with your newly acquired knowledge of where fat is concealed.

All the recipes in this book call for kosher salt, sold in big red, white, and yellow boxes in your supermarket. Kosher salt is 99.9 percent pure in order to qualify for the kosher certification; this is in contrast to our common table salt, which frequently has additives. Adding salt is usually done by eye and taste and without an accurate measure: I add kosher salt from a bowl with my fingers or pour from the box into my hand; this kind of measuring is easier to recall and reduces over-salting. Regular salt is used for all baking.

All the recipes have been written to use as little oil as possible. Adding oil when you wish—for taste, for richness, or for extra calories—is a discretionary choice.

chapter 20

BASICS
Nonfat Chicken Stock
Nonfat Vegetable Stock
Toasted Bread Crumbs
Yogurt Cheese
Our Nonfat "Mayonnaise"
Fresh Tomato Salsa
Vinaigrette Dressing
Creamy Nonfat Salad Dressing
Green Herb Sauce

PASTAS
Pasta Casserole
Pasta and Vegetables
Spaghetti with Fresh Tomato Sauce
John's Goes-with-Everything Pasta Sauce
Pasta with Red and Yellow Peppers
Pasta with Basil Sauce
Pasta with Bread Crumbs, Garlic, and Parsley
Pasta with Roasted Potatoes, Shallots, and Garlic

SOUPS
Anytime Turkey Soup
Carrot Soup
Lentil Soup with Radishes and Orange
Green Pea Soup with Cloves
Bread Soup
Fresh Corn Soup
White Bean and Broccoli Soup with Basil
Tomato Soup with Zucchini
Potato Soup with Watercress

LIGHT DISHES

Sarah's Corn Salad
Shaved Vegetable Salad
Garlic Toasts with Tomatoes and Variations
Artichokes
Flat Salads with Flowers
Romano Bean Ragout
Stewed Sweet Peppers
Cucumber and Scallion Sauce
Baked Rice Casserole
Cottage Cheese Pancakes
Corn Cakes
Pizza with Sautéed Spinach and Variations

MAIN COURSES

Lamb Grilled on Skewers
Roasted Chicken Without the Skin
Grilled Spice-Rubbed Beef, Mushrooms, and Eggplant
Baked Vegetables in Packages
Baked Chicken Breasts
Burritos
Cornmeal "Pizza" with Salad
Potato Stew with Garlic-Almond Sauce
Chili
Potato and Shrimp Paella

DESSERTS

Biscotti with Nuts

Sliced Oranges with Cinnamon

Gorp Candies

Christmas Walnuts

My Mother's Date and Nut Bread

Yogurt Cheese with Honey

Dried Calmyra Figs with Walnuts and Tangerines

Baked Pineapple with Brown Sugar

Winter Fruit Salad

Lizzy's Cocoa Meringue Cookies

Summer Compote of Nectarines and Peaches

Dried-Fruit Sauce

Bread Pudding from Bette's Diner

Jam Soufflés

BASICS

Nonfat Chicken Stock

Dispelling a myth—especially a much loved one—is always difficult. But chicken soup as it is usually prepared, served, and esteemed has too much fat. Unskimmed homemade chicken soup is often between 50 and 70 percent fat, depending on the type of chicken used to cook the soup and the ratio of water to chicken. I keep canned nonfat chicken broth as a staple in my kitchen, but it is much more expensive than homemade stock, which is easy to make. You can make stock from chicken pieces, such as backs and necks, reserved when cooking cut-up chicken for other dishes. You can use wing tips, chicken feet, skin, and bones that your butcher will give you without charge. Store them in a heavy plastic bag in the freezer until you have enough to make this long-simmered stock on a weekend.

This recipe produces a salt-free stock. Cooking the stock with skin and fat adds to the flavor. After chilling, discard the congealed layer of fat and you will have a totally nonfat chicken stock.

Serve this chicken stock as a soup, or use it for cooking grains, adding to sauces, preparing vegetable soups, stewing or browning onions, and making matzo balls.

Makes 12 cups

5 pounds chicken parts or bones, including backs, necks, and skin

2 large carrots, peeled and cut into pieces

1 celery stalk, cut into pieces

1 yellow onion, cut into pieces

8 whole peppercorns

2 bay leaves

3 fresh parsley sprigs

Put all the ingredients into a large soup pot. Add cold water to cover and bring to a boil. Lower heat to a slow boil and cook for 30 minutes, occasionally skimming off the foam. Reduce heat to a simmer. Cover and, in 5 minutes, check to make sure that the water is barely bubbling. Cook for 4 hours. Let cool.

Strain the stock and pour it into a large container (or two). Cover and refrigerate overnight. Remove and discard the congealed fat. The more bones you have used, the more gelatinous the stock will be; if your stock is gelatinous, briefly reheat it for easy pouring into containers for storage.

nonfat chicken stock

Store in an airtight container in the refrigerator for up to 5 days. To keep longer, bring to a boil and store for another 5 days or freeze for up to 3 months. For instant convenience, freeze some stock in ice cube trays and store in small plastic bags.

Nonfat Vegetable Stock

Nonfat vegetable stock is available in cans but it is very expensive, especially when you consider it can be made almost for free; making it at home is a simple project and it cooks in an hour. You can add other vegetables from your bin, including vegetable trimmings. Don't use strong-tasting vegetables such as Brussels sprouts, turnips, collards, beets, or mustard greens. Onions, leeks, carrots, celery, and herbs are the staples for my vegetable stock. The proportions and ingredients in this recipe should be considered general guidelines.

Makes 6 cups

1 onion, chopped

3 leeks, including the green parts, carefully washed and sliced

1 celery stalk, sliced

2 carrots, peeled and sliced

1 fennel bulb with its fronds, chopped (optional)

8 cups chopped vegetables such as zucchini or other summer squash,
    green beans, lettuce, potatoes, mushroom stems, peas, spinach, tomatoes,
    green cabbage, parsnips

8 peppercorns

6 fresh parsley sprigs

1 tablespoon minced fresh oregano, or ¼ teaspoon dried oregano, crumbled

Put all the ingredients into a large soup pot. Add water to cover. Bring to a slow boil and cook for 15 minutes, occasionally skimming off the foam. Reduce heat to a simmer and cook, uncovered, for 45 minutes. Let cool. Strain, pressing the vegetables lightly with the back of a large spoon, to get as much liquid as possible without forcing vegetable pulp into the stock.

REDUCED STOCK OR BROTH: To thicken stock or canned broth, boil the stock or broth until it is reduced by half; for an even thicker liquid with a much stronger taste, reduce by half once again.

Toasted Bread Crumbs

Homemade bread crumbs taste best because they are usually fresher than commercial crumbs. Use bakery or homemade bread if you can. Use toasted bread crumbs to top grain casseroles and pasta dishes, and untoasted bread crumbs to add to soups or sauces as thickeners. This is a good way to use stale and leftover pieces of bread.

A convenient way to freeze bread for crumbs is to cut off the crusts, cut the bread into 1-inch cubes, and store until you have time to make the crumbs.

Preheat the oven to 450°F. Grind 4 cups defrosted or stale bread cubes in a food processor in batches. (Reserve some untoasted crumbs and freeze them in small plastic bags for future use.) Spread the crumbs on a baking sheet in a layer about ¼ inch thick. Bake for 8 to 10 minutes, or until golden brown, turning the crumbs with a spatula several times. Let cool and store in airtight containers in the refrigerator; crumbs will keep forever as long as they don't get wet. Makes about 2 cups.

NOTE: If you are preparing bread crumbs for a specific recipe, you can customize the grind; if preparing a batch of bread crumbs to store in your refrigerator, remove half when the crumbs are coarse and continue processing the remainder until fine.

Yogurt Cheese

This "cheese" made from nonfat yogurt takes hardly any time at all, and it is less sour-tasting than yogurt itself. This is a very quick-to-prepare nonfat food to keep as a staple for snacks and to use in dressings and sauces. It can be spread on crackers or toast with jam and mixed with raisins or peanut butter. Mixed with chopped vegetables and spices it makes a savory spread; it is wonderful eaten with a sprinkling of Parmesan and spread on bagels instead of the usual high-fat cream cheese. Here are some more suggestions for using yogurt cheese:
- Mix it with chopped dried fruit for spreading on apple or pear slices.
- Add a little sugar and cinnamon and use it as a filling for sweet low-yolk omelets.
- Mix it with bits of smoked salmon (or even bits of ham—remember, in moderation and as a condiment, anything can be included) and minced fresh parsley, and you have a splendid lower-fat Sunday-morning food.
- Mix it with rice wine vinegar, chopped fresh herbs, and nonfat chicken or vegetable stock or broth to make a creamy salad dressing that will keep for 3 or 4 days.
- Serve it for dessert (see Yogurt Cheese and Honey, page 229).

Place a large sieve over a bowl. Line the sieve with a double layer of cheesecloth or 2 sheets of paper towels. Spoon 4 cups (1 quart) plain nonfat yogurt into the sieve. Place the bowl and sieve in the refrigerator for at least 8 hours to let the whey drip from the yogurt.

Place a plate on the top of the sieve and invert the cheese onto it. (If you are planning to bring the whole round of cheese to the table for dessert, you may want to consider unmolding the cheese onto grape leaves or other greens or simply a pretty plate.) Gently lift off the paper or cheesecloth. Cover loosely with plastic wrap until serving time or store in an airtight container. Refrigerate for up to 5 days. Makes one 6- to 8-inch round or 2 cups.

Our Nonfat "Mayonnaise"

Our "mayonnaise" is not intended to represent the real thing. It is so named only to indicate the possibilities for its use as a spread for sandwiches, or to mix with tuna, chopped chicken, shrimp, and chopped vegetables. You can reduce the amount of mustard and flavor the "mayonnaise" with lemon, capers, herbs, horseradish, chives, chopped anchovies, grated onion, minced shallots—whatever addition occurs to you that will complement the food you are serving.

Beat 1½ cups plain nonfat yogurt with a fork or whisk to eliminate any lumps. Add ½ cup Dijon mustard or less, according to taste, and mix well. Store, covered, in the refrigerator for up to 1 week. Makes 2 cups.

Fresh Tomato Salsa

The children I know all love salsa, and even children who are not partial to whole tomatoes like tomatoes this way. Salsa is a wonderful way to feed children vegetables. Miraculously, it can become a dip, not only for chips, but for vegetable rounds made from cucumbers or summer squash.

Makes 2 cups

3 tomatoes, diced

1 onion, diced

½ jalapeño chili, seeded and minced

½ cup fresh cilantro leaves, minced

¼ cup fresh parsley leaves, minced

3 garlic cloves, minced

Fresh lime or lemon juice to taste

1 tablespoon red wine vinegar

Kosher salt to taste

Combine all the ingredients in a bowl and let sit for 30 minutes before serving. Cover and store leftover salsa for up to 2 days in the refrigerator.

VEGETABLE OR FRUIT SALSA: Replace the tomatoes with other vegetables, such as celery, jícama, green or red bell peppers, scallions, cucumbers, and zucchini. Or, substitute fresh fruits such as pineapple, apples, pears, melons, papayas, seedless oranges, and tangerines. Add sweet onions, scallions, parsley, or cucumbers to fruit salsas; even garlic can be combined with various fruits.

fresh tomato salsa

Vinaigrette Dressing

Besides its typical use on green salads and raw vegetable salads, this vinaigrette can be boiled until slightly reduced and used as a sauce for roasted, steamed, and sautéed vegetables. To make a thicker dressing without adding oil, whisk in prepared Dijon mustard instead of dry mustard or add pureed or grated onion or white radish. As with all dressings, once vegetables, fresh herbs, garlic, or stock or broth has been added, this dressing must be refrigerated.

Makes 1 cup

¾ cup reduced nonfat chicken stock (page 158) or canned nonfat
    chicken broth

1½ tablespoons fresh lemon juice

1½ tablespoons plain rice vinegar, red wine vinegar, or balsamic vinegar

1 teaspoon dry mustard mixed with a few drops of water to make a paste

Kosher salt and freshly ground pepper

2 teaspoons minced fresh herbs, or ½ teaspoon dried herbs, crumbled

1 to 2 tablespoons extra-virgin olive oil

Combine all the ingredients in a bowl or a container with a tight-fitting lid. Whisk or shake to blend. Taste and adjust the seasoning. Cover and refrigerate for up to 3 or 4 days.

Creamy Nonfat Salad Dressing

This is another very basic dressing that is particularly good with chopped or steamed vegetables. It can also be used as a sauce for fresh fruit if you substitute additional milk for the stock, and omit the mustard and the salt. It is especially good over ripe sweet strawberries; a sprinkle of Praline Topping (page 129) adds more sweetness for the children who crave it.

Makes 1 cup

½ cup plus 2 tablespoons baker's cheese or Yogurt Cheese (page 160)

2 to 3 tablespoons nonfat milk

1 to 2 tablespoons nonfat chicken or vegetable stock (page 158 or 159) or
    canned nonfat broth

1 tablespoon plain rice vinegar

1 teaspoon dry mustard mixed with 1 teaspoon of water to make a paste

1 teaspoon minced fresh herbs (optional)

Kosher salt and freshly ground pepper

Put the baker's cheese or yogurt cheese in a bowl. Beat in just enough nonfat milk to bring the cheese to the consistency of thick whipped cream. Add the remaining ingredients one at a time, whisking in each one until it is blended. Taste and adjust the seasoning. Store in an airtight container in the refrigerator for up to 1 week.

VARIATION: For a thinner dressing, add a little more milk, stock or broth, or vinegar.

Green Herb Sauce

This quick sauce adds something special to grilled fish or chicken, or grilled or steamed asparagus, or potatoes; it can be the sauce for a cucumber salad or a dip for cut-up vegetables. If you are making pizza this sauce can replace a tomato sauce by spreading it generously under an assortment of lightly steamed vegetables.

Makes about 1 cup

1 to 1½ cups firmly packed spinach or watercress leaves

⅔ cup reduced nonfat chicken or vegetable stock (page 158 or 159) or
   canned nonfat broth

1 tablespoon extra-virgin olive oil (optional)

Kosher salt and freshly ground pepper

Fresh lemon juice

Combine the spinach or watercress, stock or broth, and oil, if using, in a blender. Blend at high speed for about 1 minute, or until smooth. Add salt, pepper, and lemon juice to taste. The sauce can be stored in an airtight container in the refrigerator for up to 3 days.

PASTAS

HELPFUL HINTS FOR COOKING PASTA

• Instead of only thinking "oil" when you want to extend your sauce, consider reduced chicken or vegetable stock or broth and/or a little of the pasta cooking water. The water is starchy from the pasta and binds well with other ingredients.

• Do not rinse cooked pasta unless the recipe tells you to.

• If using oil, use extra-virgin olive oil for mixing with pasta. The fragrance and taste are usually exceptional and enhance the traditional supplements to pasta.

• Fresh pasta sold in gourmet shops frequently contains whole eggs, while most dried pasta does not. (In this book "dried pasta" refers to eggless pasta.)

• Allow one pound of dried pasta for 3 adult main-course servings. For meals with substantial vegetable or salad courses, 1 pound of pasta serves 4. Cooking times will vary, depending on the brand and the type of pasta. Always taste pasta to determine when it is done.

• When salting pasta cooking water, use kosher salt if possible; kosher salt is easy to pick up with your fingers and to measure with your eye; it is also additive free.

Pasta Casserole

Ask a chef for a casserole? Never. Ask instead for a baked pasta and mushroom dish, and a delicious recipe comes forth. Michael Sullivan, who suggested this recipe, doesn't cook professionally any longer. He and his wife Sylvie import superb French wines to the United States from France, and cook simple and delicious food like this for family and friends. As an accompanying vegetable a green such as broccoli, green chard, or spinach would be delicious, and of course, any green salad.

Makes 5 servings

2 yellow onions, cut into ⅛-inch-thick slices

1 pound fresh mushrooms, sliced

3 or 4 dried porcini mushrooms, rehydrated and sliced

2 garlic cloves, minced

2 tablespoons balsamic vinegar

2 cups reduced nonfat chicken or vegetable stock or broth (page 158 or 159)

I pound plus a handful of dried farfalle, fusilli, gemelli, or penne pasta

Kosher salt and freshly ground pepper

2 tablespoons olive oil

I teaspoon minced fresh thyme, or ¼ teaspoon dried thyme, crumbled

3 tablespoons minced fresh parsley

I cup toasted coarse bread crumbs (page 160)

¼ cup grated Parmesan cheese

Preheat the oven to 375°F. Add ¼ inch water to a wide deep pan large enough to hold the mushrooms and cooked pasta. Add the onions and cook over medium heat until the onions are translucent, adding more water if necessary, about 5 to 7 minutes. Add the fresh and rehydrated mushrooms, and continue cooking over medium-high heat. The mushrooms will produce some liquid in the pan. Continue cooking and stirring until the liquid has evaporated.

Add the garlic and continue to cook for 2 minutes. Add the balsamic vinegar and cook another 2 minutes. Very gradually stir in I cup of the stock or broth and cook for 3 to 5 minutes. Set aside.

In a large pot, cook the pasta in salted boiling water until al dente; drain well but do not rinse. Add the cooked pasta to the mushroom mixture and toss. Add the salt and pepper to taste, olive oil, thyme, and 2 tablespoons of the parsley and toss to mix. Taste and adjust the seasoning.

Spoon the mixture into an oiled 3-quart casserole dish. There should be approximately ½ inch of liquid in the bottom of the dish to keep the pasta moist during cooking; add more stock or broth to bring the liquid to this level, if needed. Top the casserole with the bread crumbs and bake uncovered until the crumbs are brown, 30 to 40 minutes.

Sprinkle the Parmesan over the bread crumbs and return the dish to the oven until the cheese is lightly browned, about 10 to 15 minutes.

Let the dish rest for 15 minutes before serving. Sprinkle with the remaining I tablespoon parsley and serve.

The basic sauce in this recipe can be flavored in many alternate ways with different spices, thickened by reducing it further, changed in color by adding roasted tomatoes or basil sauce (page 173). Adding shrimp or scallops to the pasta along with the vegetables produces yet another transformation.

Makes 4 servings

SAUCE

1 cup nonfat chicken or vegetable stock or broth (page 158 or 159) or
    canned nonfat broth, plus more if needed

Kosher salt

Freshly ground pepper

Red pepper flakes

2 garlic cloves, thinly sliced

2 tablespoons extra-virgin olive oil

1 teaspoon minced fresh oregano or thyme

1 teaspoon fresh lime juice

1 pound dried pasta

3 to 4 cups vegetables, such as spinach leaves, snow peas, chopped chard,
    celery sticks, sliced carrots, asparagus pieces, broccoli florets, thinly sliced
    cauliflower, summer squash slices

¼ cup grated Parmesan cheese

½ cup toasted bread crumbs (page 160)

In a small saucepan, cook the stock or broth over high heat to reduce it by half. Add the salt, pepper, red pepper flakes to taste, garlic, and oil and cook for 1 to 2 minutes over medium-high heat. Add the herbs and the lime juice. Set aside and keep warm.

    Add the pasta to a large pot of salted boiling water and cook until al dente. While pasta is cooking, briefly steam or sauté the vegetables you have chosen and season to taste.

Drain the pasta; do not rinse. Put the pasta in a warm bowl and toss with the vegetables and the warm sauce. Sprinkle with a combination of toasted bread crumbs and Parmesan. Serve at once.

VARIATIONS

• In place of red pepper flakes, use ground coriander, paprika, and minced garlic to taste.

• Cook scallops or shrimp (1 pound) quickly over medium-high heat until the scallops are opaque and the shrimp are pink, about 4 or 5 minutes. If combining shellfish with vegetables, choose celery sticks, snow peas, green peas, or asparagus, vegetables that will not overpower the gentle shellfish taste.

• Add roasted tomatoes to the pan after the stock has been reduced, lower heat to medium, and cook until the tomatoes begin to "melt," adding water, stock, or broth only as necessary. Pass the tomatoes and the liquid through a food mill or a sieve to make a smooth sauce.

Spaghetti with Fresh Tomato Sauce

When tomatoes are really delicious, buy a whole bagful and cook this pasta dish. No peeling, seeding, and barely any cooking. This dish is really nice with some spicy black olives added to the sauce at the last minute and lots of warm bread to sop up the tomato sauce.

Makes 4 servings

12 ripe tomatoes, chopped

¼ cup plain rice wine vinegar

½ cup nonfat chicken or vegetable stock (see pages 158 or 159) or

    canned nonfat broth, or more as needed

4 garlic cloves, minced

1 bay leaf

1 pound dried linguini or spaghetti

½ teaspoon dried oregano, crumbled

Kosher salt and freshly ground pepper

A handful of black olives, pitted (see note)

Minced fresh parsley for garnish

In a large sauté pan or skillet, combine the tomatoes, vinegar, stock or broth, garlic, and bay leaf. Bring to a boil and immediately turn down heat to a simmer. Cover and cook for 40 minutes, checking occasionally to make sure the liquid has not evaporated; as the tomatoes cook there should always be enough liquid so that the tomatoes are halfway submerged. Add additional stock or broth if necessary.

Cook the pasta in a large pot of salted boiling water until al dente. Meanwhile, uncover the tomatoes, raise the heat to medium-high, remove the bay leaf, and add the dried oregano. As it cooks, the tomato sauce will thicken; keep the sauce at the consistency you want by adding some stock or broth, if necessary. Add salt and pepper to the tomatoes and continue cooking. Drain the pasta but do not rinse. Just before serving, add the olives to the sauce, and toss with the pasta. Garnish with parsley and serve.

NOTE: If you can purchase oil-cured or garlic-and-herb black olives in bulk, the richness of their taste will reward your search.

John's Goes-with-Everything Pasta Sauce

Our son John snacks on cold pasta with sauce and cold sauce with anything. This sauce, which he first cooked when he was thirteen, is still a family favorite. Any vegetable can substitute for the vegetables suggested in the recipe. This sauce can be spread on toasted English muffins or toasted baguettes, used as a pizza sauce or a dip for tortilla chips, eaten as soup, or poured over grain dishes, or—as it was originally intended—served over hot pasta! This recipe makes 5 quarts of sauce—2 for the refrigerator and 3 for the freezer.

Makes 5 quarts

Two 16-ounce cans no-sugar-added tomato sauce

Six 28-ounce cans chopped peeled tomatoes

2 onions, diced

8 ounces mushrooms, thinly sliced (2 to 3 cups)

8 garlic cloves, minced

2 bay leaves

1½ teaspoons dried oregano, crumbled

3 green bell peppers, seeded, deribbed, and coarsely chopped

1 teaspoon minced jalapeño chili

1 teaspoon red pepper flakes

Kosher salt

½ cup red wine vinegar

In a very large non-aluminum stockpot, combine the tomato sauce, tomatoes and their juice, onions, mushrooms, garlic, bay leaves, and oregano. Cover, bring slowly to a boil, reduce the heat, and simmer for 30 minutes. Stir occasionally to keep the sauce from sticking. Add the green peppers, chili, red pepper flakes, and salt.

Simmer uncovered, for 30 minutes more, or until thick enough to coat a spoon. Add the vinegar and set aside. Remove and discard the bay leaf.

Just before serving, cover and warm over very low heat. If the sauce has been refrigerated, let it come to room temperature for 1 hour before reheating. Store in airtight containers in the refrigerator for up to 1 week or freeze.

Pasta with Red and Yellow Peppers

A 10-minute preparation, a 30-minute maceration, and a few minutes to cook the pasta. Everybody loves this dish, especially the cook.

Makes 4 servings

1 yellow and 1 red bell pepper, halved lengthwise, seeded, deribbed, and cut into very thin slices

2 garlic cloves, thinly sliced

4 tablespoons extra-virgin olive oil

¼ cup reduced nonfat chicken stock (page 158) or canned broth

Kosher salt and freshly ground pepper

1 pound dried linguini or spaghetti

2 tablespoons grated Romano cheese

2 tablespoons minced fresh herbs, such as oregano, thyme, tarragon, savory

In a medium bowl, combine the peppers, garlic, olive oil, and stock or broth and let sit for 30 minutes. The peppers will "cook" in the marinade and the flavors will meld. Add salt and pepper to taste.

Cook the pasta in a large pot of salted boiling water until al dente. Drain but do not rinse. Add the pasta to the peppers and gently toss. Top with the Romano and herbs before serving.

Pasta with Basil Sauce

This basil sauce can also be spread on grilled-vegetable or chicken-breast sandwiches, used as a sauce for grilled fish, or stirred into a risotto. Keeping some in the refrigerator or in very small freezer containers has been the perfect way for us—and our children—to have the taste of basil at hand.

Makes 4 servings

BASIL SAUCE

8 garlic cloves, chopped

4 fresh basil bunches, stemmed and coarsely chopped

¼ cup walnuts, finely chopped

1 tablespoon fresh bread crumbs

¾ cup reduced nonfat chicken or vegetable stock or broth (page 158 or 159)

2 tablespoons extra-virgin olive oil (optional)

Kosher salt and freshly ground pepper

2 tablespoons grated Parmesan cheese

1 pound dried pappardelle, linguini, or spaghetti

TO MAKE THE SAUCE: Puree the garlic in a blender or food processor. Add the basil and puree to a coarse paste. Add the nuts and bread crumbs and puree until blended, adding stock or broth as needed to make a smooth, thick sauce. Remove from the blender or processor. If using, add the oil. Season to taste with salt and pepper.

Cook the pasta in a large pot of salted boiling water until al dente. Drain well but do not rinse. Place the pasta in a large warmed bowl and toss with the sauce. Add a little of the pasta cooking water, if necessary. Garnish with Parmesan.

NOTE: This sauce can be thickened with additional bread crumbs.

Pasta with Bread Crumbs, Garlic, and Parsley

In 1970 we toured Portugal when our children were very young. At that time it was rare for little ones to be found eating in restaurants or cafes in the tiny coastal towns of Portugal; menus, the proprietors indicated, did not take into consideration the needs of children (nor, these proprietors suggested, did their American parents!). "We will take care of your children the way we take care of ours," they said, "and we will cook them rice mixed with bread crumbs, garlic, and parsley." We cook this dish at home both with pasta and with rice; each has its own uniqueness. When you prepare this dish, don't hesitate to use more oil; it will give it a luscious richness well worth the fat.

Makes 4 servings

1 cup toasted bread crumbs (page 160)

4 garlic cloves, finely sliced

½ cup fresh parsley leaves, minced

1 pound dried pasta

3 tablespoons extra-virgin olive oil, plus more if you like

Kosher salt and freshly ground pepper

In a bowl, mix the bread crumbs, garlic, and parsley. Set aside. Cook the pasta in a large pot of salted boiling water until al dente. Drain, reserving a little of the pasta water.

In a large warm bowl, toss the pasta with the 3 tablespoons oil, and 2 tablespoons of the pasta water. Add salt and pepper to taste. Add a little more oil or pasta water if you like. Add half the bread crumb mixture and mix well. Serve the pasta in bowls and sprinkle the remaining bread crumb mixture on top.

VARIATION: Substitute steamed medium-grain rice for the pasta.

Pasta with Roasted Potatoes, Shallots, and Garlic

Potatoes, shallots, and garlic is a favorite combination of mine but you can use other vegetables that hold their shape during roasting: turnips, sweet potatoes, parsnips, onions, carrots. If you double the amount of vegetables you will have enough for a wonderful soup the next night.

Makes 4 servings

4 potatoes, cut into bite-sized pieces or sliced

4 large shallots, sliced

8 garlic cloves, coarsely chopped

3 tablespoons extra-virgin olive oil

¼ teaspoon kosher salt

Freshly ground pepper

4 tablespoons nonfat chicken or vegetable stock (page 158 or159) or canned
   nonfat broth

4 small fresh thyme sprigs, or ½ teaspoon dried thyme, crumbled

1 pound dried linguini, spaghetti, or spaghettini

¼ cup fresh parsley leaves, minced

Preheat the oven to 500°F with a baking sheet on the middle shelf.

To cook the vegetables: In a medium bowl, toss the potatoes, shallots, garlic, 1 tablespoon of the oil, the salt, and pepper. Tear off four 15-inch-long sheets of aluminum foil. Place the potato mixture on the foil sheets in equal portions, keeping the vegetables in one layer and to one side of the foil. Add 1 tablespoon stock or broth and 1 sprig or pinch of thyme to each portion.

To make sealed packets, fold the foil in half, fold the edges of the foil over twice, and crimp tightly.

Place the sealed packets on the hot baking sheet on the middle shelf of the oven and turn the oven down to 350°F. Bake for 30 to 45 minutes, shaking the baking sheet halfway through to shift the contents. When removed from the foil the vegetables will be glazed and there will be sauce in each package to add to the pasta.

Cook the pasta in salted boiling water until al dente. Drain well, place in a warm bowl, and toss with the vegetables and the remaining 2 tablespoons of oil. Taste and adjust the seasoning. Garnish with parsley.

VARIATION: While the pasta is cooking, lower a colander filled with 3 cups chopped fresh spinach leaves into the pasta water. Cook for 2 minutes. Drain, pat dry with paper towels, roughly chop, salt and pepper to taste, and toss with the pasta and vegetables.

SOUPS

Anytime Turkey Soup

Use a leftover turkey carcass from Thanksgiving, or one purchased cheaply from a local hofbrau or delicatessen. Look the carcass over inside and out, and discard *any* fat or skin.

This is a delicious one-dish meal that gets better with each reheating, and it freezes well. A few drops of balsamic or red wine vinegar adds a piquant taste to each portion of soup. Toasted bread and a side dish of fresh green beans with vinaigrette make this a satisfying meal.

Makes 4 to 5 quarts

1 turkey carcass from a 15- to 20-pound turkey

2 cups pearled barley

½ cup short-grain white rice

6 large carrots, peeled and quartered

4 celery stalks, peeled and thinly sliced

1 onion

3 fresh parsley sprigs, 2 bay leaves, 3 fresh thyme sprigs or

  ½ teaspoon crumbled dried thyme, and 10 peppercorns, tied in a

  square of cheesecloth

Kosher salt and freshly ground pepper

Balsamic or red wine vinegar, or drained capers to taste (optional)

2 tablespoons minced fresh parsley

Put the carcass in a large soup pot, cutting up the carcass if necessary. Add water to generously cover and bring to a boil. Reduce heat to a high simmer and skim several times to remove the foam.

Add the barley, rice, carrots, celery, onion, and the herb bundle. Add salt and pepper and return to a boil, skimming 2 or 3 times more. Lower heat to a low simmer, cover, and cook for 4 hours.

Remove the carcass and reserve on a platter. Discard the herbs and spices. Remove and reserve the carrot and the onion. Let cool for 15 minutes. Puree the onion in a blender with 2 cups of the soup, including some barley and rice. Return the puree to the pot and mix with the soup. Taste for seasoning.

Strip the meat from the carcass, shred, and return it to the soup. Slice the carrot and add it to the soup. Add the vinegar or capers to each portion, if you like. Garnish with parsley and serve.

Carrot Soup

You can turn almost any vegetable into a wonderful soup. Even if your children tend to shun vegetables, they may discover they like vegetables as soup. Preparing a basic vegetable soup takes minutes. Cooking vegetables with a hint of a spice such as cloves, cumin, curry, coriander, cinnamon, or red pepper flakes adds an exotic taste. The vegetable variations suggested at the end of this recipe are not fixed, but rather ideas that may inspire you to invent other combinations.

Makes 6 servings

1¼ pounds (8 to 9) carrots, peeled and chopped

1 celery stalk, peeled and chopped

1 small onion, chopped

1 bay leaf

4 to 5 cups warm nonfat vegetable or chicken stock (page 158 or 159) or
   canned nonfat broth

Several gratings of nutmeg

Kosher salt and freshly ground pepper

Minced fresh mint for garnish

Combine the carrots, celery, onion, and bay leaf in a large saucepan and add water to just barely cover. Bring to a boil, reduce heat to a simmer, and cook until the vegetables are tender, about 6 to 8 minutes. Remove and discard the bay leaf. In a blender or food processor, puree the vegetables with a little of the cooking water and 1 cup of the stock or broth. Return the puree to the soup pot and add the remaining hot stock or broth. Add the nutmeg, salt, and pepper. Adjust the consistency of the soup with more stock or broth if you wish. Reheat the soup, but do not boil. Garnish with mint and serve.

VARIATIONS In place of the carrots, celery, and onion, use one of the following combinations of vegetables:
   • 2 cups green peas, 2 cups shredded lettuce, ½ cup sliced onion, 2 garlic cloves. Cook and proceed as in the main recipe.
   • 3 cups roasted butternut or Kabocha squash, 1 roasted onion, or 6 roasted shallots. Puree and proceed as in the main recipe. (To roast the vegetables, place halved squash and whole onion or shallots in a shallow baking dish

with ¼ inch water. Cover with aluminum foil and bake in a 375°F oven for 1 hour. Peel the vegetables.)

   • 2 fennel bulbs chopped; ½ onion, chopped; 2 garlic cloves; and 1 potato, peeled and cut up. Cook and proceed as in the main recipe. Do not puree the potato; mash or break up in the finished soup with a fork.

   • 4 cups chopped zucchini; 1 potato, peeled and chopped; ¼ cup fresh basil leaves. Cook the potato and zucchini as in the main recipe. Add basil leaves when pureeing the other vegetables.

   • 3 cups cooked white beans, ½ cup roasted tomatoes, and 3 garlic cloves cooked as above. Sauté 1 cup chopped green chard leaves in 2 tablespoons water and 1 tablespoon extra-virgin olive oil. Stir the sautéed chard into the soup after all the ingredients are pureed.

SUGGESTED GARNISHES Whole basil leaves; croutons with olive oil and garlic; shaved Parmesan; Green Herb Sauce (page 165); nonfat yogurt mixed with grated or prepared horseradish; Cucumber and Scallion Sauce (page 199).

carrot soup

Lentil Soup with Radishes and Orange

Everyone loves lentil soup. Lentils can be endlessly varied—even eaten like salad when they were intended as soup. Served cold with chopped red onion, minced fresh mint leaves, and a drop of rice vinegar, lentils are a cooling hot-weather dish; pureed with toasted cumin seeds, ground turmeric, and a pinch of red pepper flakes, and served with warm, crusty bread, they are a definite cold-weather food.

The following basic lentil soup will accommodate many garnishes. Try steamed potato slices and minced fresh parsley; cucumber sticks and minced fresh oregano; toasted coarse bread crumbs and grated Romano cheese; chopped tomatoes, cucumber, and fresh marjoram; or spinach sautéed in olive oil with garlic.

Makes 5 servings

2 carrots, peeled and finely diced

2 shallots, finely diced

1 celery stalk, peeled and finely diced

2 cups dried lentils, rinsed and picked over

5 cups water

2 sprigs fresh thyme or ½ teaspoon dried thyme, crumbled

1 bay leaf

Kosher salt and freshly ground pepper

2 to 4 cups nonfat chicken or vegetable stock (page 158 or 159) or canned
    nonfat broth

1 bunch radishes, stemmed and cut into thin slices

1 orange, peeled and finely diced

Minced fresh parsley for garnish

Add ¼ inch water to a large soup pot. Add the carrots, shallots, and celery and cook over medium heat until tender, about 5 minutes, adding more water if necessary.

Add the lentils, water, thyme, and bay leaf. Bring to a boil, skimming the soup several times, and reduce heat to a simmer. Add salt and pepper, cover, and cook for 40 minutes, or until the lentils are tender. Remove and discard the bay leaf and thyme sprigs.

Puree 1 or 2 cups of the cooked lentils and return them to the pot. Add 2 cups of the stock or broth. Taste and adjust seasonings. If you prefer a thinner soup, add more stock or broth.

Adjust the seasoning. Sprinkle each serving with radishes, orange, and parsley.

Green Pea Soup with Cloves

A winter favorite in our house, split pea soup is another easy-to-prepare vegetable soup to serve as part of dinner, as a snack, accompanied by a salad, or as a complete meal. Clove is characteristic of our pea soup and happened as a result of one of those moments of experimentation when the invention really worked.

Makes 6 to 8 servings

9 cups water

2 cups split green peas

1 carrot, peeled

1 whole onion, stuck with 6 whole cloves

6 garlic cloves

12 peppercorns, 1 bay leaf, and ½ teaspoon dried marjoram,
    tied in a cheesecloth bundle

1½ teaspoons kosher salt

Minced parsley for garnish

Put all the ingredients except the parsley in a large soup pot and bring to a boil; reduce the heat to a simmer and skim several times to remove the foam. Cover and continue to simmer for 45 minutes, or until the peas are soft and falling apart.

Remove and discard the cheesecloth bundle and reserve the garlic, carrot, and onion with cloves. Let cool for 15 minutes. Puree the soup, garlic, carrot, and onion *with* cloves in batches in a blender. Add water or stock, if needed, to thin soup to the desired consistency. Taste and adjust the seasoning. Garnish with parsley and serve.

VARIATIONS: In addition to parsley, garnish the soup with crunchy toasts with melted nonfat cheese and hot sauce; minced shallots and red onion soaked in rice vinegar; toasted sesame seeds; steamed julienned carrot; minced fresh herbs; or chopped avocado and tomatillo.

NOTE: Chilled, this soup will thicken and need some thinning; use water, stock, or canned broth.

Bread Soup

I love soup-drenched toasted bread and I suppose all my children do too because I served it to them without apologies. One of our favorite combinations is the recipe that follows, but you can substitute other vegetables for the cannellini beans; try zucchini, black beans, broccoli, cauliflower, or tomatoes. This soup can also be made with canned beans (see note).

Makes 6 servings

2 cups dried cannellini beans, soaked overnight

10 garlic cloves

1 bay leaf

One 3-inch rosemary sprig

6 to 8 cups nonfat chicken or vegetable stock (page 158 or 159) or

    canned nonfat broth

1 teaspoon kosher salt

Freshly ground pepper

½ lemon

6 large thick bread slices

4 cups chopped spinach, watercress, arugula, or turnip greens (optional)

1 to 2 tablespoons olive oil

Shaved Parmesan for garnish

Minced fresh parsley for garnish

In a soup pot, combine the soaked beans, garlic, bay leaf, and rosemary. Add at least 6 cups stock or water, or a combination, or more if needed to cover the beans. Bring to a boil, then lower heat to medium and skim several times. Cover and simmer for 45 minutes. Add the salt and several grinds of pepper. Cover and cook another 45 minutes, or until tender. Remove from heat, add 2 squeezes of lemon juice, and mix in.

    While the beans are cooking, toast the bread and cut each slice in half diagonally. If using the greens, add ¼ inch water to a large pan. Add the greens and sauté over medium heat for several minutes, or until wilted; turnip greens will take longer to cook. Add salt, pepper, and oil to cooked greens and reserve.

bread soup

When the beans are tender, puree 2 cups beans and soup in a blender. Return to the pot and stir in. For a thinner soup, add additional stock or water. Taste and adjust the seasoning.

Place 2 halves of toast in each soup bowl and ladle the soup over the bread. Divide the greens and sprinkle over the top of each serving. Shave some Parmesan over the greens and garnish with parsley.

NOTE: To prepare with canned beans, use 5 cups beans. Simmer the garlic in ½ cup of water for 15 minutes and puree with 1 cup of the beans. Add to the remaining beans along with 4 to 5 cups of stock or broth. Warm over medium heat and simmer. Cook, covered, for 10 minutes. Taste and adjust the seasonings.

A friend of ours, Paul Bertolli, formerly chef at Chez Panisse in Berkeley, California, makes the best corn soup our family has ever eaten. It is a wonderful, sweet and creamy soup pretending to be full of fat! This is an adaptation of his recipe; I think it is a close second to eating just-picked corn on the cob. Serve a crusty warm sweet baguette with the soup.

Makes 6 servings

6 fresh ears corn

4½ cups water

1 onion, chopped

Kosher salt and freshly ground pepper

Minced fresh parsley for garnish

6 teaspoons extra-virgin olive oil for garnish (optional)

Cut the kernels from the cobs. In a medium saucepan, bring the water to a boil and drop in the corn kernels. Reduce the heat to a simmer, cover, and cook for 5 minutes. Do not add salt to the water; corn is toughened by salt during cooking.

Add ¼ inch water to a medium saucepan. Add the onion and sauté over medium high heat until translucent, about 8 minutes. Puree the corn, its cooking water, and onion in 3 batches in a blender, allowing the blender to run a full 3 minutes for each batch. Pour each batch through a fine-meshed sieve to catch the kernel skins. Season with salt and pepper. Garnish with parsley. If you like, trickle 1 teaspoon olive oil over the top of each serving.

White Bean and Broccoli Soup with Basil

Many years ago there was a small, steamy take-out food shop near Boston, called the Night Kitchen. Here, Sally Nirenberg-Sampson made soup on portable electric burners. This is one of her soups we ate so long ago and all still love.

Sandwiches of sweet onions and fresh or marinated peppers on crusty bread can turn this soup into dinner.

Makes 6 servings

1 red onion, chopped

6 garlic cloves, chopped

1 carrot, peeled and chopped

1 head broccoli, stalks peeled and cut into ¼-inch-thick slices, florets reserved

7 cups nonfat chicken or vegetable stock (page 158 or 159) or
   canned nonfat broth

Kosher salt and freshly ground pepper

2 cups cooked cannellini beans, rinsed if canned

2 teaspoons fresh lime juice

½ tablespoon Dijon mustard

¼ cup basil leaves, chopped, plus 6 leaves for garnish

2 strips lemon zest, cut into fine julienne

Thinly shaved Parmesan cheese

Rice vinegar (optional)

Add ¼ inch water to a medium soup pot. Add the onion, garlic, carrot, and broccoli stalks and cook over medium heat for about 5 minutes, or until the onion is softened.

Increase heat to high, add the stock or broth, and bring to a boil. Reduce heat to medium and cook until the broccoli stalks are tender, about 10 minutes. Season with salt and pepper. Add the broccoli florets and cannellini beans and cook for 15 minutes. Whisk the lime juice and mustard with a fork and add to beans. Add chopped basil and cook for 1 more minute.

Let cool for 10 to 15 minutes. Transfer the mixture, in batches, to a blender or food processor and puree. Reheat, but do not boil. Garnish with lemon zest, Parmesan cheese, and basil leaves. If you like, add a few drops of rice vinegar to each serving.

Tomato Soup with Zucchini

You can make this soup with fresh or canned tomatoes; it is delicious either hot or cold. For a light weekend lunch or summertime supper, add just a crumbling of a mild feta, a salad, and some warm bread; in wintertime, serve it with croutons baked with sesame seeds.

Makes 4 to 5 servings

12 fresh tomatoes, halved, or two 23-ounce cans tomatoes

2 unpeeled shallots

4 unpeeled garlic cloves

Nonfat chicken or vegetable broth (page 158 or 159) or canned nonfat broth
   as needed

3 small zucchini, grated, or 1 cup frozen baby lima beans

Kosher salt and freshly ground pepper

Plain rice vinegar or fresh lemon to taste (optional)

Minced fresh parsley for garnish

Preheat the oven to 400°F. Place the fresh or canned tomatoes in one layer in a large ovenproof dish. If using fresh tomatoes, place them cut-side down. Add the shallots and garlic; add water to a depth of ½ inch. Bake, uncovered, for 30 minutes. Add hot water if necessary to maintain the ½-inch of liquid. Continue cooking until the tomatoes just begin to turn black on top, about 20 minutes.

   Using a slotted spoon, remove the vegetables from the pan, reserving the juices, and puree the vegetables through a food mill. Pour into a large saucepan. Add the broth or stock, reserved liquid, and the zucchini or lima beans.

   Stir and taste for seasoning. Cook over medium heat without boiling until the zucchini or limas are tender, about 5 minutes. Add a few drops of vinegar or lemon juice if you like. Garnish with parsley.

Potato Soup with Watercress

Use any potatoes you wish for this soup and keep the skins on. I like to use watercress in soup because it is so high in calcium (almost twice that of spinach), although this soup can be made with any kind of greens. Serve this soup cold in the summertime with a small handful of finely chopped sweet tomatoes and fresh oregano leaves.

Makes 4 servings

1½ cups finely chopped leeks, including some light green portions

2 garlic cloves, finely minced

4 unpeeled potatoes, chopped

4 to 5 cups nonfat chicken or vegetable stock (page 158 or 159) or
   canned nonfat broth

Kosher salt and freshly ground pepper

2 bunches watercress, stemmed and chopped

1 tablespoon extra-virgin olive oil

Coriander seeds, toasted and ground (see note), optional

Watercress leaves for garnish

Add ½ inch water to a soup pot and sauté the leeks over medium heat until tender but not browned, about 7 to 10 minutes. Add the garlic, potatoes, and just enough lightly salted water to cover the potatoes. Bring to a boil and lower heat to a simmer. Cover and cook until the potatoes are tender, about 20 minutes depending on the type of potato and the size of the pieces.

Break up the potato pieces in the pot using a wooden fork or spoon. Remove from heat. Add the stock or broth by the cup until the soup is the consistency you desire. Add salt and pepper to taste. Cover pot.

In a medium saucepan, cook the watercress briefly in ¼ inch water and the oil until just wilted, 2 to 3 minutes; season. Add to the soup pot. Reheat without boiling. Taste and adjust the seasonings. Sprinkle with coriander, if using, and garnish with a whole watercress leaf.

VARIATION: In place of the watercress, stem and chop 1 bunch kale. Steam in ½ inch water until wilted. When cooked, add 1 tablespoon of extra-virgin olive oil.

TO TOAST SEEDS: Put the seeds in a very hot dry pan and cook, shaking the pan every now and then, until the seeds begin to pop or jump. Remove from heat and let cool. Toasted seeds can be stored for up to 3 weeks and ground or chopped when needed.

potato soup with watercress

LIGHT DISHES

Sarah's Corn Salad

Our daughter Sarah lives in Southern California, where it is quite warm much of the year; preparing foods without the heat from a stove is a high priority for her. This dish tastes best in late summer when corn is abundant and sweet, and tomatoes are ripe and luscious.

Makes 6 servings

6 ears fresh white corn

4 ripe red or golden tomatoes, diced

½ red onion, diced

½ bunch fresh cilantro, stemmed and minced

1 tablespoon olive oil

Juice of 1 lime

Kosher salt and freshly ground pepper

Cut the kernels from the cobs with a large sharp knife and put them in a medium bowl. Add all the remaining ingredients and toss gently. Let rest for 30 minutes and serve at room temperature.

Shaved Vegetable Salad

This salad from my friend Christopher Lee, who cooks at Chez Panisse restaurant, is a favorite of ours and is adored by everyone who eats it at our house. For me this is an example of the simplicity and magic made by great cooks. This salad must be served and eaten immediately or the vegetables will lose their crispness. Use a Meyer lemon if available.

It is essential that the vegetables for this salad be cut paper thin. If you are an expert at using sharp knives, by all means slice the vegetables that way. If not, the Japanese slicer made by Benriner (page 83) or a mandoline will do the job beautifully and quickly.

Makes 6 servings

2 yellow bell peppers, halved crosswise, seeded, and deribbed

1 celery stalk, peeled

1 small pattypan (scallop squash) yellow summer squash (optional)

1 fennel bulb, stripped of tough or bruised outer leaves

1½ tablespoons minced fresh parsley leaves

Kosher salt and freshly ground pepper

½ fresh lemon

2 tablespoons extra-virgin olive oil

Parmesan cheese for shaving

Cut each of the vegetables into paper-thin slices using a Japanese slicer, a mandoline, or a large sharp knife. Put in a large glass or stainless steel bowl. Scatter the parsley over the vegetables and season with salt and pepper. Add several squeezes of lemon juice and drizzle on the olive oil. Toss everything together very gently with your hands.

Transfer immediately to a large serving platter or to individual salad plates. Shave the Parmesan into thin shards with a vegetable peeler and place 2 or 3 shards (per serving) on the salad. Serve at once.

shaved vegetable salad

Garlic Toasts with Tomatoes and Variations

The tomatoes for this dish are not cooked, but there are no absolutes to this kind of food: the tomatoes can be grilled or roasted and sauceless or the sauce can be very soupy. This is an easy dish to serve as a first course for a special dinner or summer barbecue or as a light supper served with a platter of sautéed greens, green beans, and olives. To serve as hors d'oeuvres, cut the garlic toasts into small triangles.

Makes 6 first-course servings

6 slices crusty French bread, toasted and rubbed with olive oil and garlic

12 tomatoes

2 garlic cloves, finely sliced

Kosher salt and freshly ground pepper

Fresh marjoram or oregano leaves or minced parsley for garnish.

Cut the tomatoes over a bowl to catch the juice. Mix in the garlic, salt, and pepper to your taste. Let sit for 15 minutes. Cut the garlic toasts in halves, placing 2 halves on each plate or all the halves on 1 serving platter. Spoon the tomatoes, including the juice, over the toasts. Garnish with herbs of your choice.

POTATOES AND ANCHOVY VARIATION: Drain and rinse 6 anchovy fillets. Soak the anchovies in cold water for 5 minutes; drain, pat dry, and julienne.

Peel and chop 6 small potatoes into small pieces. In a 10-inch sauté pan or skillet, bring 2 cups water to a boil. Add ½ teaspoon salt and the potatoes. Lower heat to a high simmer, cover, and cook for 20 minutes, or until almost softened. Pour off all but the barest amount of water. Add just enough chicken or vegetable stock (page 158 or 159) or canned nonfat broth and toss gently so that the liquid mixture coats the potatoes. Cook, covered, over medium heat for another 10 minutes to make a sauce. Season with salt and pepper to taste.

In a small bowl, toss the anchovies with ½ teaspoon minced fresh parsley. Spoon the potato mixture over the toasts, and garnish with the anchovy-parsley mixture.

PEPPER OR ONION VARIATION: Seed, derib, and cut 3 bell peppers into thin slices, or cut 2 onions into thin slices. Add ¼ inch nonfat chicken or vegetable stock (page 158 or 159) or canned nonfat broth or water to a medium sauté pan or skillet. Add the vegetable and cook over medium heat until tender, about 3 to 5 minutes. Season to taste with salt; pepper, red pepper flakes, or cayenne; minced fresh herbs, or crumbled dried herbs. Spread the mixture over the toasts.

MUSHROOM VARIATION: Coarsely chop 1 pound mushrooms, lightly salt them, and cook in water or stock over medium-high heat in a medium sauté pan or skillet until their moisture has evaporated and they just begin to brown. For a stewlike sauce, add ½ to 1 cup nonfat chicken or vegetable stock (page 158 or 159) or canned nonfat broth and cook until the sauce thickens. For a drier dish, add only 2 to 3 tablespoons stock or broth and 1 minced garlic clove and cook for 1 or 2 minutes. Stir in a handful of toasted bread crumbs (page 160) and spread over the toasts.

Artichokes

I am always searching for new ways to cook artichokes since my family loves them. This recipe was inspired by a seventeenth-century Dutch cookbook, *The Sensible Cook*. These baby artichokes can be served at room temperature or hot; if serving hot, this is one time sweet butter is almost a necessity.

Makes 4 to 6 servings

24 to 36 baby artichokes

2 to 3 cups nonfat chicken stock (page 158) or canned nonfat broth

2 tablespoons extra-virgin olive oil

Kosher salt and freshly ground pepper

Freshly grated nutmeg to taste

Pinch of ground mace

½ cup fresh bread crumbs

1 tablespoon unsalted butter (optional)

Minced fresh parsley for garnish

Pull off the outer leaves of the artichokes, but keep on any stems. In a large pot of salted boiling water, cook the artichokes until tender, but not soft, about 10 to 15 minutes. (The artichokes are cooked when a small knife or pointed skewer goes through one easily.) Cut each artichoke in half and, if there are chokes, remove them with a small spoon.

Put the artichoke halves in a large sauté pan or skillet and add stock or broth to a depth of ¼ inch. Add the olive oil, salt, and pepper to taste, and cook over medium heat until the liquid is almost evaporated. Add several gratings of nutmeg and the mace. Add more stock or broth to cover the bottom of the pan and continue cooking for about 7 to 10 minutes, or until the artichokes are about to fall apart but there is still some sauce in the pan. Remove from heat.

Mash the bread crumbs with some stock or broth to make a paste. Add to the pan and mix with the artichokes. Taste and adjust the seasonings. If serving hot, add butter if you like, and stir gently. Garnish with parsley.

Flat Salads with Flowers

Flat salads, said Laurie Colwin, are vegetables and fruits that lie down, *platters* of salad, rather than bowls. Flat salads in our house become dinner when we add sliced chicken or smoked fish, and delicious bread. When our daughters were in the kitchen, flat salads were sprinkled with petals from our flower garden or even petals from our weeds, such as dandelions. If you like the idea of flower petals you must be sure they are edibles, such as unsprayed rose, geranium, cornflower, and viola petals. The four flat salads below are some of our favorite combinations.

- Red and yellow tomato slices; red and yellow cherry tomatoes, halved; balsamic vinegar; olive oil; minced fresh rosemary leaves and rosemary flowers
- Smoked salmon slices or gravlax, red onion rings, thinly sliced cucumber, lemon slices, and snipped fresh chives and chive flowers
- Papaya and cantaloupe, thinly sliced; celery stalks, thinly sliced; vinaigrette with snipped fresh dill; and dandelion petals
- Blood orange slices; grapefruit slices; julienned scallions; vinaigrette with grated lemon zest and orange juice; and viola flowers

flat salads with flowers

Romano Bean Ragout

During the three years I apprenticed at Chez Panisse restaurant I worked next to some extraordinary chefs. Jeff Stoffer was one. His spring vegetable garden is full of green Romano, or Italian, beans, and this is one of the delicious ways he cooks them. Look for the smallest beans in your market in springtime, and cook them the same day. For an irresistible dish, serve the beans with risotto.

Makes 4 servings

1 cup reduced chicken or vegetable stock (page 158 or 159) or canned broth

3 cups chopped Romano beans

2 garlic cloves, minced

1 large rosemary sprig, pounded slightly to release the scent

Kosher salt and freshly ground pepper

Add ½ inch of the stock or broth to a medium saucepan. Add the beans, garlic, and rosemary. Cover and cook over medium heat for 10 minutes, or until the beans are tender.

Reduce the heat to a simmer and cook another 15 minutes more, covered, checking the beans every few minutes to make sure there is enough liquid to cover the bottom of the pot. Add stock or broth by the tablespoon to maintain a thin film of liquid on the bottom of the pan.

The beans are done when they are soft and the flavors are combined in the sauce. Remove and discard the rosemary. Add salt and pepper. Ladle the ragout into a serving bowl or onto individual plates and serve immediately.

Stewed Sweet Peppers

Make a pot of these peppers for meatless sandwiches, to top hamburgers, to eat with rice, or to stuff potato skins. For a light supper, pour some spaghetti sauce on crusty bread or a toasted English muffin and pile peppers on top.

Makes 4 servings

About 1 cup nonfat chicken or vegetable stock (page 158 or 159) or
 canned nonfat broth

2 onions, thinly sliced

8 large green and/or bell peppers, seeded, deribbed, and thinly sliced

1 jalapeño chili or an assortment of chilies including Anaheim or Pasilla chilies,
 seeded and minced (optional)

8 garlic cloves, thinly sliced

Kosher salt and freshly ground pepper

1 or 2 tablespoons extra-virgin olive oil (optional)

Add ¼ inch stock or broth to a large sauté pan or skillet. Add the onions and cook over medium heat, adding additional stock or broth as necessary until the onions are softened, about 5 to 7 minutes. Add the peppers and the optional chili. Cook until the peppers are wilted and are just beginning to brown. Add the garlic and a little more stock or broth. Continue to cook until garlic is soft but not brown, about 3 minutes. Remove from heat. Add salt and pepper and optional oil. Serve in whatever way appeals to you, or just bring the pan to the table.

stewed sweet peppers

Cucumber and Scallion Sauce

This is a variation on raita, a sauce from northern India. In India sauces like this are offered in small portions as the cooling accompaniment to rather hot and spicy dishes; here, and often in my kitchen, sauces like this are eaten by the bowlful as dips for cut-up veggies and homemade chips (page 97). This raita is a nice accompaniment to Broken Potatoes (page 107), or as a side dish to a casserole of wild rice with almonds.

Makes about 2½ cups

2 cups plain nonfat yogurt

1 or 2 cucumbers, seeded and finely chopped

2 scallions, white and light green parts, cut finely into rounds

1 garlic clove, minced (optional)

Kosher salt and freshly ground pepper

Beat the yogurt with a fork until smooth. Add all the remaining ingredients. Let the sauce rest for 1 hour before serving.

VARIATIONS: Add toasted and crushed cumin or fennel seeds, paprika, red pepper flakes, or minced fresh mint to taste.

Baked Rice Casserole

Rice is a dish everyone knows how to cook but everyone cooks differently. When I have the time to sauté a few aromatic vegetables, and especially when I am baking or roasting squash, chicken, or tomatoes, I cook rice this way using a shallow flameproof casserole or ovenproof skillet, moving it from the burner right into the oven and then to the table.

Makes 6 servings

3 cups chicken or vegetable stock (page 158 or 159) or canned nonfat broth

3 tablespoons finely chopped onion or shallots

1 carrot, peeled and finely chopped

3 garlic cloves, thinly sliced

1½ cups long-grain white rice

1 tablespoon extra-virgin olive oil

1 small bay leaf

Kosher salt and freshly ground pepper to taste

¼ teaspoon dried thyme, crumbled

Minced fresh parsley for garnish

Preheat the oven to 375°F. Set the stock or broth over high heat to bring to a boil. Add ¼ inch water to a large flameproof casserole or ovenproof skillet. Add the onion or shallots and carrot and cook over medium heat until the onion or shallots are translucent.

Add the garlic, rice, oil, and 1 or 2 tablespoons stock or broth. Stir just until the rice turns opaque. Add the remaining stock or broth, bay leaf, salt, pepper, and thyme. Bring to a boil and turn off the heat. Cover tightly with a lid or aluminum foil and bake for 40 minutes, or until the rice is tender. Remove from the oven and let sit, covered, for 10 minutes before serving. Fluff with a fork, add parsley, and serve.

VARIATION: Add ground cinnamon, curry powder, cayenne, or saffron to taste during cooking. Add sautéed peppers, toasted chopped almonds, or rehydrated slivered sun-dried tomatoes to the rice after cooking.

Cottage Cheese Pancakes

When I was little my grandma and I made fritters, or beignets, with cottage cheese. Although these pancakes are not fried and puffed like those fritters, they have become a family favorite for breakfast or, with a cheese variation, for a quick lunch or light supper.

Makes 8 to 9 small pancakes

4 tablespoons cottage cheese

Pinch of kosher salt

3 tablespoons granulated sugar

½ teaspoon vanilla extract

3 tablespoons flour

3 egg whites

Olive oil, for cooking

Confectioners' sugar for garnish

Mash the cottage cheese with a fork until it is smooth. Add the salt, sugar, and vanilla and mix well. Add 1 tablespoon of the flour and mix again.

In a deep bowl, beat the egg whites until they turn white and are thickened. Fold the egg whites into the cottage cheese mixture. Gradually stir in the remaining 2 tablespoons flour until the mixture is the consistency of a thick pancake batter.

Heat a large skillet over medium heat and when hot add 1 teaspoon of olive oil to the pan, spreading the oil by tipping the pan back and forth. Pour the batter into a pitcher for easy pouring and cook 4 small pancakes at a time (or what your pan can contain). Cook until bubbles appear on the top and the bottom is golden brown. Flip and cook the other side. (If you are doubling or tripling this recipe, you may want to keep the pancakes warm in a 250°F oven.) Sieve confectioners' sugar over the hot pancakes and serve at once.

VARIATION: For savory pancakes, omit the sugar, vanilla, and confectioners' sugar. Mix 2 tablespoons grated Parmesan or Emmenthaler cheese or a crumbled blue cheese such as Gorgonzola into the batter after the flour is mixed in. Add freshly ground pepper or cayenne to taste. Serve with a mild sauce such as marinated peppers pureed with a few drops of water or nonfat milk.

Corn Cakes

My children loved corn pancakes when they were growing up, and they still do. Serve these as snacks, breakfast, or as a quick supper with soup. These pancakes are very light, and as appetites grow, so will quantities consumed. The recipe is easily doubled or tripled, and these pancakes never fail even when you approximate the ingredients.

Makes 6 to 7 small pancakes; serves 2

1 cup fresh or frozen corn kernels (2 to 3 ears corn)

2 tablespoons flour

Kosher salt and freshly ground pepper

1 tablespoon nonfat milk or water

2 egg whites

Cook fresh corn for 1 minute or so in boiling water. Or put frozen corn kernels in a sieve and hold under hot running water for 1 minute. Drain and pat dry with paper towels.

In a small bowl, combine the flour, salt, pepper, and milk or water and mix until smooth. Add the corn and mix well.

In a deep bowl, beat the egg whites only until they turn white and are thickened. Fold the corn mixture into the beaten whites and gently mix. Pour the entire mixture into a pitcher for easy pouring into the pan.

Heat a large nonstick skillet over medium-high heat and lightly wipe the pan with oil using a wadded-up paper towel. Pour in just enough batter so that you can cook 3 or 4 small pancakes at a time. Cook until browned, then turn and cook the other side. Serve immediately.

Pizza with Spinach and Variations

Pizza is always a respite from usual cooking for me, because of the simplicity of the meal and the simplicity of the preparation. Picking up partially baked pizza shells from the market or using ready-made dough from my local pizza restaurant makes pizza an almost effortless weekly food. For last-minute pizzas, English muffins or a sweet baguette from your freezer is a perfect base for assorted vegetables and sauces. Making your own dough, of course, is an option you might choose.

The recipe that follows and its variations are for pizza without cheese. If you are cooking with cheese, try mixing ½ cup grated nonfat mozzarella with several gratings of Parmesan or your favorite cheese. If possible, bake pizza on a preheated pizza stone or a layer of bricks; the crust will be crisper and the pizza will cook more evenly and quickly.

Consider preparing some pizzas for snacks and freezing them in individual slices; the family can eat your pizza rather than the market's.

Makes one 10-inch pizza or two 6-inch pizzas

2 large bunches fresh spinach or 2 bunches green chard, stemmed and coarsely
    chopped, or one and a half 10-ounce packages frozen chopped spinach

6 garlic cloves, slivered

¾ cup nonfat chicken or vegetable stock (page 158 or 159) or canned broth

2 tablespoons extra-virgin olive oil

Kosher salt and freshly ground pepper

Red pepper flakes

Pizza Dough (recipe follows), or pizza shells

Preheat the oven to 500°F with a pizza stone or a layer of bricks in the upper third of the oven, if using.

Add ½ inch water to a large sauté pan or saucepan. Add the greens, cover, and cook over medium heat for 5 minutes or until wilted. If you are using chard, the cooking time will be increased by up to 15 minutes, depending on the freshness of the vegetables. Drain, pat dry with paper towels, and set aside. Add the garlic and stock or broth to the pan. Cook over low heat for 5 to 7 minutes, or until the garlic is tender but not browned. Remove the garlic and set aside. Continue cooking down the liquid remaining in the pan until there is a scant ⅛ inch of liquid; remove the pan from heat. Return the greens and garlic to the pan and toss with the remaining liquid. Add the oil, salt, pepper, and red pepper flakes.

If using pizza dough, form a ball for each pizza. On a floured surface, flatten and stretch each ball into a ⅛-inch-thick disc with your hands. (If you use a rolling pin the dough will be crackerlike when baked.) Transfer the dough to a baking sheet or a baker's peel if you have one.

If using cheese, spread on dough. Spread the greens over the cheese. If using a stone or bricks, slide the pizza(s) off the baker's peel or baking sheet directly onto the stone or bricks. Otherwise, place the baking sheet in the upper third of the oven. Bake the pizzas for 12 to 15 minutes, or until the edges and bottom of the pizzas are nicely browned.

VARIATIONS:
- Sliced fresh tomatoes, green and red peppers, and onion tossed with 2 tablespoons oil and kosher salt and pepper to taste.
- Sautéed green bell peppers, onions, sunflower seeds, garlic, kosher salt and pepper to taste.
- A thin layer of pureed rehydrated sun-dried tomatoes topped with red onion slices tossed with 1 tablespoon oil, anchovies, green olives, and pepper.
- Cooked red and yellow onions and apple slices, fennel, and cayenne.
- Thinly sliced steamed potatoes cooked with a green leaf vegetable, garlic, rinsed capers, some stock or broth, olive oil, grated lemon zest, and pepper.

Pizza Dough

This recipe can be doubled.

Makes dough for one 10-inch pizza or two 6-inch pizzas

½ cup warm (105° to 115°F) water

½ package active dry yeast

1 tablespoon olive oil

¼ teaspoon kosher salt

¼ teaspoon pepper

3 tablespoons rye flour or unbleached all-purpose flour

About ¾ cup unbleached all-purpose flour

In a large bowl, combine the water and yeast and stir until the yeast dissolves. Add the olive oil, salt, pepper, and the 3 tablespoons flour. Gradually stir in the ¾ cup flour. Knead the dough on a floured surface for 5 to 7 minutes, or until smooth and elastic, adding more flour only if the dough sticks.

Lightly oil the dough all over and place it in a large bowl. Cover the bowl with a dish towel or cloth and let the dough rise in a warm place until doubled, about 40 minutes. If you have the time, punch down the dough and let it rise once again for 40 minutes. This is not necessary, but the dough will be a bit lighter and more pliable.

Form the dough into 1 ball for a 10-inch pizza, or 2 balls for 2 smaller pizzas. On a floured surface, press the dough into ¼-inch-thick disks with your hands. Press and stretch and rotate the dough to form the crusts.

MAIN COURSES

Lamb Grilled on Skewers

Children love a picniclike meal of skewered lamb with bowls of vegetables and grains and salsas to eat with the lamb. A couscous vinaigrette with chopped red onion, a black bean salad with chopped yellow peppers, a summer fruit salsa (papayas, peaches, nectarines), a winter fruit combination (pears, apples, pineapples, raisins, figs), or Dried Fruit Sauce (page 235) are all possibilities.

Makes 6 servings

SPICE PASTE

4 garlic cloves, minced

Juice of ½ lemon

1 teaspoon sugar

1 teaspoon ground coriander

½ teaspoon ground cumin

½ teaspoon fennel seeds, crushed

½ teaspoon red pepper flakes

½ cup marinated red peppers, pureed

½ teaspoon kosher salt

Freshly ground pepper

About ½ cup nonfat chicken stock (page 158) or canned nonfat chicken broth

1¼ pounds boned leg of lamb, cut into thin strips for threading on skewers

Soak 18 bamboo skewers in water to cover for at least 15 minutes; soaking will keep the skewers from burning when broiling or grilling. Thread the lamb on the skewers.

TO MAKE THE SPICE PASTE: In a stainless steel or glass bowl, combine the garlic, lemon, and sugar. Add all the remaining ingredients except the stock or broth and mix well. Add just enough stock or broth to make a thick paste. Rub the spice paste evenly over the skewered lamb. Cover and refrigerate for at least 2 hours or overnight. Bring to room temperature before broiling or grilling.

Grill the lamb quickly over white coals or under a preheated broiler for about 3 minutes on each side for medium rare. Serve hot.

lamb grilled on skewers

Roasted Chicken without the Skin

A violation of the senses; a crime of omission! Skin the chicken? Take away the best part? That crisp and slightly crunchy, deliciously fatty part of that never-go-wrong meal? The part that covers the soft, tender, delicate meat, protecting it from the harsh drying of the oven and delivers it moist and silky?

We committed the unforgivable: We fooled around with perfection. But cooked this way, chicken has approximately 50 percent less fat than when roasted with its skin and fat intact.

Ask the butcher to skin the chicken—not that you can't, but it does take a sharp knife and a good bit of patience. When you return home, use your kitchen scissors to cut off any skin that remains and snip off any visible fat.

While the chicken is roasting, bake the potatoes at the same time. Put the cooked chicken in a covered casserole with the potatoes, roughly broken up, and keep everything warm in a low oven until ready to serve.

Makes 4 to 5 servings

Kosher salt and freshly ground pepper

One 4- to 5-pound chicken, skinned and trimmed of fat

I lemon, cut into quarters

4 fresh tarragon sprigs, or ½ teaspoon dried tarragon, crumbled

2 carrots, peeled

I leek, halved lengthwise and sliced crosswise (white part and some pale green)

2 onions, cut into eighths

6 garlic cloves, halved

½ cup water

1½ cups nonfat chicken stock (page 158) or canned nonfat broth

Handful of currants or raisins (optional)

Preheat the oven to 400°F. Salt and pepper the chicken inside and out. Stuff the chicken with the lemon and three-fourths of tarragon. Place the chicken on a roasting rack in a roasting pan or Dutch oven and arrange the cut vegetables, the remaining tarragon, and garlic around the chicken. Pour the water and I cup of the stock or broth into the roasting pan. If using, add the currants or raisins.

Cover the breast of the chicken with a small piece of aluminum foil, parchment paper, or wet cheesecloth. Cover the pan with a tight-fitting lid or with aluminum foil sealed tightly around the edges. Reduce the oven heat to 300°F and bake the chicken for 3 hours, or until very tender. The cooked chicken will be moist and be very lightly browned on top.

Discard the lemon and tarragon, separate the vegetables from the sauce, and skim the fat from the sauce. Reserve the carrots. Pass the skimmed pan juices and other vegetables through a food mill or sieve. Reheat the sauce and add stock or broth to make more sauce or reduce sauce if necessary; taste and adjust the seasoning and slice the carrots into the sauce.

VARIATION: While the chicken is roasting, cut and core 8 to 12 apples. Put the apples in a pan and add 1 cup nonfat chicken stock (page 158) or canned nonfat chicken broth. Cover and cook over low heat for 30 minutes. Uncover and cook for about 20 minutes longer, or until most of the liquid has evaporated but enough remains to coat or glaze the apples. Toss gently with minced fresh oregano or a bit of crumbled dried oregano, kosher salt, and pepper. Serve along with the roasted chicken.

Grilled Spice-Rubbed Beef, Mushrooms, and Eggplant

When cooking for vegetarian guests we often prepare this dinner without the meat, substituting additional Portobello mushrooms. Portobellos are ordinary brown mushrooms left to grow for an extra few days. Serve this dish with a saffron rice or spicy millet and a homemade fresh-fruit salsa.

Makes 6 to 7 servings

2 eggplants, halved lengthwise

Kosher salt for sprinkling

2 pounds flank steak, trimmed of fat

6 to 8 Portobello mushrooms, stemmed

SPICE RUB

4 teaspoons cumin seeds

4 teaspoons fennel seeds

One 2-inch piece cinnamon stick, broken into pieces

10 peppercorns

3 whole cloves

½ teaspoon kosher salt

8 teaspoons sesame seeds

8 garlic cloves, minced

¼ cup minced peeled fresh ginger

Lay the eggplant cut-side down on a cutting board and cut into thick crosswise slices, leaving the skin on. Lightly salt the eggplant slices on both sides. Score both sides of the steak almost but not quite through to the other side. Cut each mushroom cap in half horizontally to make 2 thick slices about ½-inch thick.

TO MAKE THE SPICE RUB: Grind the cumin, fennel, cinnamon stick, peppercorns, cloves, and salt in a spice grinder and transfer to a small bowl. Add the sesame seeds, garlic, and ginger to the spice mixture and mix well.

Rub the excess salt from the eggplant with your fingers or a paper towel and pat the eggplant dry with paper towels. Coat the eggplant, steak, and mushroom slices with the spice rub. If the spice rub doesn't adhere to the food, add a bit of water or stock to make more of a paste and smear it over all surfaces of the vegetables and meat. Place the eggplant, meat, and mushrooms on a platter. Cover and refrigerate for at least 2 hours.

Remove the eggplant, meat, and mushrooms from the refrigerator 45 minutes before cooking. Light a fire in a charcoal or gas grill, or preheat a broiler with a broiler pan. Put the vegetables on the grill over a hot fire or under the broiler 6 inches from the heat and cook for 2 to 3 minutes. Add the meat. Cook for 3 to 4 minutes on each side, or until vegetables are browned and tender and the meat is medium rare. Slice the steak diagonally across the grain. The vegetables can be served directly from the grill or broiler, or cut into smaller pieces and served in a bowl.

Everyone likes to open packages, and these can be opened right at the table. These packets are so quick to prepare and can almost be last minute thoughts from what is in your fridge. Arrange the vegetables loosely and use just a little liquid; the vegetables will give off their own juices even in this brief cooking time.

Makes 6 servings

4 carrots, peeled and cut into 4-inch julienne

2 large celery stalks, cut into 4-inch julienne

½ small onion, thinly sliced

1 tablespoon extra-virgin olive oil

½ teaspoon dried thyme, crumbled, or 6 fresh thyme sprigs

Kosher salt and freshly ground pepper

½ fresh lemon

6 teaspoons water

Preheat the oven to 425°F. Place a baking sheet in the oven to heat.

Lay six 16-by-12-inch rectangles of aluminum foil or parchment paper on a work surface. In a bowl, combine the carrots, celery, onion, olive oil, dried thyme if using, salt, and pepper. Toss to mix. Place one sixth of the mixture on one half of each sheet, spreading the vegetables slightly apart. Squeeze 1 drop of lemon juice and sprinkle 1 teaspoon water over each batch of vegetables. If using fresh thyme, lay 1 sprig on the vegetables. Fold the foil in half over the vegetables and crimp the edges to make a secure seal. If using parchment paper, fold one half of the paper over the half with the vegetables and, starting at one corner, fold the edges back over themselves, inch by inch, working your way around the package; twist the end firmly to keep the seal in place. The package will resemble a turnover in shape.

Lower the oven heat to 400°F. Place the packets on the heated baking sheet and bake for 7 minutes. Transfer each packet to a platter or individual plates. Carefully open each packet by piercing it with a knife to let the steam escape, then cut the packet open.

VARIATIONS Replace the ingredients in the main recipe with one of the following combinations:

• Steamed cut-up potatoes, paper-thin garlic and shallot slices, minced fresh rosemary, grated lemon zest, olive oil, kosher salt, and pepper. Uncooked potatoes must be sliced thinly and baked for 25 minutes.

• Very thinly sliced cauliflower, julienned leek, baby snow peas, kosher salt, pepper, olive oil, ground coriander.

• Very thinly sliced raw baby artichokes, thinly sliced red onion, kosher salt, pepper, and a few drops of balsamic vinegar.

• Peeled and finely julienned broccoli stems, julienned celery, paper-thin garlic slices, olive oil, pepper, and crumbled dried tarragon.

Baked Chicken Breasts

This dish can quickly become a family favorite. Baked chicken chills nicely and can be prepared the day before for picnics and outdoor parties. Serve it hot with a barley or brown rice casserole that can bake at the same time, or baked whole winter squash or potatoes. Sautéed greens or steamed carrots and broccoli would be perfect colors to add to this dinner.

Makes 6 servings

12 skinless chicken breast halves, bone-in

3 cups toasted coarse bread crumbs (page 160)

3 tablespoons sesame seeds

2 tablespoons mixed dried tarragon, marjoram, and thyme, crumbled

1 tablespoon curry powder

½ teaspoon kosher salt

½ teaspoon freshly ground pepper

Nonfat milk for dipping

Preheat the oven to 425°F. Cut any visible fat from the chicken breasts. Mix the bread crumbs, sesame seeds, herbs, curry powder, salt, and pepper in a bowl. Dip each chicken piece in the milk and roll in the bread crumb mixture to coat evenly.

On a nonstick or lightly oiled baking sheet, place the chicken pieces so they are just touching but not overlapping. If there isn't enough chicken to fill the pan, cover the bare part with aluminum foil to prevent burning.

Lower the oven heat to 375°F. Bake, uncovered, for 40 minutes. Let cool on the baking sheet for 20 minutes before serving. The chicken will be moist and delicious.

VARIATION: Substitute 5- to 6-ounce white fish fillets—cod, rockfish, or halibut—for the chicken. Bake for about 15 minutes, or until opaque and flaky.

baked chicken breasts

Burritos are on most children's top-ten list of favorite foods, and consequently are frequently my choice for visiting children. They are also filling and, best of all, require very little time and attention. After assembling the burritos they can be quickly wrapped in foil and warmed in a hot oven for a few minutes. For festive dinners or party buffets, add platters of broiled chicken, roasted potatoes, and a bowl of sliced avocado, red onion, and orange.

Makes 6 servings

Kernels cut from 4 fresh ears of corn, or

    one 10-ounce package frozen corn kernels

12 nonfat flour tortillas

2 cups cooked black beans, rinsed and drained if canned

2 cups cooked rice or another kind of cooked beans

2 red bell peppers, seeded, deribbed, and sliced, or 1 cup marinated bell peppers,

    thinly sliced

1 cup shredded nonfat mozzarella cheese

2 cups shredded cabbage

Fresh Tomato Salsa (page 162) or bottled salsa

Nonfat quark, or plain nonfat yogurt

8 scallions, sliced into rounds

Bottled hot sauce

If using fresh corn, cook the kernels in boiling water for 2 or 3 minutes; drain. If using frozen corn kernels, put them in a sieve and hold under hot running water for 1 minute, then drain. Place the corn and all the remaining ingredients in separate bowls and bring to the table or set out on the kitchen counter. Let each person put together his or her own burrito. Eat the burritos at room temperature, or wrap in aluminum foil and heat in a preheated 400°F oven for 10 minutes.

NOTE: To crisp the tortillas, sprinkle generously with water and toast or bake for several minutes in a 400°F oven until brown and puffed. For very soft tortillas, wrap them in aluminum foil and heat in a preheated 400°F oven for 8 minutes. Tortillas can also be steamed 6 at a time in a bamboo steamer for 1 to 2 minutes.

Once, when our son Charles was visiting, he offered to prepare dinner and served us all a very simple meal that deserves sharing. Serve this "pizza" with a pureed Lentil Soup (page 105) or a gazpacho. Note: The oven should not be preheated.

Makes 6 servings

CORNMEAL

2 cups cornmeal

2 teaspoons kosher salt

3 tablespoons grated Parmesan cheese

½ cup shredded nonfat mozzarella cheese

Cayenne to taste

1 tablespoon extra-virgin olive oil

Kosher salt and freshly ground pepper

3 red bell peppers, seeded, deribbed, and thinly sliced

½ large onion, thinly sliced

4 handfuls (4 ounces) mixed salad greens

4 to 6 tablespoons Vinaigrette Dressing (page 163)

TO PREPARE THE CORNMEAL: Bring 8 cups water and 2 teaspoons kosher salt to a boil. Add the cornmeal gradually, whisking all the while. Cook over low heat so the cornmeal is just barely bubbling; stir frequently until thick and creamy, about 15 minutes. Stir in the Parmesan, transfer to a bowl, and set aside to cool.

Lightly oil a 9-by-13-inch glass baking dish. Line the baking dish with the cooled cornmeal, pressing down to make a compact crust. The crust should be 1 inch thick. Mix the mozzarella cheese with the cayenne and sprinkle it evenly over the cornmeal.

In a medium bowl, combine the olive oil, salt and pepper to taste, two thirds of the pepper slices, and the onion. Spread the vegetables over the cheese.

Place the dish on the second shelf from the bottom of the oven and turn the oven to 500°F. Bake for 25 minutes, then place a sheet of aluminum foil, smaller than the dish but large enough to cover the vegetables, over the top of the "pizza" and bake for an additional 15 minutes. Let the "pizza" rest for 20 minutes before serving.

Toss the remaining pepper slices with the salad greens and the vinaigrette, and serve with the "pizza." Use a spatula or large cake knife to serve the "pizza."

Potato Stew with Garlic-Almond Sauce

This recipe is adapted from a Catalonian dish that includes sausage. The stew is a splendid, simple-to-prepare one-dish meal. The Garlic-Almond sauce (page 219) and the onion and tomatoes can be prepared one day ahead. Serve this as a main course or as an accompaniment to an oven roast.

Makes 3 main-course servings or 6 side servings

2 onions, sliced

6 cups nonfat chicken stock (page 158) or canned nonfat chicken broth

5 canned peeled tomatoes, chopped and juice reserved

6 to 7 unpeeled white potatoes, sliced (6 cups)

4 garlic cloves, sliced

Kosher salt and freshly ground pepper

Garlic-Almond Sauce (recipe follows)

4 thick bread slices, toasted

Minced fresh parsley, oregano or tarragon leaves for garnish

Add ½ inch water to a large saucepan. Add the onions and cook over medium heat until softened. Add ¼ cup of the stock or broth and continue cooking until the liquid has almost evaporated. Watching carefully, repeat this process until the onions are light brown, about 15 minutes. Add the tomatoes and a bit more stock or broth. Stir until the onions and tomatoes melt into one another, about 5 minutes. If preparing ahead, cover and refrigerate.

To a medium saucepan or sauté pan add the potatoes, garlic, salt and pepper to taste, and enough stock or broth to barely cover the potatoes. Bring to a boil and reduce heat to a high simmer, adding stock when necessary to maintain an ample sauce. Cover and cook until the potatoes are tender, about 30 minutes. Add the tomato mixture to the potatoes and cook briefly. Turn off the heat and mix the garlic-almond sauce into the stew. Cut the toast in half diagonally and place 2 halves in each of 4 shallow soup bowls. Ladle the potato stew over the bread. Sprinkle with the parsley or oregano.

Garlic-Almond Sauce

Makes ½ to ⅔ cup

10 walnut halves, toasted (see below)

10 blanched almonds, toasted (see below)

1 large slice French bread, crusts removed, toasted, and broken into pieces

Scant ¼ teaspoon kosher salt

2 peppercorns

2 garlic cloves, minced or crushed

4 fresh parsley sprigs, stemmed and minced

1 tablespoon extra-virgin olive oil

Grind the nuts, toasted bread, salt, and peppercorns in a spice grinder. Remove to a bowl. Add the garlic, parsley, and oil and mix well. Cover tightly and refrigerate overnight. Store for up to 3 days.

TOASTING NUTS: Preheat the oven to 400°F. Spread the nuts in one layer on a baking sheet and toast them, shaking the pan once or twice, for 5 to 6 minutes, or until fragrant.

Chili

Most children, and adults, love chili; I like to cook a large pot. This recipe is easily doubled or tripled for large groups. Serve with an assortment of garnishes children love, warm bread, and a platter of steamed or liquid-sautéed assorted greens as a side dish.

Makes 6 generous servings

Nonfat chicken or vegetable stock (page 158 or 159) or

    canned nonfat broth (optional)

2 red onions, chopped

1 tablespoon dried oregano, crumbled

2 teaspoons chili powder

2 teaspoons red pepper flakes

1 tablespoon ground cumin

2 teaspoons cayenne

1 jalapeño chili, seeded and minced

8 garlic cloves, minced

2 red bell peppers, seeded, deribbed, and chopped

2 green bell peppers, seeded, deribbed, and chopped

10 cups cooked black beans

½ cup bulgur wheat (optional)

2 cups canned peeled tomatoes, coarsely chopped, and 1 cup juice

Kosher salt

Two 6-inch orange zest strips

Minced fresh parsley for garnish

Nonfat plain yogurt for serving

Add ½ inch stock, broth, or water to a large soup pot. Add the onions, oregano, chili powder, red pepper flakes, cumin, and cayenne. Cover and cook over medium heat until the onions are softened, about 10 minutes.

Stir in the jalapeño, garlic, half the red and green peppers, beans, bulgur if using, tomatoes, juice, salt, and orange zest. Cover and cook over very low heat, stirring occasionally, for 30 minutes. Taste and adjust the seasoning. Add stock, broth, additional tomatoes, or water if you like.

Serve in warm bowls, garnished with parsley and the remaining chopped red and green peppers. Pass the yogurt separately.

Potato and Shrimp Paella

Paella, as originally prepared in Spain, was a Lenten dish. In Spain, each area has its own special paella; a paella in Barcelona will be very different from one in Granada, both different from one in Cadiz. Here, as well, paella has become a dish that welcomes innovation from the cook. Substitute your children's favorite fish, shellfish, and vegetables, or create an all-vegetable dish.

Makes 6 servings

4¼ cups nonfat chicken or vegetable stock (page 158 or 159) or

   canned nonfat broth

2 red onions, chopped

1 pound small red or white potatoes, cut into ¼-inch-thick slices (3 cups)

1½ cups Arborio rice

1 teaspoon paprika

2 pinches saffron threads, crushed

Kosher salt and freshly ground pepper

4 garlic cloves, slivered

18 to 24 large shrimp in the shell

2 tablespoons minced fresh parsley

Green Herb Sauce (page 165), optional

Put ¼ cup of the stock or broth to a 15- or 18-inch skillet or shallow flameproof casserole dish. Add the onions and potatoes and cook over low heat until the onions soften, about 10 minutes. Meanwhile, heat the remaining 4 cups stock or broth.

Add the rice, paprika, saffron, salt, pepper, half the garlic, and 3¾ cups of the hot stock or broth. Simmer, uncovered, for 15 minutes. Cook another 8 to 10 minutes, without stirring, until the potatoes are softened but not falling apart. Add the shrimp and cook for 5 minutes, or until the shrimp are pink and opaque, and the rice is tender but firm. Remove from heat, cover, and let rest for 5 minutes.

Meanwhile, simmer the remaining garlic in the remaining ¼ cup stock for 3 to 5 minutes, or until translucent. Stir this mixture into the rice along with the parsley just before serving. Pass the herb sauce separately, if using.

DESSERTS

Fresh seasonal fruit is always the easiest dessert: bowls of ruby cherries, velvet-skinned peaches, firm Bosc pears, fragrant tangerines. Apples and pears can be baked in 20 minutes, sweet orange slices can be sprinkled with balsamic vinegar, and ripe nectarines can simply be sliced into pretty bowls.

In addition to several special fruit desserts, I have included recipes for cookies, a soufflé, and a lush bread pudding. Some take only minutes to prepare; others longer. All of them are lower in fat and will provide a sweet ending to a meal.

Biscotti with Nuts

These cookies are baked twice, like all biscotti. This recipe is modified from several relatively higher fat ones. I was determined to do this one as a birthday gift for my husband to satisfy his urge for a crunchy dipping cookie. For an even lower-fat version, see the variation.

Makes about 50 biscotti

2¼ cups unbleached all-purpose flour

½ teaspoon baking powder

½ teaspoon baking soda

¼ teaspoon salt

4 egg whites

1½ cups sugar

1 teaspoon vanilla extract

1 teaspoon aniseed, chopped

1 cup unblanched almonds or mixed hazelnuts and almonds, toasted and coarsely
  chopped (see page 219)

2 tablespoons grated orange zest

1 egg white, mixed with 1 tablespoon nonfat milk

Preheat the oven to 325°F. Lightly oil a baking sheet. In a medium bowl, combine the flour, baking powder, baking soda, and salt. In a large bowl, beat the 4 egg whites with the sugar, vanilla, and aniseed until the mixture is thick and shiny. Fold in the flour mixture, nuts, and orange zest.

Knead the dough on a lightly floured surface for about 3 minutes, or until well blended. Divide the dough into 2 pieces. Shape each piece into a log about 10 inches long, 4 inches wide, and 1 inch high. Lightly flour the logs for easy handling. Place the dough logs parallel to each other on the prepared baking sheet. Whisk the egg white and milk together and brush the top of each log with the mixture.

Bake on the middle shelf of the oven for about 30 minutes, or until the logs are an even golden brown and a knife inserted into the center of one comes out clean. This first baking is crucial; the dough must be cooked through.

Transfer the logs to a cutting board and let cool to the touch. With a very sharp knife, cut the loaves into ½-inch-thick diagonal slices. Lay the slices on their sides on 2 baking sheets and bake for about 10 minutes, or until barely colored, turning them once halfway through. Let cool on racks. Store in an airtight container for up to 6 weeks.

CURRANT VARIATION: For no-added-fat biscotti, use 1¼ cups sugar and replace the nuts with 1 cup currants.

biscotti with nuts

Sliced Oranges with Cinnamon

This is our nonfat alternative to pies at Thanksgiving. This dish is crisp and cold and refreshing after a sumptuous meal. When preparing this dessert for adults, I use dry red table wine in place of the grape and cranberry juice.

Makes 6 servings

¾ cup sugar

1 cup water

¾ cup unsweetened white grape juice

¼ cup unsweetened cranberry juice

2 cloves

One 1-inch piece cinnamon stick

One 1-inch piece vanilla bean, sliced lengthwise

6 lemon slices

6 large seedless oranges

In a heavy, medium saucepan, combine the sugar and water and cook over medium-high heat, stirring, until the sugar is dissolved. Add the juices, cloves, cinnamon stick, vanilla bean, and lemon slices. Bring to a boil, reduce heat to medium, and cook for 15 minutes. Strain the liquid and let cool for 10 minutes.

    Meanwhile, using a large, sharp knife, cut off the top and bottom of each orange down to the flesh. Stand each orange on end and cut off the peel in strips down to the flesh, making sure to remove all the white pith. Cut the oranges into thin slices and arrange them in your prettiest glass bowl. Pour the syrup over the orange slices and refrigerate for at least 4 hours. This dessert is best when eaten the same day.

These are simple enough for most young children to make with adult supervision. If they last longer than a day or two without being eaten, they can be wrapped in waxed paper (not plastic wrap) and kept in the refrigerator for several days more.

Makes about 32 balls

1 egg white

1 cup rolled oats

½ cup raisins, chopped

¼ cup almonds, chopped

¼ cup M&M's, chopped

½ cup sesame seeds

Preheat the oven to 325°F. In a medium bowl, beat the egg white just until it turns pure white (just before peaks begin to form). Add all the remaining ingredients except the sesame seeds and mix well with your hands. Roll the dough into balls the size of large marbles and roll each in the sesame seeds.

Place the balls on a nonstick or a lightly oiled baking sheet and bake for 20 minutes. Let cool.

Christmas Walnuts

As well as being holiday and party treats, these walnuts can accompany or garnish a dessert such as Yogurt Cheese with Honey (page 229). As our children were growing up this was the Christmas recipe we prepared together for friends. For slightly savory walnuts to serve at an adult party with sherry, port, or vodka, see the variation.

Makes 2 ½ cups

One 5-inch piece cinnamon stick, broken up

1 nutmeg

14 allspice berries

½ teaspoon kosher salt

10 peppercorns

2 cups sugar

½ cup water

2½ cups walnut halves

Grind the cinnamon stick in a spice grinder and measure 1½ tablespoons into a small glass. Grate 2 teaspoons nutmeg and add to the same glass. Grind the allspice, salt, and peppercorns together in a spice grinder and add to the glass, mixing well.

In a heavy, medium saucepan, combine the sugar and water and cook at a slow boil, without stirring, until a candy thermometer reaches 320°F, or until a drop of the syrup dripped onto a metal surface is glass hard, 10 to 15 minutes.

Immediately remove the pot from the heat and quickly stir in the spices with a wooden spoon. Add the walnuts and mix until the nuts are coated. Turn out onto a pastry marble or a baking sheet, spreading the nuts out as thinly as possible. Let cool, then pull apart. Store in an airtight container in a cool place for up to 6 weeks.

SAVORY VARIATION: Increase the salt to 1 teaspoon and add ½ teaspoon cayenne.

My Mother's Date and Nut Bread

When I was a little girl my mother and grandfather made this sweet bread for B. Altman & Co., a grand old-fashioned department store in New York. I have fond memories of "our bread" stacked in pyramids of colored cellophane tied with raffia. Sliced into thin rounds, this dense, sweet bread is delicious by itself. Spread it with yogurt cheese for dessert sandwiches; mix the yogurt cheese with minced fresh mint or parsley and chopped cucumber for an afternoon adult snack. To bake the bread as I do, use two 16-ounce soup or bean cans.

Makes 2 cylindrical loaves, about 30 slices

2 cups unbleached all-purpose flour

½ cup sugar

1 heaping teaspoon baking soda

¼ teaspoon salt

½ teaspoon freshly ground pepper

1½ cups walnuts, coarsely chopped

1 cup Dromedary pitted dates, chopped

1½ cups boiling water

Preheat the oven to 350°F. Remove one end from each of two 16-ounce cans. Lightly grease the inside of each can with olive oil. Cut 2 rounds of aluminum foil or parchment paper, using the can as a template. Place a round in the bottom of each can.

In a large bowl, combine the flour, sugar, baking soda, salt, and pepper. Add the nuts and dates to the flour mixture. Stir to blend all the ingredients. Gradually stir in the boiling water and beat until well mixed.

Pour the batter into the prepared cans, filling each three-fourths full.

Bake for about 40 minutes, or until a skewer inserted in the center of each bread comes out clean. Run a blunt knife around the inside of each can. Let the bread cool in the cans for 20 minutes. Gently bounce the bottom of each can on a folded dish towel on the counter. The bread should slip out easily. Let cool completely on a rack.

Yogurt Cheese with Honey

Inventing desserts free of added fat for our family in the days before fat-free Ben & Jerry's required a lot of thought once a fruit-only dessert had been vetoed as the evening's treat. This fat-free dessert is simple, and pleasing to both children and adults. The fruit slices are used as "crackers" for the cheese. Variations can include julienned lemon or orange zest, and fruits such as sliced Fuyu persimmons, nectarines, or melon.

Makes 6 servings

½ cup candied ginger (optional)

6 tablespoons honey

2 unpeeled apples or pears

Few drops fresh lemon juice

Yogurt Cheese (page 160)

Fresh mint, basil, or oregano leaves for garnish

Cut the candied ginger into julienne with a scissors or a knife; you should have 36 to 48 strips. Pour the honey into a small pitcher. Core and slice the unpeeled fruit, and toss with a few drops of lemon to keep it from discoloring.

Place a 2-inch wedge of yogurt cheese on each plate. Drizzle some honey over the cheese and in squiggles on the plate. Arrange the fruit slices on the plates and place several ginger strips over the fruit. Garnish and serve.

VARIATION: Replace the ginger with Christmas Walnuts (page 227) or plain walnuts.

Dried Calmyra figs, available in bulk in some markets, are a staple food in our household. We use them for nibbling, adding to stuffings and grain dishes, cooking with roast chicken, poaching in wine, and for a dessert such as this. For this dessert, plan on 4 figs for each person's plate, and some extra. For a festive dinner, serve this dish with a sparkling cider for the children and a sweet dessert wine such as a Vin Santo, or Barsac, for the adults.

Makes 6 servings

1 tablespoon fennel seeds

30 dried Calmyra figs

30 walnut halves, toasted (see page 219)

Confectioners' sugar for dusting

Fresh oregano sprigs for garnish (optional)

Bowl of tangerines

In a small dry skillet, toast the fennel seeds over high heat until they begin to smoke or "jump." Immediately remove from heat and let cool (see note).

Make a slit in each fig and stuff the fig with 5 to 6 fennel seeds and a walnut half. Place the figs on pretty plates or a platter and sieve confectioners' sugar over all. Garnish with oregano, if you like, and serve with a bowl of tangerines.

NOTE: Fennel seeds can be toasted and stored for up to 2 weeks.

Baked Pineapple with Brown Sugar

Our friend Lynn Milberg served us this dessert after a glorious Mexican feast. Everyone will eat more of this sweet and slightly tart dish than you plan for. The pineapple can be peeled and cored earlier in the day, making the preparation at dinner almost effortless.

Makes 4 to 5 servings

1 ripe large pineapple

1 cup loosely packed brown sugar

1 teaspoon ground cinnamon

1 tablespoon granulated sugar

¼ cup water

¼ teaspoon orange extract

½ lemon

Fresh mint leaves, cut into shreds

Preheat the broiler. Peel, quarter, and core the pineapple on a platter to catch the juice. Cut the quarters into ¾-inch-thick slices. Squeeze the peel to extract the juice and reserve the juice. Place the pineapple slices in a shallow flameproof baking dish. Mix the brown sugar and cinnamon together and sprinkle the mixture over the pineapple.

Broil 2 inches from the heat until the pineapple is lightly caramelized and can be easily pierced with a fork. Do not turn the slices.

Transfer the pineapple to a large serving platter.

Add the reserved pineapple juice, granulated sugar, water, orange extract, and 2 squeezes of the lemon to the baking dish. Cook over low heat on top of the stove for 2 to 3 minutes, stirring in all the caramelized bits from the pineapple.

Spoon the sauce over the pineapple, garnish with the mint leaves, and serve at once.

VARIATION: For adults, substitute ¼ cup brandy for the water and omit the orange extract.

Everyone prepares fruit salad in summertime, but the tart, crisp fruits of winter make fine salads also. More fruits are becoming available in the winter all over the country. Look for Bosc or Comice pears, Satsuma or Fairchild tangerines, and pippin, Gravenstein, or Arkansas Black apples.

Makes 6 servings

½ cup sugar

½ cup water

3 peppercorns

2 lemons (Meyer if possible)

1 unpeeled tart, crisp apple, cored and sliced

2 unpeeled pears, cored and sliced

2 Fuyu persimmons, peeled, halved, and cut into thin slices

2 Satsuma tangerines, peeled, and separated into segments or sliced into rounds

⅓ cup pomegranate seeds

3 tablespoons pomegranate juice

In a small, heavy saucepan, combine the sugar, water, and peppercorns. Cook for 10 minutes at a slow boil. While the syrup is cooking, cut 1 of the lemons into thin slices. Reduce heat to a simmer, add the lemon slices, and poach for 3 to 4 minutes.

Using a slotted spoon, remove the lemon slices and peppercorns. Reserve the lemon slices, discard the peppercorns, and pour the sugar syrup into a small bowl to cool.

Toss the apple and pear slices with several squeezes of lemon. Place the apples, pears, persimmons, and tangerines in a large glass bowl. Add the pomegranate seeds and poached lemon slices.

Add the pomegranate juice to the sugar syrup. Taste and adjust the flavoring with lemon juice, if you like. Pour the liquid over the fruit. Cover and refrigerate for at least 2 hours, but not longer than 6, so the fruit will stay crisp.

Lizzy's Cocoa Meringue Cookies

A platter of these cookies disappears almost immediately. They are simple to prepare and impossible to keep on hand. I don't bake very often, but when I do our daughter Lizzy's cookies are always on my list.

Makes 50 cookies

5½ cups unsifted confectioners' sugar

4 heaping tablespoons Dröste's or Hershey's unsweetened cocoa powder

2 cups hazelnuts, almonds, or a combination, toasted and chopped
  (see page 219)

Pinch of salt

4 grinds of fresh pepper

1 teaspoon orange extract

5 egg whites

Preheat the oven to 350°F. Line 2 baking sheets with parchment paper or use nonstick pans.

In a large bowl, combine the sugar, cocoa, nuts, salt, and pepper. Add the orange extract to the egg whites and beat lightly with a fork until white. Fold the egg whites gently into the sugar mixture until blended.

Place teaspoonfuls of batter 2 inches apart on the baking sheet. Bake on the middle shelf of the oven for 20 minutes. Transfer the cookies to dinner plates or a platter to cool.

The only sugar in this dessert comes from the fruit itself. For the sweetest compotes, buy fruit at the height of its season, and even ask to taste it in the market. The only problem with this dessert is that there never seems to be enough.

Makes 6 servings

5 white or yellow peaches

5 nectarines

Juice of 1 orange

Raspberries, small purple grapes such as Concords, or

    fresh or dried currants for garnish (see note)

Holding the fruit over a bowl to catch the juices, peel the peaches and cut them into thick slices. Slice the unpeeled nectarines to the same thickness.

    Place the peaches and nectarines in a pretty glass bowl. Pour the orange juice and reserved fruit juice over the fruit. Let sit for 5 minutes. Garnish with berries, grapes, or currants and serve.

NOTE: If using dried currants, plump them in warm water or for 20 minutes.

Dried-Fruit Sauce

This sauce can be prepared days ahead and will keep in the fridge indefinitely. As a dessert topping it is wonderful over nonfat vanilla ice cream or sorbet, or any sliced crisp fruit. As a main-course accompaniment, it's great with curry, saffron rice pancakes with peppers, or spicy grilled chicken or meat.

Makes 2 cups

8 dried figs, Calmyra if available, thinly sliced

15 dried apricot halves, thinly sliced

½ cup large raisins, plumped in warm water for 15 minutes

1 tablespoon finely julienned lemon peel

Juice of 1 orange

Juice of 1 lemon

⅓ cup sugar

2 tablespoons water

Put the figs, apricots, raisins (plumping water discarded), and lemon peel in a medium bowl. Combine the orange and lemon juice in a glass.

In a small, heavy pan, combine the sugar and water and boil over high heat for 5 minutes. Remove from heat and let cool for 10 minutes. Add the sugar syrup by the tablespoonful to the orange juice mixture until the juice is sweetened to your taste. Pour just enough liquid over the dried fruit to cover it. Toss gently. Cover and let sit for 2 hours before serving. Store in tightly lidded glass jars in the refrigerator.

Bread Pudding from Bette's Diner

Bette's Diner in Berkeley has a take-out shop right next door. One very special offering has always been the soft, scintillating, always warm bread pudding, rich with eggs and butter. Angel that she is, Bette worked with me to come up with this lower-fat version.

Makes 8 servings

2 loaves stale eggless white bread, crusts removed, cut into 1½-inch-cubes

    (about 12 cups)

1 cup golden raisins

1 egg

2 egg whites

2 tablespoons extra-virgin olive oil

2 tablespoons sugar

½ teaspoon freshly grated nutmeg

1 teaspoon vanilla extract

6 cups nonfat milk

Preheat the oven to 325°F. Lightly coat an oval or rectangular 3-quart baking dish with oil. Layer the bottom of the dish with half the bread. Sprinkle the raisins over the bread. Layer the remaining bread over the raisins.

In a large bowl, whisk the egg, egg whites, and olive oil together. Whisk in the sugar, then the nutmeg, vanilla, and milk until blended.

Pour the milk mixture over the bread and press down on the top gently with your hand. The milk mixture should come just to the top of the bread; add more milk, if necessary. Cover the dish with aluminum foil, sealing the edges and making a dome to keep the foil from sticking to the bread.

Place the dish in a larger baking pan. Fill the larger pan with hot water to within 1 inch of the top of the baking dish. Bake for 1 hour and 45 minutes, or until the pudding is very lightly browned and slightly crisped. Uncover and let cool in the baking dish. Serve warm.

Jam Soufflés

This is one of those dishes that was invented out of desperation on a long and stormy day when we ran out of puzzles, patience, and electricity. A really good jam makes this an exceptional dessert; if your children have a favorite jam then of course that is what makes these soufflés best.

Makes 4 servings

4 tablespoons jam at room temperature

Unsalted butter, for coating custard cups

Sugar, for dusting

4 egg whites

Preheat the oven to 400°F. Stir the jam with a fork to soften it. Lightly coat the insides of 4 6-ounce custard cups or ramekins with unsalted butter and sprinkle with sugar.

In a large bowl, beat the egg whites until soft peaks form. Fold in the jam thoroughly and divide among the dishes. Bake on the middle shelf of the oven for 15 minutes, or until puffed and golden brown. Serve immediately.

some noteworthy low-fat foods

This is a listing of some of the very low fat or nonfat foods mentioned in the book and some specialty foods we have found to be of particularly unusual quality. They are, by no means, the *only* high-quality, lower-fat or fat-free packaged foods in the marketplace to deserve recognition, just some we are partial to and know well. Each manufacturer has been contacted and is pleased to assist you in finding where their products can be purchased. If the manufacturer has an 800 phone number, it is listed below.

QUARK FROM APPEL FARMS

Appel Farms in Ferndale, Washington, produces three types of quark: nonfat, low-fat, and whole-milk. Nonfat quark from Appel Farms is made from 100 percent nonfat milk and is sold in pint-sized containers in states west of the Mississippi River.

Appel Farms, 6605 Northwest Road, Ferndale, WA 98248

(360) 384-4996

FROMAGE BLANC FROM THE VERMONT BUTTER & CHEESE CO.

Fromage Blanc is the name for this company's *nonfat* product similar to quark (the product sold as quark by this company is 11 percent fat). Fromage Blanc is nonfat and is packaged in half-pint containers for shipments to states east of the Mississippi. Call Allison Hooper (mother of three) for the location of your nearest store and for recommended cooking suggestions.

The Vermont Butter & Cheese Co.

(800) 884-6287

BAKER'S CHEESE
Friendship Dairy Co., Friendship, NY
(518) 271-0322

ALMONDINA BRAND COOKIES
No-added-fat-except-for-the-nuts cookies. These delicate and delicious, handmade cookies can truly take the place of your own. Call Jack Hunter at Almondina if you can't find them where you live.
Almondina
(800) 736-8779

MUIR GLEN (ORGANIC) CANNED TOMATO FOODS
All sorts of delicious tomato products: peeled and stewed tomatoes; soup; salsas; spaghetti sauces. All in cans or jars; most are fat-free. Ask for recipes and serving suggestions.
Muir Glen
(800) 832-6345

WAX ORCHARD CHOCOLATE SAUCES
CHOCOHOLICS CHOCOLATE SAUCES
These extraordinary dessert sauces made by different companies come in a variety of flavors, and in chunky 11-ounce jars. Except for a trace of fat from pure cocoa powder, all are nonfat and both manufacturers will mail order if their products are not sold where you live.
Wax Orchard (800) 634-6132
Chocoholics (800) 760-2462

ALAINE'S KITCHEN RAINFOREST CAKE
This is a fat-free (except for the nuts) cake of fruit that is absolutely delicious and for-tunately bears no resemblance to what is commercially produced and called "fruitcake." The cake comes simply packaged in a burlap bag and is sold through mail-order.
(800) 718-1115

SANTA FE OLE
A superb maker of salsas, chutneys, marinara sauces, marinades, and bean sauces. Except for nut sauces and a chili peanut butter, all are nonfat and delicious. Look for their salt-, sugar-, and oil-free Roasted Red Pepper puree in your market; mixed with just a little quark or yogurt this is a perfect mayonnaise substitute for sandwiches.
(800) 570-0724

JUST TOMATOES, ETC.
The vegetable candy! Dehydrated tomatoes and bell pepper pieces, and freeze-dried corn, peas, and carrots—that's all. An incredible totally fat-free snack for the entire family. If you can't find it, call; Karen or Bill Cox will tell you where you can.
(800) 537-1985

SNYDER'S NO-ADDED FAT PRETZELS

This company pioneered nonfat pretzels and has been consistently producing the best-tasting, sugar-free, fat-free pretzels in the marketplace. One of their pretzel varieties has added fat; check the label.

Snyder's
(800) 233-7125

G. L. MEZZETTA ROASTED RED PEPPERS

Absolutely delicious, juicy, fat roasted peppers packaged in water, but never tasteless. Distributorship is broad in the west and is in the process of being expanded nationwide. In the interim, call for your products by phone and they will be shipped immediately.

G. L. Mezzetta
(800) 941-7044

DRYER'S NONFAT ICE CREAM

This is a delicious frozen dessert without the taste of yogurt and almost the taste of real ice cream. The chocolate flavor has veins of syrupy chocolate fudge amply running through it, also nonfat. Dryer's brand is called Edy's east of the Mississippi River. Both names are easy to find in your supermarket.

SAUCES AND PASTES

Epicurean International packages some of the most practical to use and delicious-tasting products under the brand name Thai House. Try the Yellow Curry Paste, Green Curry Paste, Red Chili Paste, Plum Spring Roll Sauce, or Lemon Grass Salad Splash, among many. All the products are available in supermarkets and specialty stores. Except for just a little added oil in several, many are fat-free. If you can't locate these products call Alexandra at the company office.

Epicurean International
(800) 967-8424

acknowledgments

To the people who first became interested in this project in the very early days, whose enthusiasm and encouragement was so important, thank you. You helped to establish the context out of which this book was born.

Throughout I had the opportunity to follow the dedicated and thoughtful research, the epidemiological outcomes, and the preventive programs of giants: to Walter Willet, M.D., John Deitschy, M.D., Gerald Berenson, M.D., Peter Kwiterovich, M.D., Michael Brown, M.D., Mary Enig, Ph.D., William Castelli, M.D., Nathan Pritikin, M.D., Dean Ornish, M.D., Bruce Ames, Ph.D., and so many others, I am forever thankful for the light.

To Jane Brody, my appreciation for making *JAMA* and the *New England Journal of Medicine* come to life.

To Peter Kwiterovich, M.D., I am indebted for your wise and considered scrutiny of my ideas.

To Leonard Michaels, teacher and friend, thank you.

Were it not for the valor of my friend Peter Kunkel, M.D., Medical Director of Mt. Diablo Heart Health Center in Walnut Creek, California, this book might not have been.

To Katherine Thanas, who long ago taught me about patience and inclusion, you have helped me more than you know.

James (Jim) Levine, my agent, knew what was necessary to publish this book; I am forever appreciative as I am to Richard Simon, friend and colleague, for my "blind date" with Jim; it changed everything.

Gerald Saunders, Librarian at the Alta Bates Medical Library in Berkeley, was an unfailing resource.

To Naomi Lucks, master of titles and organization, thank you.

Lisa Howard diligently produced numerous clean drafts of the manuscript from barely readable pages. She is a miracle worker.

Bill LeBlond, Editor at Chronicle Books guided me, with quiet determination, through the steps of translating my manuscript into a book. I am thankful to the others at Chronicle who helped this process, notably Leslie Jonath and Sarah Putman.

Julie Snyder's friendship and penchant for order and for ordering me, was a gift, still is, and shall always be.

Rita Allhoff Mitchell, R.D., gifted nutritionist, asked all the right questions.

Christopher Lee, masterful cook and longtime chef at Chez Panisse restaurant in Berkeley, translated the recipes from my kitchen scribbles into cups and measures with great patience, elegance, and thoughtfulness.

Takao Minatoya, sushi chef at Akira Komine's wondrous Kirala Restaurant in Berkeley, taught me over many years to know the clean and exquisite flavors of fresh fish and how small tastes can be explosions.

Paul Bertolli, chef at Oliveto restaurant in Oakland, California, taught me so much about cooking; the best was always cooking something splendid out of nothing special.

And in our conversations of cabbages and kings and other important things, not the least of which was writing, marriage, children, and food, were it not for Cathleen Fraser, Jane Dillenberger, Sue Bender, Linda Bertolli, Leonard Karpman, Toby Gidal, Brandy Engel, Lynn Milberg, Richard Strohman, Sally Sampson, David Bersin, my cousins Leah and Herman Schwartz, Lincoln Diamant, Charles Munitz, and Lenore Munitz, and my sister Roselynn Sokol, this would have been a lesser book. To my mother and dad, thank you for everything.

To my cousins Leah and Herman Schwartz, who made Bolinas my private Yaddo, there are no words; they know of my appreciation for that and everything else.

For the love, devotion, and grit of our children, Sarah, Charles, John, and Lizzy, I am more grateful than I know how to say. To my husband Bob—mentor, truth teller, inspiration, keeper of our humor, and sometimes saint—you are a rare being and I am blessed.

general index

a

Alaine's brand fruitcake, 239
Almondina brand cookies, 239
American Academy of Pediatrics recom-
    mendations, 4, 12
Antioxidants, 23
Asian restaurants, 146–47
Atherosclerosis, 17
Avocados
    fat in, 13, 22, 40, 41, 143
    as garnish, 40
    in sandwiches, 143

b

Bacon sandwiches, 119, 143
Bagels, 79
Baked beans, 127
Baker's cheese
    adding to, 68–69
    buying, 69
    cooking with, 92
    low fat content of, 68
    sources, 239
Bakery goods, 52
Balsamic vinegar, 76
Bamboo steamers, 84
Beans
    baked, 127
    buying, 53, 103
    fiber in, 121
    making more appealing to children, 93–94
    protein in, 132
    spreads, 121
    sugar added to, 56
Birthday parties, 150–51
Bisquick, 34
Bread
    buying, 52
    flour used in, 39
    high-fiber, 120–21
    lower-fat, 69–70
    sugar added to, 56
Bread crumbs
    cooking with, 92
    as a substitute for cream, 92
Breakfasts, 112–17
    high-fat, 18
    lower-fat, 18, 116–17

Broths, nonfat, 72
Buckwheat
    about, 100
    protein in, 132
Bulgur, protein in, 132
Bulk foods, 70–71
Burritos, 147
Butter
    alternatives to, 22, 58, 90, 124
    saturated fat in, 13, 15
Buttermilk, fat in, 44

c

Cakes
    birthday, 150–51
    fat-free, 72, 239
    lower-fat, 150
Calcium
    children's requirement for, 133
    sources of, 133
    in vegetarian diets, 131–32
Calories
    in 1 gram of fat, 38
    replacing, from fat, 20–21
Canned foods
    buying, 53–54
    healthy, 70–72
Cereals
    with added fats, 66
    buying, 54, 76
    fat in, 54, 76
    sugar in, 56, 76
Change, resistance to, 25, 26–27, 30
Cheese
    alternatives to, 133–34
    baker's, 68–69, 92, 239
    buying, 52
    as a condiment, 59
    cottage, 44, 132
    deleting half of, 59
    fat in, 52, 63–64, 133
    Fromage Blanc, 238
    mozzarella, 52
    nonfat, 52
    quark, 69, 238
    in sandwiches, 143–44
    saturated fat in, 13
    yogurt, 92

general index

using more whites for yolks, 52–53, 59,
68, 90, 113
Equipment, 81–84
Exercise, 9–10

f

Fast-food restaurants, 140–42
Fat. *See also* Saturated fats; Trans fatty acids;
Unsaturated fats
added, 40–41
American Academy of Pediatrics recommendations for, 12
animal foods high in, 41
calories in 1 gram of, 38
camouflaged, 43–47
chilling to remove, 15, 58, 94
computing percentage of, in packaged
foods, 32–38
computing percentage of, in recipes,
38–39
importance of, for growth, 7, 12
intrinsic, 40–41
plant foods high in, 41
popularity of, 11
replacing calories from, 20–21
right amount of, 20
saturated, 13
unsaturated, 22–23
"Fat-free," definition of, 46
Fiber
in bread, 120–21
foods high in, 121
importance of, 121
Fish
buying, 109–10
calcium in, 133
including in family meals, 109, 110
Flavorings, lower-fat, 74–75, 94
Freezer
removing high-fat foods from, 65
restocking with healthy food, 70–71
French fries, 106
Fromage Blanc, 238
Frozen foods
buying, 54–55
fat in, 34–36
less than 15 percent fat, 36, 59
lower-fat desserts, 53
Frozen yogurt
nonfat, 53
saturated fat in, 13

Fruits
canned, 56
fiber in, 121
increasing children's consumption of, 79
stocking, 73

g

G. L. Mezzetta Roasted Red Peppers, 240
Gorp, 80
Grains
casseroles, 93
fiber in, 121
making more appealing to children, 93–94
protein in, 132
sauces for, 101–2
spreads, 121
varieties of, 74
Granolas
buying, 54
fat content of, 54, 76
Growth, 12, 21

h

Hamburgers. *See also* Fast-food restaurants
cheeseburgers, 143
cooking in ridged skillet, 82
in high-fat dinner, 125–26
in low-fat dinner, 126
vegetarian alternatives to, 126–27
Ham sandwiches, 144
Hash browns, 106
HDLs. *See* Cholesterol
"Health" food restaurants, 139–40
Heart disease, 13, 17
Holidays, 148–50
Hot dogs, 127
alternatives to, 53
buying, 53
fat in, 53
misleading labels on, 53
Hydrogenated oils, 13. *See also* Trans fatty acids
effects of, 13, 16–18
in ingredient listings, 13
in margarine, 22
prevalence of, 2–3
recognizing, 14, 15
sources of, 13, 15

i

Ice cream
alternatives to, 53

Nuts
	buying, 76
	fat in, 13, 22, 41
	fiber in, 121
	roasted in oil, 65
	for snacking, 40

o

Obesity, 9
Oils
	coconut, 13
	deleting half from recipes, 59, 89, 90
	fat in, 41
	hydrogenated, 2–3, 13
	olive, 22–24
	tropical, 13
Olive oil, 22–24
	buying, 24
	extra-virgin, 22, 23
	monounsaturated fatty acids in, 23
	sautéing in, 58
	storing, 24
Olives, 13, 22, 41
Omelets, 59, 90
Organ meats, 41

p

Packaged foods
	buying, 53–54
	computing percentage of fat in, 32–38
	healthy, 70–71
	hydrogenated fat in, 15, 66
	labels on, 32–38
	less than 15 percent fat, 36
	"97 percent fat-free," 45–46
Palm kernel oil, 13
Pancake mixes, 116
Pantry
	removing high-fat foods from, 65–66
	restocking with healthy food, 70–72, 74–75
Passover, 149
Pasta
	canned, 53
	in restaurants, 146
Peanut butter
	buying, 61, 120
	fat in, 41, 60
	mixtures, 79
	sandwiches, 40, 60–61, 120, 123
	sugar added to, 56
Peanuts, 22, 41

Pediatrician, consulting, 4
Peer pressure, 27
Pepperidge Farm Goldfish, 36
Peppers
	dehydrated, 239
	puree, 239
	roasted, 240
Percent Daily Value, 32–33
Picnics, 123–24
Pizza restaurants, 146
Plaque, arterial, 17
Polyunsaturated fats, 22
Popcorn, 79
Potatoes
	French fried, 106
	hash browned, 106
	instant, 53
	salad, 93, 106
Pretzels
	no-added-fat, 240
	sugar added to, 56
Protein
	children's requirement for, 132
	complete, 132
	in eggs, 113
	sources of, 132
	in vegetarian diets, 131–32

q

Quark, 69, 238
Quinoa, 100

r

Recipes
	computing percentage of fat in, 38–39
	problems with, 92–93
	revising to make lower-fat, 86–97
	revising to make vegetarian, 134
Refrigerator
	removing high-fat foods from, 63–64
	restocking with healthy food, 70–71
Restaurants, 137–48
	Asian, 146–47
	fast-food, 140–42
	"health" food, 139–40
	Mexican, 147–48
	pizza and pasta, 146
	sandwich shops, 142–44
	taking children to, 145–46
Rice, 132. *See also* Wild rice
Ritz Crackers, 37

recipe index

a

Almond Sauce, Garlic-, 219
Anchovies, Garlic Toasts with Potatoes and, 193
Apples
    Roasted Chicken without the Skin (variation), 209
Artichokes, 195
Arugula
    Bread Soup, 184–85

b

Baked Chicken Breasts, 214
Baked "Fries," 106
Baked Pineapple with Brown Sugar, 231
Baked Potatoes with Toppings, 107
Baked Rice Casserole, 200
Baked Vegetables in Packages, 212–13
Baker's cheese
    cooking with, 92
    Creamy Nonfat Salad Dressing, 164
Barley
    Anytime Turkey Soup, 177–78
    cooking, 100
Basic Recipe for Green or Brown Lentils, 105
Basic Recipe for Soaked Dried Beans, 104–5
Basil Sauce, Pasta with, 173
Beans
    Basic Recipe for Soaked Dried Beans, 104–5
    Bread Soup, 184–85
    Burritos, 215
    buying and cooking dried, 103
    buying and cooking fresh shell, 102–3
    Chili, 220–21
    cooking times for, 104
    High-Fiber Sandwich Spread or Dip, 122
    hummus, 121
    Romano Bean Ragout, 197
    soaking, 103
    toppings for, 127–28
    White Bean and Broccoli Soup with Basil, 187
Beef, Mushrooms, and Eggplant, Grilled Spice-Rubbed, 210–11
Biscotti with Currants, 224
Biscotti with Nuts, 223–24
Biscuits, Puffed, 96–97
Bob's Egg-White and Tomato Omelet, 115

Bread
    Bread Pudding from Bette's Diner, 236
    Bread Soup, 184–85
    Garlic Toasts with Tomatoes and Variations, 193
    My Mother's Date and Nut Bread, 228
    Puffed Biscuits, 96–97
Bread crumbs
    cooking with, 92
    Pasta with Bread Crumbs, Garlic, and Parsley, 174
    Toasted Bread Crumbs, 160
Broccoli and White Bean Soup with Basil, 187
Broken Potatoes without Butter, 107
Broths. See Stocks
Buckwheat, 100
Bulgur wheat, 100
Burritos, 215

c

Carrot Soup, 179–80
Cheese
    Cottage Cheese Pancakes, 201
    Yogurt Cheese, 160–61
    Yogurt Cheese with Honey, 229
Chicken
    Baked Chicken Breasts, 214
    Nonfat Chicken Stock, 158–59
    Roasted Chicken without the Skin, 208–9
Chili, 220–21
Christmas Walnuts, 227
Cookies
    Biscotti with Currants, 224
    Biscotti with Nuts, 223–24
    Lizzy's Cocoa Meringue Cookies, 233
Cooking techniques, low-fat
    "deletion and substitution" method, 57–60, 86–87, 95–97
    dry-browning meat, 88
    liquid-sautéing, 87–88
Corn
    Burritos, 215
    Corn Cakes, 202
    Fresh Corn Soup, 186
    Sarah's Corn Salad, 191
Cornmeal
    cooking, 100
    Cornmeal "Pizza" with Salad, 216–17

recipe index

recipe index

table of equivalents

The exact equivalents in the following tables have been rounded for convenience.

US/UK

oz=ounce
lb=pound
in=inch
ft=foot
tbl=tablespoon
fl oz=fluid ounce
qt=quart

METRIC

g=gram
kg=kilogram
mm=millimeter
cm=centimeter
ml=milliliter
l=liter

OVEN TEMPERATURES

Fahrenheit	Celsius	Gas
250	120	½
275	140	1
300	150	2
325	160	3
350	180	4
375	190	5
400	200	6
425	220	7
450	230	8
475	240	9
500	260	10

WEIGHTS

US/UK	Metric
1 oz	30 g
2 oz	60 g
3 oz	90 g
4 oz (¼ lb)	125 g
5 oz (⅓ lb)	155 g
6 oz	185 g
7 oz	220 g
8 oz (½ lb)	250 g
10 oz	315 g
12 oz (¾ lb)	375 g
14 oz	440 g
16 oz (1 lb)	500 g
1½ lb	750 g
2 lb	1 kg
3 lb	1.5 kg

LIQUIDS

US	Metric	UK
2 tbl	30 ml	1 fl oz
¼ cup	60 ml	2 fl oz
⅓ cup	80 ml	3 fl oz
½ cup	125 ml	4 fl oz
⅔ cup	160 ml	5 fl oz
¾ cup	180 ml	6 fl oz
1 cup	250 ml	8 fl oz
1½ cups	375 ml	12 fl oz
2 cups	500 ml	16 fl oz
4 cups/1 qt	1 l	32 fl oz

LENGTH MEASURES

⅛ in	3 mm
¼ in	6 mm
½ in	12 mm
1 in	2.5 cm
2 in	5 cm
3 in	7.5 cm
4 in	10 cm
5 in	13 cm
6 in	15 cm
7 in	18 cm
8 in	20 cm
9 in	23 cm
10 in	25 cm
11 in	28 cm
12 in / 1 ft	30 cm

EQUIVALENTS FOR COMMONLY USED INGREDIENTS

All-Purpose (Plain) Flour / Dried Bread Crumbs / Chopped Nuts

¼ cup	1 oz	30 g
⅓ cup	1½ oz	45 g
½ cup	2 oz	60 g
¾ cup	3 oz	90 g
1 cup	4 oz	125 g
1½ cups	6 oz	185 g
2 cups	8 oz	250 g

Whole-Wheat (Wholemeal) Flour

3 tbl	1 oz	30 g
½ cup	2 oz	60 g
⅔ cup	3 oz	90 g
1 cup	4 oz	125 g
1¼ cups	5 oz	155 g
1⅔ cups	7 oz	210 g
1¾ cups	8 oz	250 g

Brown Sugar

¼ cup	1½ oz	45 g
½ cup	3 oz	90 g
¾ cup	4 oz	125 g
1 cup	5½ oz	170 g
1½ cups	8 oz	250 g
2 cups	10 oz	315 g

White Sugar

¼ cup	2 oz	60 g
⅓ cup	3 oz	90 g
½ cup	4 oz	125 g
¾ cup	6 oz	185 g
1 cup	8 oz	250 g
1½ cups	12 oz	375 g
2 cups	1 lb	500 g

Raisins / Currants / Semolina

¼ cup	1 oz	30 g
⅓ cup	2 oz	60 g
½ cup	3 oz	90 g
¾ cup	4 oz	125 g
1 cup	5 oz	155 g

Long-Grain Rice / Cornmeal

⅓ cup	2 oz	60 g
½ cup	2½ oz	75 g
¾ cup	4 oz	125 g
1 cup	5 oz	155 g
1½ cups	8 oz	250 g

Dried Beans

¼ cup	1½ oz	45 g
⅓ cup	2 oz	60 g
½ cup	3 oz	90 g
¾ cup	5 oz	155 g
1 cup	6 oz	185 g
1¼ cups	8 oz	250 g
1½ cups	12 oz	375 g

Rolled Oats

⅓ cup	1 oz	30 g
⅔ cup	2 oz	60 g
1 cup	3 oz	90 g
1½ cups	4 oz	125 g
2 cups	5 oz	155 g

Jam/Honey

2 tbl	2 oz	60 g
¼ cup	3 oz	90 g
½ cup	5 oz	155 g
¾ cup	8 oz	250 g
1 cup	11 oz	345 g

Grated Parmesan/Romano Cheese

¼ cup	1 oz	30 g
½ cup	2 oz	60 g
¾ cup	3 oz	90 g
1 cup	4 oz	125 g
1⅓ cups	5 oz	155 g
2 cups	7 oz	220 g